Interiors in the Era of Covid-19

Interiors in the Era of Covid-19

Interior Design between the Private and the Public Realms

PENNY SPARKE, ERSI IOANNIDOU, PAT KIRKHAM, STEPHEN KNOTT, JANA SCHOLZE

BLOOMSBURY VISUAL ARTS
LONDON · NEW YORK · OXFORD · NEW DELHI · SYDNEY

BLOOMSBURY VISUAL ARTS
Bloomsbury Publishing Plc
50 Bedford Square, London, WC1B 3DP, UK
1385 Broadway, New York, NY 10018, USA
29 Earlsfort Terrace, Dublin 2, Ireland

BLOOMSBURY, BLOOMSBURY VISUAL ARTS and the Diana logo
are trademarks of Bloomsbury Publishing Plc

First published in Great Britain 2023

Selection and editorial material © Penny Sparke, Ersi Ioannidou, Pat Kirkham,
Stephen Knott, Jana Scholze, 2023
Individual chapters © their authors, 2022

Penny Sparke, Ersi Ioannidou, Pat Kirkham, Stephen Knott and Jana Scholze
have asserted their right under the Copyright, Designs and Patents Act, 1988,
to be identified as Editors of this work.

Cover design: Eleanor Rose
Cover image © Joanna Rosado

All rights reserved. No part of this publication may be reproduced or transmitted
in any form or by any means, electronic or mechanical, including photocopying,
recording, or any information storage or retrieval system, without prior
permission in writing from the publishers.

Bloomsbury Publishing Plc does not have any control over, or responsibility for,
any third-party websites referred to or in this book. All internet addresses given
in this book were correct at the time of going to press. The author and publisher
regret any inconvenience caused if addresses have changed or sites have
ceased to exist, but can accept no responsibility for any such changes.

A catalogue record for this book is available from the British Library.

A catalog record for this book is available from the Library of Congress.

ISBN: HB: 978-1-3502-9422-6
PB: 978-1-3502-9421-9
ePDF: 978-1-3502-9423-3
eBook: 978-1-3502-9424-0

Typeset by Integra Software Services Pvt. Ltd.
Printed and bound in India

To find out more about our authors and books visit www.bloomsbury.com
and sign up for our newsletters.

Contents

List of illustrations viii

Notes on contributors xv

Introduction   *Penny Sparke, Ersi Ioannidou, Pat Kirkham, Stephen Knott, Jana Scholze* 1

SECTION ONE   Homes, health and well-being 11

1. Live gym classes at home: Lea Daan and broadcast body movement in 1930s Belgium   *Selin Geerinckx and Els de Vos* 13

2. Dancing across the threshold: Privacy and the home in the time of Covid-19   *Alice T. Friedman* 25

3. Achieving well-being in simple ways: Cosy, comfortable and contented domestic interiors in interwar Vienna   *Michelle Jackson-Beckett* 35

4. The quest for health and well-being in Japanese homes from late nineteenth century to Covid-19   *Izumi Kuroishi* 47

5. A space of their own: A case study advocating appropriation of the domestic interior for well-being   *Eliza Sweeney and Sebastian Messer* 61

SECTION TWO   The unstable home 73

6. The re-materialization of everyday life: New aesthetic experiences of staying at home in Sweden during the Covid-19 pandemic   *Maja Willén* 75

7 Room for independence: Home-based women workers and their interiors   *Fiona Del Puppo and Paule Perron* 87

8 Working at home: Architects during the pandemic in China   *Ye Xu, Katharina Borsi and Jonathan Hale* 101

9 From *Caseta* to *Cuarto*: The spaces of restorative and transitional justice in Colombia before and during the Covid-19 pandemic   *Cynthia Imogen Hammond, Greg Labrosse, Vanessa Sicotte and Marcela Torres Molano* 113

10 Games without frontiers – Covid living in refugee camps   *Mark Taylor and Iris Levin* 127

SECTION THREE   Representing the (in)visible 139

11 Tell don't show: The invisible plague in Dutch seventeenth-century paintings of the domestic interior   *Irene Cieraad* 141

12 Lockdown portraits: Resituating the self   *Inga Bryden* 155

13 Fiction: IKEA's saleable living for pandemic life   *Rebecca Carrai* 167

14 Nice white spaces: Race and class in domestic cleaning ads during Covid-19   *Rachele Dini* 181

15 Uncanny on display: Musée Dom-Ino. A virtual museum of domesticity in lockdown   *Nina Bassoli and Roberto Gigliotti* 195

SECTION FOUR   Collecting the interior in the era of Covid-19 207

16 Changing scenes: Image-making from parlour to screen   *Patrick Lee Lucas* 209

17 Shelter in Place Gallery: Exhibiting contemporary art and creating community in a pandemic   *Michelle Millar Fisher, Eben Haines and Courtney Harris* 221

CONTENTS

18 *The Domestic Body   Stefania Napolitano* 233

19 *Interior Archipelago – postcards from our islands   Lois Weinthal, Patrick Macklin, Wen Liang and Alice Huang* 247

20 Stay Home – rapid response collecting project at the Museum of the Home   *Danielle Patten* 259

Index 271

Illustrations

Figures

1.1 The Icosohedran in use at the Lea Daan School, 1938, Collection City of Antwerp, Letterenhuis 17

1.2 Lea Daan during a radio class, two female dancers in action, c. 1938, Collection City of Antwerp, Letterenhuis 18

1.3 Cover for *Wie Turnt er mee … met het N.I.R?* Radio programme brochure 28, NIR 19

1.4 Practitioner exercising close to the open window in the sun, no date. Courtesy Archive Lea Daan, Collection City of Antwerp, Letterenhuis 21

2.1 The living room transformed for Zumba fitness classes 28

2.2 Multiple computer screens for teaching 29

2.3 Participants on one of many Zoom screens 30

2.4 Modelling a hat after class 32

3.1 Was in Wien Modern ist? Die wohlangewandte Ecke (What is modern in Vienna. Modern Spatial Art: The Well-Used Corner), *Wiener Bilder*, 7 September 1930. ANNO/Österreichische Nationalbibliothek. Public domain 41

3.2 Fritz Gross, 'Einwohnraum' (A single multi-use room for living, dining, working and sleeping). *InnenDekoration* (January 1929). Universitätsbibliothek Heidelberg. Public domain 42

3.3 Ernst Plischke, 'Das Blumenfenster' (design for a windowsill

ILLUSTRATIONS

	garden), *Profil: Monatsschrift für bildende Kunst* (April 1934). ANNO/Österreichische Nationalbibliothek. Public domain 43
3.4	Liane Zimbler, 'Trennungswand in der Diele' (Partition wall in the hallway of an apartment). *InnenDekoration* (August 1931). Universitätsbibliothek Heidelberg. Public domain 44
4.1	Japanese historical dwelling depicted in 'View of dwelling from garden, Tokio' in Edward S. Morse's *Japanese House and their Surroundings* (1886). Edward S. Morse 51
4.2	Plan of the first prize design, Healthy Housing Competition, organized by Osaka Mainichi Newspaper, 1930. Osaka Mainichi Newspaper 53
4.3	Uzo Nishiyama's axonometric sketch of the interior of his small dwelling designed by Dojunkai in the 1930s. Courtesy Nishiyama Bunko Archive 54
4.4	Uzo Nishiyama's sketch of a typical n+LDK dwelling in the 1970s. Courtesy Nishiyama Bunko Archive 56
5.1	A scenographic spaceship: A table with recycled materials and personal belongings. Sebastian Messer. Drawing by Sebastian Messer 66
5.2	A space helmet: Paper grocery bag, aluminium foil, coloured card stars. Sebastian Messer. Drawing by Sebastian Messer 67
6.1	Laptop table, illustration from IKEA catalogue, 2021 78
6.2	A living room working space, illustration from IKEA catalogue, 2021 79
6.3	Women working from home, photo from *Hemmakontor* by Daniel Nilsson, 2021 80
6.4	Couple working from home, photo from *Hemmakontor* by Daniel Nilsson, 2021 81

7.1	Interpretative sketch of Virginia Woolf's and Laura's workrooms, 2022. Drawing by Paule Perron and Fiona Del Puppo	91
7.2	Interpretative sketch of Pia's, Dalila's and Laura's workrooms, 2022. Drawing by Paule Perron and Fiona Del Puppo	93
7.3	Interpretative sketch of Alice's and Sophie's border-objects, 2022. Drawing by Paule Perron and Fiona Del Puppo	95
7.4	Interpretative sketch of Sylvie's inhabited hallway, 2022. Drawing by Paule Perron and Fiona Del Puppo	96
8.1	A minimal home of one's own. Drawn by Ye Xu	103
8.2	Drawing architecture studio office. Drawn by Drawing Architecture Studio	105
8.3	A tale of two apartments. Drawn by Drawing Architecture Studio	106
8.4	Living by interface. Drawn by Feng Lu	107
9.1	Interview room, Truth Commission office, Bogotà, Colombia, 2018. Design by DUCON Disenos y espacios productivos	116
9.2	*El Mochuelo*, Itinerant Museum of Memory and Identity of Montes de María, Colombia (2008). Photograph by Sergio Gómez	117
9.3	The *cuarto* of Alejandra Gutiérrez Gómez in Bogotà, Colombia (2021)	118
9.4	The *cuarto* of Alejandra Gutiérrez Gómez (2021). Hand drawing by Alejandra Gutiérrez Gómez. Reproduced with permission of Alejandra Gutiérrez Gómez	121
10.1	A Jewish woman and her two children outside a makeshift hut, Poland, 1920	128

ILLUSTRATIONS

10.2 Moria Camp Refugees fear possible Coronavirus outbreak, Lesbos, Greece, March 2020, 2020   132
10.3 Refugee camp on Lesbos, Greece – stock photo, 2020   133
10.4 Melbourne in lockdown as Victoria works to contain Covid-19 Spread, 2020. Courtesy of Getty Images AsiaPac, © Darrian Traynor/Stringer   135
11.1 Painting by Theodoor van der Schuer, *Pest Victims in a Pest House* 1682. Museum De Lakenhal, Leiden   142
11.2 Painting by Hendrick ten Oever, *The slaughtered pig* 1670. Collectie Overijssel, Zwolle   143
11.3 Watercolour by Gesina ter Borch, *Death at Ramshorst* 1660. Rijksmuseum Amsterdam   144
11.4 Painting by Samuel van Hoogstraten, *The Slippers* 1658. Musée du Louvre, Paris   145
12.1 'Sally' by Fran Monks, *Social Distance – Lockdown Mark I*, 2020   159
12.2 *Hold Still: A Portrait of Our Nation in 2020* – 'Justin, from the outside in' by Sara Lincoln. National Portrait Gallery, London   162
12.3 'Tesco Value Dad' by Enda Burke, *Homebound with My Parents*, 2020   163
13.1 Backstage for 1974/75 catalogue   169
13.2 IKEA Place App commercial from 2017   171
13.3 IKEA Italia, (2020) [Instagram] 15 March   175
13.4 Third 2020 Life at Home Report, *The Big Home Reboot*   176
14.1 In 'House Proud' Dettol turns so-called diversity into a quirk   185
14.2 The closing shot of Dettol 'House Proud' (2021)

14.3 Fairy's white baby mascot surrounded by white plates plays on longstanding racist tropes 188

14.4 Finish '#SkipTheRinse' frames the environmental crisis as a problem for reified, atomized individuals to solve from home 189

15.1 Roberto Bartolacci, *Small pleasures of life*, 2020 197

15.2 Asia Maria Andreolli, *Stuck in the domestic landscape. 750 minutes at the desk*, 2020 199

15.3 Nicolaï Martini, *Bossa (Casa) Nova*, 2020 201

15.4 Nina Bassoli, Davide Tommaso Ferrando, Roberto Gigliotti, *Museé Dom-Ino*, 2020 203

16.1 The Quilting Frolic, John Lewis Krimmel, Philadelphia, Pennsylvania, United States, 1813, Oil on canvas, 1953.0178.002 A, B, Museum purchase 212

16.2 Wallace Nutting. *At the Fender, ca.* 1904. Wallace Nutting, Public domain, via Wikimedia Commons 213

16.3 The author's own room, with its background from a 1902 Colonial Revival House. Screen capture by author, 2021 216

16.4 The anonymous author of Bookcase Credibility provides pithy reviews of the bookcases that appear in the Twitter feed. Here activist Angela Davis appears, as featured on 19 June 2020 218

17.1 Shelter in Place gallery, seen from exterior in the artists' living room 223

17.2 'Another show down as another show arrives! Miles Jaffe's crates are acclimatising in the gallery as we break for

ILLUSTRATIONS   xiii

coffee and eat our wheaties. Gonna be some heavy lifting, thank god he provided dollies!' 224

17.3 The first post on @shelterinplacegallery Instagram 225

17.4 Terrestrial globe compass, around 1675–1685 in Dieppe, France, engraved ivory. Gift of the heirs of Bettina Looram de Rothschild (2015.109a-b). Photograph © Museum of Fine Arts, Boston 227

17.5 Ron Ho (American, 1936–2017), TV Guide, 1992, silver, patinated copper, polymer clay; silk cord. The Daphne Farago Collection, 2006.251. Reproduced with permission. Photograph © Museum of Fine Arts, Boston 228

17.6 Eben Haines's 'Shelter in Place Gallery' on view in the exhibition New Light: Encounters and Connections at the Museum of Fine Arts, Boston, 28 July 2021. Photograph © Museum of Fine Arts, Boston 230

18.1a, b, c Still from the tutorial of *The Domestic Body* workshop: Pre-quarantine map, quarantine map and dynamic diagram 237

18.2 Contribution to *The Domestic Body* workshop from a Milanese heterosexual couple with a new-born child: Pre-quarantine and quarantine maps 238

18.3a, b Contribution to *The Domestic Body* workshop from a Parisian couple of young heterosexual professionals: Pre-quarantine and quarantine maps; individual dynamic diagrams 240

18.4a, b, c Filippo's contribution to *The Domestic Body* workshop: Pre-quarantine and quarantine maps 243

19.1a, b, c, d top left: Liu Meiming (AADTHU), One Day; bottom left: Joanna Rosado (GSA), The table- my universe centre;

top right: Ruixue Wang, (AADTHU); bottom right: Daniela Nicole Ellero (TMU) 253

19.2a, b, c, d top left: Spatial Configurations, Jiao Zha (AADTHU); bottom left: Dennis Lum, (GSA); top right: Alice Huang, (TMU), Ritual Artifacts: Laundry; bottom right: Linghang Cai, (AADTHU) 254

19.3a, b, c, d top: Representation, Shuxin Yin (AADTHU); middle left: David Ross (GSA); middle right: Paul Armand Georgescu (GSA); bottom: Xuefei Chen (AADTHU) 255

19.4a, b, c Images of the Exhibition of *Interior Archipelago* at Academy of Art and Design, Tsinghua University. Photographs by Wen Liang 257

20.1 Lahiru's family exercising in their living room, 2020 261

20.2 Chantelle painting her mural, 2020. Courtesy of the Museum of the Home 263

20.3 G holding her son to the window behind a sign saying thank you to all key workers. 2020 265

20.4 Our Home Our Stories display by Alaa Alsaraji, 2021 268

Table

5.1 EPR framing of the *Exploration in Space* programme 65

Notes on Contributors

Nina Bassoli is an architect and curator and Research Assistant at the Free University of Bozen-Bolzano. She has curated exhibitions and events, including 'Take Your Seat' (2021), 'Reconstructions' (2018), the Turin Architecture Festival (2017), 'Architecture as Art' (2016), 'City after the City – Street Art' (2016), and 'Innesti/Grafting' at the 14th Venice Biennale, with Cino Zucchi (2014). Since 2008 she has been a member of the editorial staff of *Lotus International*.

Katharina Borsi is Associate Professor of Architecture at the University of Nottingham. She teaches design and architectural and urban theory. Her research focuses on the intersection between housing, domesticity and urbanism. She has lectured and published extensively on the history and theory of housing and urbanism.

Inga Bryden is Professor of Cultural History and Head of Research in the Faculty of Arts at the University of Winchester, UK. Her research interests span literary, visual and material cultures, with a focus on interdisciplinary ways of interpreting places and spaces. She has published on medievalism in Victorian culture, the Pre-Raphaelites, domestic space, Indian domestic interiors, literature and architecture, mapping urban space, graffiti, fashion and food. Publications include *Reinventing King Arthur* (2005) and, edited with Janet Floyd, *Domestic Space: Reading the Nineteenth-Century Interior* (1999).

Rebecca Carrai is a PhD researcher and teacher at KU Leuven University. She was a visiting scholar at the Architectural Association. Her PhD project is entitled *The IKEA Home*. She graduated from the Faculty of Architecture in Florence.

Irene Cieraad is a cultural anthropologist and affiliated Senior Researcher in the Faculty of Architecture and the Built Environment of Delft University of Technology, the Netherlands. She is the editor of *At Home: An Anthropology of Domestic Space* (e-book 2021) and the author of articles on the Dutch domestic interior.

Els de Vos, engineering architect and urban planner, is Professor at the University of Antwerp, where she chairs the interior architecture programme. Her research is situated in the field of history and theory of (interior) architecture, home culture, gender and public space in the second half of the twentieth century.

Fiona Del Puppo is an architect and PhD student at the Urban Sociology Laboratory of Ecole Polytechnique Fédérale de Lausanne. Her thesis focuses on the transformations of the home, influenced by a flexible labour market, especially for the young generation in London and Geneva. She is also involved in a research project with a multidisciplinary team working on *Domotopie*, aiming to define a contemporary science of the home interior.

Rachele Dini is Senior Lecturer in American Literature at the University of Roehampton, London. Her publications include *Consumerism, Waste, and Re-use in 20th-Century Fiction: Legacies of the Avant-Garde*, *'All-Electric Narratives': Time-Saving Appliances and Domesticity in American Literature, 1945–2000*, and *Queer Trash & Feminist Excretions: New Directions in Literary and Cultural Waste Studies*.

Michelle Millar Fisher is currently the Ronald C. and Anita L. Wornick Curator of Contemporary Decorative Arts at the Museum of Fine Arts, Boston. Her work focuses on the intersections of people, power and the material world. At the MFA, she is working on her next book, tentatively titled *Craft Schools: Where We Make What We Inherit*, and on a book (MIT Press 2021), exhibition, curriculum and programme series called *Designing Motherhood: Things That Make and Break Our Births*. She is currently completing her doctorate in art history at The Graduate Center at the City University of New York (CUNY).

Alice T. Friedman is the Grace Slack McNeil Professor of the History of American Art and Co-Director of the Architecture Program at Wellesley College. Her research focuses on the contributions of clients to the evolution of modern architecture and design. Her publications include *Women and the Making of the Modern House* (1998) and *American Glamour and the Evolution of Modern Architecture* (2010). She is currently working on a book titled *Poker Faces: Modern Architecture, Performance and Private Life*.

Selin Geerinckx is an interior architect affiliated with the interior architecture programme at the University of Antwerp. Through a focus on modern dance theory and methodologies, her research centres on the bodily and mental effects of modernist housing.

Roberto Gigliotti holds an MLA degree in architecture. He is Associate Professor of Interior and Exhibit Design at the Free University of Bozen Bolzano. His research interests focus on the exhibition of architecture and the public space of the contemporary city. He is currently working on the research project *Architecture in the Age of Display* with Nina Bassoli and Léa-Catherine Szacka. He is vice-president of ar/ge kunst Bolzano and founding member of Lungomare. In 2015 he collaborated with Studio Lupo&Burtscher on the exhibition design of the *Casa Semirurale* in Bolzano.

Eben Haines is an artist and designer living in Boston, MA. His work investigates the life of objects through works that emphasize the constructed nature of history. He is also a contributor and co-director of Shelter in Place Gallery, a miniature community gallery brought about by the Covid-19 pandemic. He is also a recipient of the 2021 James and Audrey Foster Prize from the Institute of Contemporary Art, Boston.

Jonathan Hale is an architect and Professor of Architectural Theory in the Department of Architecture and Built Environment, the University of Nottingham. He is Head of the Architecture, Culture and Tectonics research group. He has published extensively on architectural theory and criticism; phenomenology and the philosophy of technology; the relationship between architecture and the body; museums and architectural exhibitions.

Cynthia Imogen Hammond is Professor of Art History at Concordia University. Her work focuses on women and the history of the built environment, urban landscapes, research-creation and oral history. Her publications include studies of the spatial history of the suffrage movement, public art, gardens and the politics of urban change. She is leading research projects on the spaces of restorative and transitional justice and on the urban knowledge of senior citizens.

Courtney Harris is Assistant Curator, Decorative Arts and Sculpture, Art of Europe at the Museum of Fine Arts, Boston. She is currently working on an exhibition called *Tiny Treasures*. Her recent projects at the MFA include the reinstallation of over 150 decorative arts objects in new galleries of Dutch & Flemish art. She contributes regularly to academic journals. She received her MA from the Courtauld Institute of Art in London and her BA from Johns Hopkins University in Baltimore.

Alice Wenyi Huang studied Interior Design at Toronto Metropolitan University and previously completed an BA (Hons) from the University of Toronto. She is a multidisciplinary designer with wide-ranging interests that include the intersectionality of design and digital technologies and storytelling through interiors.

Ersi Ioannidou is a design educator and researcher at Kingston School of Art, where she holds the position of PGR Student Director for The Design School. Her research deals with the machine as design paradigm in twentieth-century domestic architecture. Her recent work, reflecting her fascination with space travel, explores real and fictional space interiors; utopian domestic architecture of the 1960s and 1970s; and interiors in science fiction film.

Michelle Jackson-Beckett is a design historian specializing in critical histories of modernism in Central Europe and the United States. She holds an MPhil and PhD in Decorative Arts, Design History, and Material Culture from Bard Graduate Center, New York, and an MA in the History of Design and Decorative Arts from the Cooper Hewitt, Smithsonian Design Museum/Parsons School of Design, New York.

Pat Kirkham is Professor of Design History and member of the Modern Interiors Research Centre (MIRC), Kingston University, and Professor Emerita, Bard Graduate Center, New York. She has written widely on design, gender and film. Her publications include *A View from the Interior: Feminism, Women and Design* (1989, with Judy Attfield), *The Gendered Object* (1996) and *Screen Interiors* (2021, with Sarah Lichtman).

Stephen Knott is a writer, researcher and lecturer in craft theory and history. He is author of *Amateur Craft: History and Theory* (Bloomsbury, 2015) and is one of the editors of *The Journal of Modern Craft*. He lectures at Kingston University where he is a member of the Modern Interiors Research Centre (MIRC).

Izumi Kuroishi is an architect and Professor at Aoyama Gakuin University, Japan. Her publications include *Constructing the Colonized Land: Entwined Perspectives of East Asia around WWII* (2014); 'Social Resilience in Disaster Recovery Planning for Fishing Port Cities', *Journal of Urban History* (2019) and 'Cultural Politics of the Cold War and Living a Shibui Life', Lee & Rajguru (eds.) *Design and Modernity in Asia* (2022).

Greg Labrosse is an interdisciplinary PhD candidate at Concordia University. His research focuses on spatial agency, social aesthetics, youth narratives and representations of urban memory. He has published on the relationship between children, play and public space in Cartagena, Colombia. He has worked as an editor on literary projects, including Territorio Fértil, which received the María Nelly Murillo Hinestroza award for Afro-Colombian literature.

Iris Levin is Lecturer in the Sustainability and Urban Planning Department, RMIT University (Australia). Her research interests focus on issues of home, housing and the impact of migration on urban environments. She has published on various aspects of housing and diversity in the city. Her first book was *Migration, Settlement, and the Concepts of House and Home* (2016, Routledge), and she has recently co-edited *Migration and Urban Transitions in Australia* (2022, Palgrave Macmillan).

Patrick Lee Lucas is Associate Professor at the University of Kentucky. An award-winning teacher, Lucas leads seminars, teaches lecture courses, offers education abroad opportunities and facilitates studio interactions by engaging in community conversations and encouraging students to think about the place of design in the world. His research interest in historic interiors led to the speculation of the continuities in collecting across time.

Wen Liang is Associate Professor in the Department of Environmental Art Design at Tsinghua University. Her activities vary from architecture design, interior design to spatial information design. Wen is known for her iconological-based building environment analysis. She uses visualization and hermeneutics as a telescope into unseen building environment realities.

Patrick Macklin is Reader in Interior Design and acting Deputy Head of the School of Design at The Glasgow School of Art. He co-founded pop-up innovators Lapland, was associate artist and designer with the award-winning theatre company Suspect Culture and practised as Frozen River and, more recently in the partnership SpaceKraft. He is a trustee of Interior Educators (IE), the National subject association for interiors in the UK.

Sebastian Messer is an architect and Senior Lecturer and leader of the Master of Architecture programme at Northumbria University. His interdisciplinary research is concerned with the multiple forms of narratives in the production, representation, uses of and lived experiences in the built environment.

Marcela Torres Molano is a PhD candidate in the Department of Art History at Concordia University. From Colombia, she has a background in architectural design and community activism and holds a master's degree in Building and Urban Design from the Bartlett School of Architecture. Her research interests include socially engaged art, collaborative activism in post-conflict scenarios, collectively produced art and art in the built environment.

Stefania Napolitano studied Architecture at La Sapienza University of Rome. After working as an architect in several Italian and international firms, she is currently employed at the MAXXI museum education department. She has participated in several iterations of *Museum Among the School Desks* and contributed to the *Kids Museum and* the *Captions in the Collection* projects. She co-curated the first two editions of the international congress dedicated to education through the built environment, *Leggere lo spazio/*Reading the Space.

Danielle Patten is Head of Creative Programming and Collections at the Museum of the Home. She has worked on the development and production of the Museum's new displays and galleries as well as initiatives to increase the Museum's contemporary collections of people's homes. Since April 2020 she has worked on the *Stay Home* digital collecting project, which seeks to explore how Covid-19 has changed the way we live, and to think about the future of home life.

Paule Perron is an architect and teaches at HEAD – Genève, CH. She develops a practice between research and project to question the perpetuation of domination patterns through the study of mutual influences between spaces and bodies, especially focusing on gender studies. She recently co-founded minor, a collective practice. Her work has been published and exhibited in various magazines and institutions such as *Plan Libre, Architecture d'Aujourd'hui* and the *Villa Noailles*.

Jana Scholze is a design curator and Associate Professor at Kingston University where she heads the MA Curating Contemporary Design in partnership with the Design Museum. She has been a curator at the Victoria and Albert Museum and recently co-curated the exhibition *At Home* for the International Design Biennial St Etienne 2022. Her transdisciplinary research covers questions around formats of interaction and contemporary design practice engaging with society, technology and the environment.

Vanessa Sicotte is an MA candidate in the Department of Art History at Concordia University. She is an author, speaker, columnist and podcaster in the fields of architecture and decorative arts. She holds a Bachelor of Commerce with a major in Marketing from Concordia's John Molson School of Business, and she studied Industrial Psychology in Los Angeles. Sicotte is the author of two books on design published by Les Éditions Cardinal.

Penny Sparke is Professor of Design History and the Director of the Modern Interiors Research Centre (MIRC) at Kingston University, London. Her main research interest is modern interiors and their relationship with gender and identity. Her publications include *As Long as It's Pink: The Sexual Politics of Taste* (2010 [1995]), *The Modern Interior* (2008) and *Nature Inside: Plants and Flowers in the Modern Interior* (2021).

Eliza Sweeney has worked for ten years as a designer-scenographer and, since 2017, in drama and expressive arts therapy in which she makes use of scenography and place-making practices as artistic tools for mental health and wellness. A PhD candidate at the University of Northumbria, her research explores the cultivation of architectural and scenographic spaces through participatory and community-led projects, which lead to well-being.

Mark Taylor is Professor of Architecture at Swinburne University of Technology, Australia. He researches the modern interior through a cultural and social perspective. His publications include both traditional and non-traditional research outputs. Current projects include the co-edited anthologies *Domesticity under Siege* (2022) and *Place and Parametricism: Critical, Archival and Digital Approaches to Contemporary Design* (2023).

Lois Weinthal is Professor in the School of Interior Design at Toronto Metropolitan University. Her research and practice investigate the relationship between architecture, interiors, clothing and objects. Her edited books include *Toward a New Interior: An Anthology of Interior Design Theory*. She is the co-editor of *After Taste: Expanded Practice in Interior Design* and *Digital Fabrication in Interior Design: Body, Object, Enclosure*. Currently, she holds the position of Honorary Professor at the Glasgow School of Art.

Maja Willén is an art historian currently working at the *University of Arts, Craft and Design* in Stockholm. Her main research interest is contemporary housing and dwelling ideals from an everyday user perspective. Willén has published texts on the breakthrough of the open plan designed home in the early Swedish twenty-first century and on the use and construction of history in contemporary kitchen catalogues. She is now working on a larger project on how the staying at home situation of the pandemic is rechoreographing the home materially, socially and spatially.

Ye Xu is a PhD student in Architecture at the University of Nottingham. She graduated from Peking University with a master's degree in Geography (urban and regional planning). Her research interests include housing, domesticity and urbanism, as well as drawing and critical visual practice.

Introduction

Penny Sparke, Ersi Ioannidou, Pat Kirkham, Stephen Knott, Jana Scholze

Interiors in the Era of Covid-19: Interior Design between the Public and Private Realms is a cross-disciplinary anthology of twenty chapters which provides accounts of interiors as they responded to the extraordinary times in which we have found ourselves living since early 2020, namely the era of the Covid-19 pandemic.

The pandemic caused people, worldwide, to be confined to their homes for longer periods of time than previously, causing many changes to take place within them, while many other interiors beyond the home have had to respond to the new priorities in a variety of ways.

Homes have had to accommodate their additional roles as schools, gymnasia, restaurants, cinemas, offices, making spaces and more besides. Above all, the home has been looked to as a site to support and enhance the well-being of its inhabitants in a variety of ways. At the same time, many of the work, retail, leisure and hospitality spaces in the buildings in our city centres have sat empty constituting a threat to the future urban environment.

This project developed out of discussions that began at the first meeting of the Modern Interiors Research Centre (MIRC) at Kingston University, London, after England went into a national lockdown in late March 2020 in the hope of slowing the rapid spread of Covid-19. It was the first of many online meetings at which MIRC members discussed a wide range of issues related to the pandemic and interiors (public, private and those that blur the lines between the two). The themes we discussed ranged from additional burdens on women in relation to homeschooling, housekeeping and childcare; new and multi-purpose uses of spaces and furniture such as kitchen tables; the new importance of thresholds; the role of indoor/outdoor spaces such as balconies and garden sheds; home studios; and issues around hygiene, air purification, ventilation, square footage per inhabitant, contested spaces and mental health issues.

On 24 March 2021 MIRC hosted an international webinar on the topic of interiors in the Covid-19 era. This book grew out of that initiative, and all the chapters that follow began life as papers presented at it: they embrace a variety of types of interiors, from living rooms to architectural studios, and the main geographical spread ranges from Japan to the United States, Austria, Belgium, France, the UK, Italy, Sweden, Switzerland, China, Colombia and Australia, with additional countries referenced as points of comparison or influence. The authors range from academics (both senior and emerging scholars), mainly from/or across the fields of Design History, Architectural History, History, Cultural Studies and Curatorial Studies, to a therapist, and several design and architectural practitioners and curators, all of whose contributions we are delighted to include here.

Our call for papers specified that we were open to papers with a historical focus and the main time frame here ranges from the interwar years to the present, although several authors refer back to earlier periods in which large-scale cholera outbreaks and the devastating 'Spanish Flu' epidemic of 1918–19, which killed an estimated fifty to a hundred million people, for example, took place.

Themes and issues

We have grouped the chapters into four thematic sections, namely *Home, health and well-being; The unstable home; Representing the (in)visible* and *Collecting the interior in the era of Covid-19*. Perhaps not surprisingly during such a deadly pandemic, periods of lockdown and advice to 'Stay Home', domestic interiors feature in many of the chapters, as do notions of domesticity and home, including places/spaces of one's own (real and imagined) and those of others seen on Zoom and other digital platforms. Commercial spaces feature less frequently but those that do include a 1930s radio recording studio in Belgium transmitting fitness classes directly into people's homes, and professional workspaces, including one used by architects in China. The individual rooms and spaces that appear most frequently within the pages that follow are living spaces, home-working spaces and bedrooms, or, very commonly, multi-purpose spaces that embrace elements of all of these. Several chapters draw attention to the ways in which members of different family members and generations negotiate living closely to one another during a period of considerable anxieties and fears, while others feature the interplay between indoors and outside. Among the many issues and topics raised across the chapters are class, social stratification, age, gender, race, generational differences, interiority, memory, curation, vulnerability and therapy, all of which are woven throughout the four sections. While each section focuses on a particular area, so closely are all these themes and issues related to each other that they re-emerge in a variety of different contexts. Also, while many case studies are included to demonstrate the specificity of the ways in which Covid-19 affected interiors in a breadth of different contexts, and oral histories and ethnographic studies have been extensively undertaken to unearth the particularities of certain situations, the commonality of the themes and issues that arise are very striking.

Section One: Homes, health and well-being

We have asked much of our interiors during the Covid-19 pandemic. This section explores some of the various ways in which homes and their interiors are, among many other things, sites of health, therapy and well-being, and how they were experienced as such in the past as well as the present. With their staggering death rates and swift infection transmissions, pandemics thrust issues of health to the foreground; they literally become a matter of life or death. Homes have long functioned as places to look after the sick, and recently more homes than ever have had to cope with the additional burden of Covid-19 illness and death.

The penetration of potentially fatal disease into the home radically disrupts the nineteenth-century Western bourgeois notion of home as 'sanctuary' from the outside world and interiors as places of comfort, relaxation and familial accord – a notion far from lived reality. An interesting, albeit temporary, movement from health in the public sphere to the domestic came recently with official closures of gymnasia, swimming pools and all manner of fitness and leisure centres as millions of people sought ways to keep fit at home. At the same time, 'stay-home' directives led to a plethora of advice on well-being and health in the home, from new hobbies and indoor air-purifying plants to home fitness routines, and we open this section with the latter.

We have paired two chapters about health and fitness classes piped into domestic spaces. In Chapter 1, *Live gym classes at home: Lea Daan and broadcast body movement in 1930s Belgium*, Selin Geerinckx and Els de Vos explore Lea Daan's radio fitness classes aired in Belgium between 1935 and 1940 to home listeners. They contextualize the classes within the contemporaneous body culture movement and the promotion of the nation's health amidst high levels of poverty and chronic disease. By holding live classes in the radio station to live accompaniment, Daan hoped to offer as near as possible an authentic experience for listeners. In Chapter 2, *Dancing across the threshold: Privacy and the home in the time of Covid-19*, Alice T. Friedman reflects on her experiences when her US Zumba class went online during the Covid-19 lockdowns in 2020. Friedman's narrative offers a window into the extent to which online delivery upheld and enhanced fitness routines while gently explicating anxieties about digital etiquette, such as screen backgrounds and whether to turn on cameras when one's whole body is on show.

The need for healthy and versatile spaces within the small homes of 'ordinary' people is a recurrent theme in the next pairing. Chapter 3, Michelle Jackson-Beckett's *Achieving well-being in simple ways: Cosy, comfortable and contented domestic interiors in interwar Vienna*, outlines a new interior design culture that emphasized comfort and cosiness as well as hygiene. She shows how, as part of his plan to integrate well-being into interiors, architect-designer Josef Frank allowed the eye to 'rest' as well as other parts of the body. In such conceptions of the home, attention to 'psycho-social viewpoints' was key. She also explores initiatives attentive to the psychological experience of the home, from a special issue of *InnenDekoration* in 1930 on the sensorial inhabitation of interiors and its impact on the body, to socialist Red Vienna's improved housing conditions for working families. Izumi Kuroishi offers a long view of Japanese housing in Chapter 4, *The quest for health and well-being in Japanese homes from the late nineteenth century to Covid-19*. She seeks examples of Japanese housing that might prove useful for those involved in re-thinking the design of future dwellings, including interiors, bearing in mind problems experienced during Covid-19, especially by those confined to small urban spaces. She ranges from discourses of hygiene adapted from Western models to holistic notions of interior design for well-being informed by Confucianism and other models and offers suggestions for the way forward in Japan.

From broad considerations, we move to a specific example. Chapter 5, Eliza Sweeney and Sebastian Messer's *A space of their own: A case study advocating appropriation of the domestic interior for well-being*, presents a model of child therapy developed to mitigate against negative effects of lockdown on children, including lack of privacy. Sweeney converted to online delivery an arts therapy programme she devised for children aged five to seven living in poorer parts of Paris. Deploying the notion of 'psychoscenography' – recognizing the importance of 'spatial appropriation and place-making' in health and well-being – Sweeney and Messer describe how, through telehealth practices, children were encouraged to project their anxieties onto objects surrounding them, appropriate space, and create scenes in their homes that they could inhabit through role-play. Informed by literary precedents wherein the domestic is turned magical, the project demonstrates the power of domestic space to heal and protect in difficult times.

Section Two: The unstable home

One of the most noticeable effects of Covid-19 on interiors, especially those located within the home, was the erosion of what had, prior to 2020, been a set of relatively stable binaries, among them those of public/private, work/leisure, individual/collective and urban/domestic. The new condition of people spending more time at home and using increasing numbers of technological means to communicate with people outside it disturbed the balance between those binaries, broke down the boundaries between them and created high levels of instability.

As the home needed to accommodate new functions, previously undertaken in the public arena for the most part – including work, schooling, exercise, entertainment (that would have previously taken place in theatres and cinemas) and online shopping – people's hitherto relatively stable ways of life, and the material and spatial environment that had supported it, were adapted accordingly. These instabilities, in turn, affected people's individual and social definitions of self and the ways in which they orchestrated their lifestyles. In short, the rebalancing of the relationships between these boundaries had material, spatial, social and psychological ramifications.

These shifts in the ways in which interiors were inhabited and experienced were not limited to one geographical arena but, rather, had a global presence. The case studies in the first four chapters presented here cover examples of the effects of domestic instability in countries as diverse as Sweden, Switzerland, China and Colombia. The last chapter in the section, which addresses refugee camps, embraces examples located in Bangladesh and Greece, as well as an apartment block in Australia. While conditions inevitably varied from place to place and from home to home, the idea of instability characterizes most of the interiors described here.

In Chapter 6, *The re-materialization of everyday life: New aesthetic experiences of staying at home in Sweden during the Covid-19 pandemic*, Maja Willén examines how a group of Swedish people accommodated the new demands of Covid-19 materially and spatially in their homes; how the retail store, IKEA, depicted some of those changes; and how the Swedish photographer, Daniel Nilsson, captured the home office in his project *Hemmakontor* (home offices). She sets out to show us how the social, the material, the spatial and the aesthetic, are all linked and that the changes that are being made in homes transform our bodily practices of inhabiting it.

In Chapter 7, *Room for independence: Home-based women workers and their interiors*, Fiona Del Puppo and Paule Perron focus on ways in which seven women, most of them located in Geneva, responded to Covid-19 in their homes. They want to understand whether it has had the effect of liberating women from conventional gender domination patterns or whether it has enhanced them. If the former, they ask, has it been at the price of their work/life stability? Like Willén, they also describe some of the material strategies – such as using bookcases to create spatial boundaries – that these women have employed to try to separate work from everyday life in the home.

In Chapter 8, titled *Working at home: Architects during the pandemic in China*, Ye Xu, Katharina Borsi and Jonathan Hale address some of the same questions, this time in the context of two case studies of the interior spaces occupied by Chinese architects who wrestled with the erosion of the distinction between work and everyday life at home. Their main finding is that this is a fluid process which happens over time. Their aim is, through drawings which track the movements of the case-study inhabitants, to offer a way in which architects can understand how this process works and design adaptable spaces with that in mind.

Chapter 9, *From Caseta to Cuarto: The spaces of restorative and transitional justice in Colombia before and during the Covid-19 pandemic*, written by Cynthia Imogen Hammond, Greg Labrosse, Vanessa Sicotte and Marcela Torres Molano, focuses on the very specific case study of a Colombian Truth Commission case worker who had to move from an office, in which she had held face-to-face interviews, to interviewing people from a computer in her bedroom. She employed several strategies to make the space feel more personal and to compensate for the absence of face-to-face experiences.

While refugee camps aim to protect vulnerable people and act as temporary 'housing', as Mark Taylor and Iris Levin explain in Chapter 10, titled *Games without frontiers – Covid living in refugee camps*, they enhance their inhabitants' sense of homelessness. In the era of Covid-19 this was exacerbated by the fact that, because of the limited spaces available, the lack of privacy, the ease with which spatial boundaries are transgressed and overcrowding, they are unable to protect people from disease. The chapter references the Cox's Bazar in Bangladesh, the Moria and Mavrovouni refugee camps in Lesbos, Greece, and the Flemington and North Melbourne public housing towers lockdown in Melbourne, Australia.

Section Three: Representing the (in)visible

This section focuses on portrayals of domestic space during a pandemic in paintings, portraits, advertisements, virtual corporate worlds and drawings. Regardless of the medium used, most of these presentations do not depict real but, rather, fictional, imagined and constructed spaces which seem to ignore harsh reality and support a longing for a lost normality. Several of these constructed images are the results of clever marketing strategies that aim to benefit commercially from a distressing and life-changing situation. Few examples of this new visual culture attempt to show the overpowering nature of the pandemic and the emotional responses of people who are living in confined spaces, without contact, and experiencing fear and anxiety. These examples redefine the domestic as a space of human and non-human relations, of emotions and behaviours confirming what Baudelaire described: 'What one can see out in the sunlight is always less interesting than what goes on behind a window-pane. In that black and luminous square life lives, life dreams, life suffers' (Baudelaire 1969/1970).

In Chapter 11, titled *Tell don't show: The invisible plague in Dutch seventeenth-century paintings of the domestic interior*, the (potential) visibility of the impact of Covid-19 on the visual culture created during the pandemic is questioned and speculated about by Irene Cieraad. She analyses historical examples of seventeenth-century Dutch paintings from the period of the Plague and identifies a near invisibility of the epidemic. This could be understood as a coping mechanism through which these paintings allowed viewers to keep their dreams of a former normality alive. Cieraad describes the application of a specific iconography which references and evidences the Plague in both public and domestic life, but which conceals the devastating impact of illness, death, existential anxiety and loneliness that accompanied it.

In Chapter 12, titled *Lockdown portraits: Resituating the self*, Inga Bryden investigates notions of familiarity and unfamiliarity concerning domestic spaces in times of crisis. In response to the desertion of public urban space rendered as the uncanny, the confinement to the home, did not only limit the physical environment but the focus and attention to the interior even in the digital extensions to spaces outside of one own home. The domestic became a constant and secure reference point and portraiture, a mode of representation and stabilizing the self within this environment at a moment defined by danger and the unknown. But Bryden shows how these portraits not only have confirmed the stable and known but have rendered the familiar unfamiliar.

In Chapter 13, titled *Fiction: IKEA's saleable living for pandemic life*, the invisibility of the effects of Covid-19 on daily life and society in images is also argued by Rebecca Carrai who investigates the construction of images of domestic life during the pandemic by the furniture retailer IKEA. Building on the challenges created by the long periods of closure of most retail spaces, IKEA successfully expanded its online presence and trade by embracing digital marketing strategies, a variety of social media formats and online advice services. Evidenced by interviews, and with a focus on Italy as a case study, Carrai shows how the construction of persuasive imagery played a vital role in IKEA's success. Through references to domesticity and lifestyles, the retailer portrayed the home as a happy, frictionless and organizable space offering a dream, a hope and a break from a life that was chaotic, unsettling, stressful and decidedly unphotogenic.

In Chapter 14, *Nice white spaces: Race and class in domestic cleaning ads during Covid-19*, Rachele Dini focuses on digital commercial messages, mainly films, which demonstrate how corporations have been capitalizing on fear in this moment of crisis. In her analysis of selected advertisements of cleaning products shared by UK and US media the domestic spaces that she discusses are, she claims, defined by narrow narratives of race, class and gender. Despite ostensibly attending to diversity and inclusion through the choice of the actors used in the films, through the choices of architecture, furniture and decorations the interiors that Dini discusses present an audience that is comfortable, educated and settled. The author concludes that, while cleaning remains the territory predominantly of less educated and under-privileged people, both the United States and the UK remain invested in associating cleanliness and taste with wealth, status and whiteness.

In contrast to the attempts made to render the impact of the pandemic invisible, in Chapter 15, *Uncanny on display. Musée Dom-Ino. A virtual museum of domesticity in lockdown*, Nina Bassoli and Roberto Gigliotti introduce a project, the Musée Dom-Ino, which seeks to translate into images and spaces observations of the behaviours, feelings and perceptions that manifested themselves in domestic spaces during lockdowns. The project at the Free University of Bozen-Bolzano asked students to transform their domestic interiors into exhibition galleries and to stage a show about the house itself. Predictably, the themes that were analysed covered obsessions about security, cleaning, privacy, solitude and control, and, through drawings and installations, the students represented the home as an expression of individual and collective behaviours. The chapter sets out to chart the return of the domestic uncanny in a moment dominated by the media, the omnipresence and pervasiveness of which have radically transformed the relationship between the public and the private realms.

Section Four: Collecting the interior in the era of Covid-19

This section brings together five chapters that deal one way or another with the experience of the domestic interior during lockdown, its representation and curation via various methods and media, and its projection to the world. As Patrick Lee Lucas discusses in Chapter 16, this process of collecting images within the private space of the domestic interior and using them to construct a curated public identity is not new. However, the combination of the extreme experience of the domestic interior during lockdown with the availability of digital means of communication allowed for a unique insight into other people's lives. Wishing to capture this historic moment, galleries and museums launched collecting projects that asked participants to represent in images and text their experiences of their domestic interiors during the pandemic. These collected representations work in two ways: as means that allowed the participants to reflect on their experiences as they happened, and as valuable testimonies for future historians. Further to their personal and historical value, these representations reflect interplays between the intimate and the global, the material and the virtual, the public and the private, and the personal and the collective. They also attest to the construction of complex 'interior-scapes' (Weinthal 2011) that are called to reconcile and accommodate virtual and physical spaces of both performance and intimacy.

Chapter 16, Patrick Lee Lucas's *Changing scenes: Image-making from parlour to screen*, introduces the idea of collecting and curating images within the domestic interior as a means of constructing and projecting a personal and familial identity. It discusses the gradual proliferation of images within the domestic interior from the eighteenth century onwards in the form of prints, decorated chinaware, scenic textiles and wallpapers. He argues that our construction and projection of our identities during the pandemic, through what is presented on online platforms such as Zoom, is only the latest expression of a long-established process.

In Chapter 17, *Shelter in place gallery – Exhibiting contemporary art and creating community in a pandemic*, Eben Haines, Michelle Millar Fisher and Courtney Harris present a miniature gallery sited within a domestic interior to provide artists with both a physical and virtual platform on which to exhibit their work during lockdown. By transposing it into a private, characterful, miniature scale, intimate interior, the dolls' house-scale gallery subverted the norms of exhibiting contemporary art in public, white-cube, full scale or large spaces. Together with its virtual presence on a website platform and Instagram©, the miniature gallery represents both the physical shrinking and virtual expansion of the world and encapsulates the contrasting scales that the domestic interior was called to accommodate during lockdown.

Chapter 18, Stefania Napolitano's *The Domestic Body*, describes and analyses a project set by the Education Team at the MAXXI museum in Rome during the pandemic. To capture the individual narratives of a collective traumatic experience, the project equipped its virtual participants with simple ways of mapping the intensified use of their domestic interiors in lockdown. The entries form a collection of rich material that describes the involuntary and speedy transformation of everyday habits and highlights the material, spatial, social and psychological consequences of the extreme compression of space that people experienced in lockdown.

In Chapter 19, *Interior archipelago-postcards from our islands*, Patrick Macklin, Lois Weinthal, Wen Liang and Alice Huang describe a collaborative collecting project undertaken by three universities – The Glasgow School of Art, UK; Toronto Metropolitan University, Canada; and Tsinghua University, China. The participants were tasked with capturing the heightened sense of interiority that they experienced during lockdown and to represent it succinctly in the format of postcard. The collection of interior views and experiences that resulted from this exercise allowed people in three design communities to gain glimpses of interiors not only in other places and time zones, but also in other phases of the pandemic. Seen as a whole, this record of everyday life during the pandemic asks us to think about how the interplay of the physical and the digital shapes the experience of interiors.

Chapter 20, Danielle Patten's *Stay Home – Rapid response collecting project at the Museum of the Home*, presents a project that reached out to the museum's local community asking them to document how lockdown had reshaped their everyday lives. The project leaders asked for testimonies in the form of texts, photographs, videos, voice recordings and diaries, and the anonymity of entries allowed for candid descriptions of positive and negative experiences that testified to a radical transformation of behaviours and spaces. Together the material creates a picture not only of home life during the pandemic, but also of how neighbourhoods, local communities and digital platforms sprang into action to help people stay connected and feel supported at a troubling time.

References

Baudelaire, C. (1969/1970), 'Windows', in Louise Varèse (trans.), *Paris Spleen*, 85, New York: New Directions.

Weinthal, L. (2011), 'Interior-scapes', in L. A. Brown (ed.), *Feminist Practices: Interdisciplinary Approaches to Women in Architecture*, 139–54, London: Routledge.

SECTION ONE

Homes, health and well-being

1

Live gym classes at home
Lea Daan and broadcast body movement in 1930s Belgium

Selin Geerinckx and Els de Vos

Introduction

The Covid-19 pandemic has forced people worldwide to stay home for long periods. Our homes suddenly had to be adapted to new activities, including work, schoolwork and keeping fit. Alongside government guidelines and 'lockdowns', the lack of space for adequate social distancing and poor ventilation in many venues meant that many gymnasia, dance schools, sports clubs and fitness centres organized online courses for their members to participate in from within their own homes. Domestic interiors were thus temporarily transformed into spaces for maintaining and improving health through physical exercises that were carried out by individual participants yet who were also part of a wider fitness-conscious community. Today's online gymnastics and fitness classes may seem like a new phenomenon but there was a precedent in 1930s Belgium.

Drawing upon archival material and period literature, this chapter focuses on the radio classes taught by the Belgian modern dance and movement pioneer Lea Daan (1906–95) that were transmitted into individual Belgian homes between 1935 and 1940 by the national radio network. It introduces Daan, choreographer, dancer and dance teacher, and considers the ideas and influences behind her classes that were based upon body movements to music, as well as the impact of communications technology on the home.

The classes are discussed from the perspectives of both conception and reception, and how they addressed both the bodies and minds of those who tuned in to them. In addition, it examines the blurring of boundaries between the public sphere of national radio and the private sphere of the individual home and draws out similarities and differences between Daan's classes and online courses during the Covid-19 pandemic. Daan's national radio classes were organized at a time when radio was the only means of live democratic mass-communication technology in Belgium. Established in 1930, the Belgian National Broadcasting Institute (NIR/INR) was an important mass medium for popular education. It regulated the daily schedule of radio programmes available to home listeners during the Great Depression that followed the New York Wall Street Crash in 1929. The population needed reassurance and peace of mind above all. Besides providing politically neutral news reports several times a day, the national broadcasting body tried to fulfil a culturally uplifting, educational function (De Vijlder et al. 1994: 52, 227). There was a strong body culture movement in Europe during the interwar years, and, as part of a wider project of improving national health, well-being and morale during those difficult times, the NIR/INR decided to include a programme run by Daan that delivered a weekly dose of body culture straight into the heart of individual homes that was presented as part of a modern lifestyle. Housewives and others were encouraged to search for a suitable place within their homes and follow the instructions coming over the airwaves.

Daan grew up in Antwerp where she opened a modern dance school in 1931 after studying in Germany with the renowned German choreographer Rudolf von Laban and his pupil Kurt Jooss, and gaining a diploma in dance pedagogy. For the radio corporation, she created a unique physical and pedagogical programme that was conveyed to listeners, preferably in well-ventilated spaces within hearing distance of the radio. The communication between Daan and individual participants was largely through audio means and catalogues with images; there was no mutual visual contact.

Radio as a mass modernizing medium

The economic crisis in Belgium in the 1930s was severe, with blue-collar workers and young workers under the age of twenty suffering the most. Some estimates put the unemployment rate as high as 40 per cent during 1933–4. The labour market shrank dramatically, the working day was reduced and wages fell (De Vijlder et al. 1994: 158–9). The notion of the family wage flourished as greater emphasis was placed on married men as breadwinners and married women were encouraged to leave the workplace to focus on their responsibilities as mothers (De Vijlder et al. 1994: 227). Housewives were regarded as the creators of a *goede en reine thuis* (good and sane home). As a result, more people spent more time in their homes than previously. In the spirit of the rationalist European Modern Movement in architecture and design, especially progressive municipal housing programmes such as that in Frankfurt, Germany (Berendsen and Van Otterloo 2009: 115–38), Belgian housing reformers strived for modern, hygienic, well-ventilated and comfortable homes within a better society (De Caigny 2005: 7; De Vijlder *et al.* 1994: 197–215; Van Caudenberg and Heynen 2004: 23–49). Domestic and personal hygiene, orderliness and tidiness were deemed to be the first steps to a happy family life (De Caigny 2005: 6). The modern arrangement and furnishing of familial domestic spaces contributed to the creation of healthy and happy homes in which both the family's psychological and mental well-being were catered for. These practices were promoted by various progressive sociocultural women's organizations through courses, journals and newspapers, as well as by modern architects, designers, and social and political reformers (De Caigny 2005: 5–6).

Radio emerged as a new type of mass communication during the 1920s, and radio receivers slowly entered the home, bringing new structures to the daily life of listeners. Programme times were verified at the Royal Meteorological Institute (VRT annual reports, 1934) and thus the domestic radio functioned as a clock within the home. In the 1930s the Belgian National Broadcasting Institute, which provided bilingual broadcasts, and cheaper radios, helped broaden the reach of, and democratize, the new medium. The main objective of the national radio was to broadcast classical and contemporary music but programmes to educate women soon followed. Women were seen as a key audience sector, and some women began working as radio reporters. From late 1935, the radio institute ran daily early morning gym classes. Gust de Muynck, director of Flemish language broadcasts and a socialist member of the Belgian Labour Party, had previously hired Daan to train the socialist youth movement choir based on her skills. In order to instruct this group of dance amateurs, she applied the Laban system as a method that enabled her to link body movement to music, voice and expression. This technique became her ticket to the radio gym class.

Daan and body movement

As Thomas Crombez (2008: 56) explains, Belgium was one of the last countries in Western Europe where socio-theatrical mass events for workers (both singing and reciting choirs), as they were held by the Socialist movement in Germany, Russia and then the Netherlands, became popular and were employed not only as ways to strengthen the workers' sense of self-worth, but also as effective disciplining strategies. Interestingly, since Belgium is the only country in Europe where the largest workers' movement is Catholic, the Catholics imported the Socialist mass events such as the 'lay movement choirs'. Lea Daan was one of the young professionals from the budding modern dance scene who made use of the Laban system to train lay movement choirs in Belgium (both socialist and catholic) (Crombez 2008: 58).

As a choreographer and dance pedagogue associated with free expression through body movement in tune with music, Daan both contributed to and benefited from the increasing public interest in body movement to music. Her modern dance school in Antwerp catered for various groups, including children, young adults and schools, and welcomed amateurs as well as professionals. She also gave weekly gym classes in Catholic schools and trained professionals to become body movement teachers, performing dancers or choreographers.

Prior to a three-year classical dance training in Brussels, she took a course with modern dancer Francesca d'Aler at the avant-garde Vocational School for Craftsmanship in Antwerp. In order to specialize further in modern dance, she moved to Germany, a key centre for modern dance, in 1927 to take lessons in Essen, at the Folkwangschule, newly established by Kurt Jooss. Thereafter she trained in Hamburg with Albrecht Knust and in Berlin with Laban in Berlin where in 1931 she earned a diploma authorizing her to teach the Laban system (Demin 1996: 32–3; Vos 2012: 265–6).

Archival images of Daan reveal traces of the impact of the dance theory and techniques of Laban, who was active in the European progressive dance movement and favoured exploring movement in an open landscape, free from the restrictions of enclosed spaces. Daan's preference for a natural outdoor environment was in line with Laban's idea that the body must be liberated from its physical surroundings. Laban's principle of 'free' or absolute dance underpinned Daan's approach to structuring the body in relation to time and space, and this was reflected in her radio classes. Laban's *Choreutics*, a system that comprehends all kinds of bodily, emotional and mental movements (Laban and Ullmann 1976: 8), involved platonic volumes such as the icosahedron (Figure 1.1). The importance of the icosahedron in Daan's classes was twofold; the solid guided the dancers to find the right position in the space and their way in the inner world of emotions. Laban followers believe that the icosahedron provides an elegant framework based on patterns of nature within which dancers could create harmony within their inner space and both they and audiences could enter into a mystical or near mystical space. The solid encourages dancers to make three-dimensional movements and to develop more variations.

FIGURE 1.1 *The Icosohedran in use at the Lea Daan School, 1938, Collection City of Antwerp, Letterenhuis.*

Laban introduced Daan to the importance of the interrelations of dance-sound-word for the expression of the self and the interplay of expressive powers of gesture, song and speech (Maletic 1987: 6). In Daan's article 'Body Culture and Amateur Dance', which appeared in *Vrouwenfront* (*Women's Front*) between 1934 and 1935, she stated that the main goal of amateur dance was not to please the public eye but to enjoy the act of expressing oneself individually within a shared communal feeling enabled by means of the movement choir. She believed that dance would improve the practitioner's physical or mental condition and thus positively affect their life by offering harmony. Such convictions informed her radio gym classes in which she combined music, dance and speech.

Radio gym classes

From 1935 to 1940 Daan and Omer Woestyn, her French-speaking colleague, broadcast live morning gym classes; she broadcast in Flemish. The first classes were broadcast at 7 am on weekdays and weekends. Audience demand led to two live morning classes (6.40 am and 7.40 am) from 8 December 1935 (Het Belang van Limburg, 1935).

FIGURE 1.2 *Lea Daan during a radio class, two female dancers in action, c. 1938, Collection City of Antwerp, Letterenhuis.*

Already popular, home gymnastics was deemed more appropriate for upper- and middle-class women with servants who had more time in which to take up such activities. Some people and newspapers, including the socialist newspaper *Vooruit*, considered such activities redundant for workers' wives, arguing that housekeeping involved similar body movements if carried out in a more conscious manner (Vooruit, 1932). Daan, however, offered more than an ordinary body workout. In order to make her radio classes connect with listeners as directly as possible, she taught a live class, complete with piano accompaniment, in the broadcast studio, with students from her dance school (Figure 1.2). By supervising and correcting the rhythmic body movement of her students *in situ*, she was able to better guide listeners at home. The music set the pace for the home students, helping them vary the speed of their movements without losing the rhythm and making the whole experience more pleasant.

Woestyn versus Daan: Two approaches

Daan and Woestyn had different approaches, as is evident from the brochures for their classes which were for sale *en masse* from the late 1930s in accessible places such as bookshops, newsagents and newsroom at railroad stations. The broadcast institute viewed these publications as instruments for the 'national elevation' of the population. Both brochures featured diagrams and commentaries to aid the home-based students. Daan's 'body movement to music' approach was in stark contrast to that of Woestyn who remained seated in the studio while dictating instruction to the home listeners. The covers for both brochures each feature three human bodies immersed in radio waves (Figure 1.3). That for Daan's classes features a family practising in the open air, with the inviting title 'Who will join us for some gym?', while that for Woestyn's classes features three abstracted forms signifying people within houses represented in an equally abstracted manner. The more conventionally depicted clock can be read as signifying both 'home' and the timing of the classes, suggesting Woestyn attached importance to exact timing.

Daan's brochure covers forty-six routines which, she claimed, 'anyone could do' and explains 'only the most difficult exercises'. Each page presents a single routine with an accompanying description that explains the exercise and its purpose. The exercises aim for a complete body workout: strength, muscular flexibility, endurance, elegance, balance and agility. Attention is given to breathing. The workout considers movements from the inner physical core of the body within the orthogonal planes of a cube. The arms and legs might be positioned in diagonal planes. To a musical beat, circular rotational movements of the arms and legs are executed within the same orthogonal planes, thus providing an organic flow to the exercises. Daan called her classes a remedy

FIGURE 1.3 *Cover for* Wie Turnt er mee ... met het N.I.R? *Radio programme brochure 28, NIR. Courtesy of private collection of Selin Geerinckx.*

to 'the adverse effects of modern life', claiming they would reduce stress, increase muscular flexibility and enhance a sense of well-being, even a sense of spiritual freedom. She was against exercises performed mechanically, emphasizing paying constant attention to the breath in order to acquire a mental and physical flow throughout the whole body.

By contrast, Woestyn mainly focused on individual body parts. His brochure features 116 fragmented body positions and exercises intended to rid the gymnast of any muscular or articular stiffness, lest they cause medical problems such as an arched back or a stiffening of the spine. The second section focuses on the balancing, walking, running and jumping exercises in relation to muscles and bone structure, including the anterior and posterior muscles of the torso.

In short, Woestyn approached the gym classes in a more physiotherapeutic manner than Daan, focusing on body strength and fitness in order to prevent medical problems. Daan's classes were more flow-oriented, paying attention to dance qualities such as agility, balance and elegance, while positing a sound and healthy body as a vehicle to free the mind.

Spaces for home gym

Little is known about how listeners performed the exercises or where they did them. A 1939 image of a radio gymnast in a Woestyn's class provides some insights, notwithstanding it probably being probably staged, at least to some degree. The setting is the living room of an upper-middle-class house, given the mantelpiece and the white pillar in the corner. The listener-gymnast sits on a carpet before a stove while a radio sits on a small table in front of him, as if it is his teacher giving instructions.

No images of Flemish radio listeners in action are known, but a sketch on a business card for Daan's dance school shows a lithe female listener practising before 'an open window' to stimulate breathing during the workout as sunrays shine in. Like Daan, modernist architect Huib Hoste, who admired Daan, considered the windows the lungs of the house. It was already known that fresh air helps breathing but it was not so widely acknowledged as today; indeed, many people smoked inside (Müller, 1930: 2) and dust-generating fireplaces and coal stoves were widely used (van Overbeeke 2001). Daan's recommendations that, if possible, people exercise in the fresh air or near a window helped improve their breathing and enhanced their chances of reaching a mindful body flow.

The mirrors in an image of a German radio gym class drew our attention to the fact that the Belgian radio gym class brochures did not recommend mirrors, nor are they present in the images. In ballet studios mirrors are an indispensable feature that enables dancers to observe their own movements

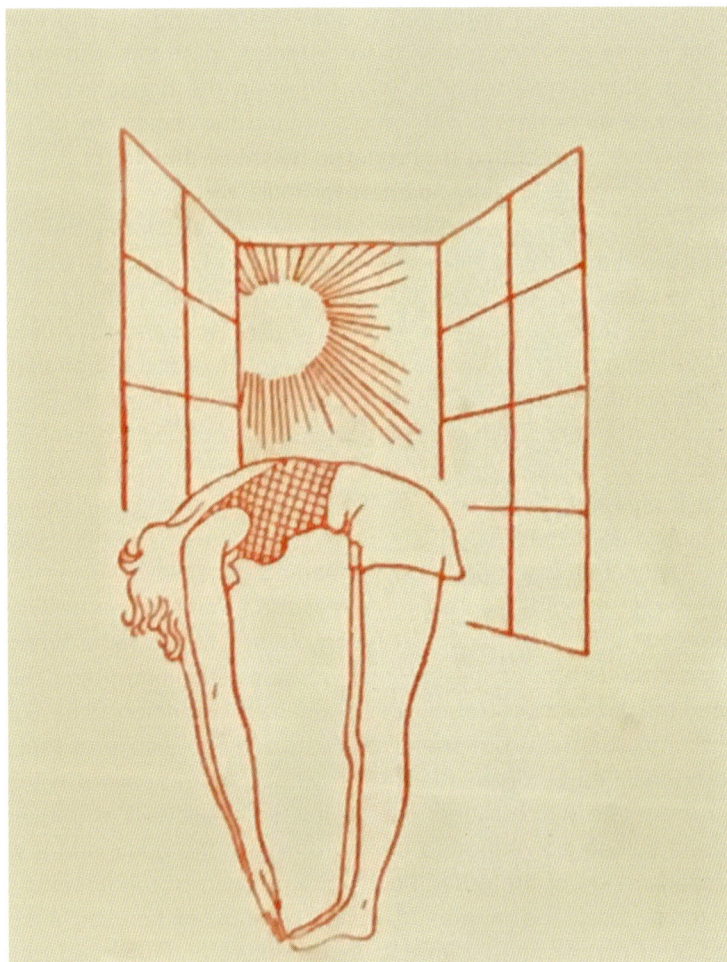

FIGURE 1.4 *Practitioner exercising close to the open window in the sun, no date. Courtesy Archive Lea Daan, Collection City of Antwerp, Letterenhuis.*

and correct them. For Daan, by contrast, it was more important that people did the movements mindfully, irrespective of how they looked.

Conclusion

At a time when many Belgians spent more time at home than previously during the Depression, which restrained their social lives, the National Broadcasting Institute helped regulate the patterns of domestic life through its time schedule while bringing listeners in contact with the outside world.

The Institute was mainly dedicated to the broadcasting of daily news and music, but it also provided a means for listeners to stretch and strengthen their bodies, either individually or with others in the household if they so wished, as well as remotely with others around the region, as part of their daily rituals, thus contributing to the public health of the nation. As a trained and skilled teacher, Daan fully adapted for radio the teaching methods she learned during her training and developed during her career. Her dance, a composed technique of sound-music-word, and use of repeated rhythmic body movements based on geometrical volumes proved well suited to the radio classes, not least because she continued to use live piano accompaniment and her live voice to communicate with both real students in the radio studio (unseen to home students) and the home students (unseen to Daan). Her approach was not dependent on a particular space or special equipment and, albeit from a distance, she was able to encourage a very large group of people to create a pleasant sense of community, belonging and well-being while helping individual listener-students create a feeling of freedom (detached from the material environment) and a sense of spirituality. The technological development from radio to computer, tablet and mobile phone has impacted the experiences of fitness and well-being classes. While radio brought the voices and soundscape of the external world into the home and television introduced the outside world audio-visually, current technologies have created two-way communications between the private and public spheres that further blur the boundaries between them. The 'virtual' room appears within each home; a room into which others can be invited or allowed on request. The camera and screen act as both a mirror reflecting the body, and a window into domestic stage of the other. People staging part of their interior for the camera today recall the nineteenth-century notion of keeping a so-called 'best room' or parlour fitted with the best furniture and intended to receive prestigious visitors. Parts of today's domestic rooms can become decor for the virtual meeting space, arguably distracting participants from the matter at hand. The position of the participants remains ambivalent, as mentally they participate in the virtual activity but physically remain in their domestic spaces. Daan could not see her listeners at home, and neither could they see her nor themselves on a screen, and we end by asking was it precisely this *lack* of surveillance that helped Daan's followers to become fully aware of their daily body movements and more readily focus on their core strength?

List of Abbreviations

NIR	Nationaal Instituut voor de Radio-omroep
INR	Institut National de Radiodiffusion

Acknowledgements

We thank the Hendrik Conscience Heritage Library, the Letterenhuis, the Local History Circle of Maaseik, and the Omroepmuseum for sharing their collections with us. We express special thanks to Rik Nulens for his assistance in data acquisition.

References

Het Belang van Limburg. (1935), December 8, p. 6.
Berendsen, M. and Van Otterloo, A. (2009), 'The "family laboratory": The Contested Kitchen and the Making of the Modern Housewife', in R. Oldenziel and A. De La Bruheze (eds), *Manufacturing Technology: Manufacturing Consumers. The Making of Dutch Consumer Society*, Amsterdam: Aksant, 115–38.
Crombez, T. (2008), 'Liturgy and Mass Spectacle: The Case of Catholic Mass Theatre in Flanders during the Interwar Period', *Performance Research*, 13(3): 55–63.
Daan, L. (1934–1935), 'Lichaamskultuur en Lekendans', *Vrouwenfront*, 1(8): 9–10.
De Caigny, S. (2005), 'Catholicism and the Domestic Sphere: Working-Class Women in Inter-War Flanders', *Home Cultures*, 2(1): 1–24.
Demin, L. (1996), 'In het spoor van Laban', *Etcetera*, 4(55): 31–6.
De Vijlder, A., R. Gobyn, N. Merckx, W. Spriet and H. Verwilst (1994), *De Jaren '30 In België: De Massa In Verleiding*, Brussel: ALSK.
INR (1939), *Radio Gymnastique*. Programme Brochure of the French Series, 29, Brussels: INR Publications.
Laban, R and L. Ullmann (1976), *Choreutics*, 2nd edn, London: MacDonald & Evans.
Leeuwarder Nieuwsblad. (1926), 'Radio en gymnastiek-onderwijs', *Leeuwarder Nieuwsblad*, June 12, 2.
Maletic, V. (1987), *Approaches to Semiotics. Body-space-expression: The Development of Rudolf Laban's Movement and Dance Concepts*, 75, Berlin: Mouton de Gruyter.
Müller, J. P. (1930), *Mijn Systeem voor Vrouwen*, Third print, Amsterdam: n.v. Syffardt's boek- en muziekhandel.
NIR (1938), *Wie turnt er mee ... met het NIR?* Programme Brochure of the Flemish Series, 28, Brussels: NIR Publications.
Van Caudenberg, A. and H. Heynen (2004), 'The Rational Kitchen in the Interwar Period in Belgium: Discourses and Realities', *Home Cultures*, 1(1): 23–49.
Vandenbreeden, J. (2020), Interview in De Modernisten 1: Huib Hoste. TV, VRT. https://www.vrt.be/vrtnu/a-z/de-modernisten/1/de-modernisten-s1a1-huib-hoste/.
van Overbeeke, P. (2001), *Kachels, geisers en fornuizen. Keuzeprocessen en energieverbruik in Nederlandse huishoudens 1920–1975*, Hilversum: Uitgeverij Verloren.
Vos, S. (2012), *Dans in België 1890–1940*, Leuven: Leuven University Press.
Vooruit (1932), 'De weg naar kracht en schoonheid', *Vooruit*, 25 January, 4.

2

Dancing across the threshold

Privacy and the home in the time of Covid-19

Alice T. Friedman

'For Ketty'

Almost two years into the current pandemic, most of us not only know our way around **Zoom©**, the popular video conferencing platform, having used it for lectures, seminars, meetings, 'zoomtails' and chats with friends and family. Some people have become adept at creating and using customized virtual backgrounds, situating themselves in the nave of San Lorenzo in Florence – or wherever else they choose to be – or on an imaginary beach in the tropics, whereas others have gone to great lengths to 'curate' the shapes and colours of objects, books, plants, family photographs and other items displayed on shelves, cabinets or mantelpieces that they deliberately position themselves in front of. Ironically, the worldwide experience of Covid-19, which has taken so much away and wreaked such havoc on our lives, has given the privileged and technologically savvy among us the rare gift of thinking of ourselves in new ways: not only potentially connected to one another through a new medium, but also bifurcated in time and space: working in the posture and dress of our virtual offices from the waist up, while staying at home, in track suits and pyjamas, from the waist down.

And that's only the most obvious way in which our communal sense of time, space and domestic boundaries has changed. Privacy concerns and the potential for unwanted intruders to 'Zoom-bomb' and otherwise enter and disrupt both institutional and private meetings soon came to the fore. These were quickly addressed by the Zoom parent company as were unsanctioned cloud recordings and other threats such as third-party access to personal data. For most users and institutional licensees, the fixes guaranteed by the software company were sufficiently reassuring to lock in continued usage despite myriad other concerns about what it meant to enter into intimate spaces like living rooms, studies and even bedrooms, or worries about the effectiveness of teaching in an online format. As the pandemic dragged on, the benefits of continued productivity and revenue – from customers, clients and tuition-paying students – and the pleasures of experiencing a sense of connection to other people after months of isolation clearly outweighed the potential costs in terms of lost privacy or the added pressures of learning a new technology for communicating and presenting oneself online (Hodge 2021).

Nevertheless, as we know only too well, cyberspace is a strange and sometimes dangerous place – if, indeed, it is a place at all. From chat rooms and online pornography sites, to telehealth consultations and Zoom classrooms, we have become accustomed to thinking of 'virtual reality' as a spatialized imaginary where role-playing, self-invention, deep emotional experiences and intense physical sensations are possible. It is a truism to say that the internet creates a feeling of physical and psychic presence for its users: as one online platform called 'Second Life' claims on its landing page, 'with thousands of virtual experiences and communities, you'll never run out of places to explore and people to meet' (Second Life 2022).

Indeed, through 'Second Life', one's custom-configured avatar can build and furnish houses, buy fashionable clothes or biker gear, change hairstyles or genders, wander through sci-fi landscapes or explore a meticulously recreated Sistine Chapel; it is even possible to 'experience' childbirth remotely – no matter one's 'real' age or sex – or take part in any of the vast range of sexual experiences that its users dream up.

Because of the potential for online anonymity and the availability of tools with which to alter our virtual identities, and despite the obvious drawbacks of IP addresses and other signature markers, we often imagine that we can be or do anything we want in cyberspace, as MIT professor Sherry Turkle has explained in her publications and widely circulated TED talks (Turkle 2022). Though Turkle has long warned of the dangers of such fictive identities and interactions for 'real-life' well-being, the pandemic has shown us that real-time, in-person conversation and emotional connection via the internet are not only possible but also pleasurable, as long as we bear in mind that online and in social media, 'things' of every description, from backgrounds and place-markers to the sounds of voices and the look of faces, are often not what they seem. Clearly, many contradictions remain, not least of all the seemingly limitless capacity of the internet to create opportunities for both total anonymity and also full-on, sense-based recognition of individuals on live communication platforms. It is to my own experience of the latter during the Covid-19 pandemic that I now turn.

I live in the United States, and in April 2020, after a long, scary month spent on my own because of the quarantine requirements of my blended family's staggered arrivals back at my partner's (and her ex's, and their partner's) suburban Boston homes from dorm-rooms and rented apartments once universities and most workplaces around the world abruptly shut down, I discovered that I could continue to take dance classes with two of my favourite Zumba© teachers through online sessions, offered, amazingly enough, for free or for a small donation. Invented in Colombia in 2001, Zumba is an exercise programme that combines fitness and dance routines, using the motivating dance party rhythms of contemporary Latin and World music to get people up and moving. Wildly popular around the world – classes are regularly offered in gyms, village halls and studios all over Europe, in the United States, and even in the Middle East (though it was banned by Muslim clerics in Iran in 2017) – Zumba is easily modified to fit any age or fitness level, making it both manageable and fun as a weekly, or even daily, workout (Erdbrink 2017). Like fitness and dance classes of all kinds, whether in-person or online, it is especially popular with women.

During the pandemic, online Zumba teachers seemed to pop up everywhere, primarily through pre-recorded workouts presented virtually in public parks, on city streets, at dance studios and in gyms. In Zumba classes, each teacher adapts their choreography to fit their own teaching style, and some are more fitness-based and some more dance-based; online, each teacher also configured their own teaching space to suit their preferences for self-presentation or desire for more or less privacy. Many teachers taught classes in their own at-home spaces: some teachers eliminated any traces of private life, removing all furniture and personal items, while others used make-shift dance studios that looked as if the teacher had simply set up a camera in their own living room or bedroom, ushering class members into domestic realms where we would otherwise never go.

Each of the teachers I got to know before Covid-19 hit took a different approach to this challenge. One, named Erin, created a space that was neutral and anonymous, stripped down to bare surfaces except for a large, quilted wall-hanging and, eventually, a wooden platform on the floor suitable for dancing: despite the obvious domestic scale, the fitted carpet and the occasional sighting of a friendly dog wandering through, the room was clearly meant to be read as a blank canvas. The other teacher, named Ketty, took a different approach, creating a studio in her cosy family room, complete with a comfy sofa and glass-topped coffee table, a large wooden bookcase stuffed

FIGURE 2.1 *The living room transformed for Zumba fitness classes.* Photo: Alice T. Friedman.

with books and photo albums, and shelves covered with greeting cards and mementos. Neatly stacked folding chairs propped up in the back corner of the room clearly indicated the regular gatherings and parties that were hosted there. Now the furniture was pushed to the side to make way for a video camera and multiple screens that enabled Ketty to see herself and all of us at once, but the sense of home – and of home as a self-portrait – was always palpable (Figure 2.1).

Erin's online class size ranged from ten to twenty attendees, down from thirty or more when she taught twice a week in person at a local community centre where numbers swelled with drop-ins during the warm months: both online and in person, Erin – a talented dancer and fitness coach – was always welcoming, enthusiastic and friendly, but also careful to maintain a professional distance, consistent with the carefully curated teaching space.

In Ketty's case, on the other hand, I was surprised to discover that a teacher whom I knew from in-person classes that attracted 20–30 people at my gym, now hosted 80–120 online students every morning except Saturdays and sometimes even twice a day. Most of the students were seniors – single women, some couples, occasionally family members and friends – who knew each other from at a class they had attended in person, some for many years, suburban Jewish Community Centre. Now dispersed around the world, they logged on faithfully from California, Cali, Amsterdam or Berlin, and greeted each other by name. The online format seemed to cause the long distances to evaporate. For many, social boundaries disappeared as well. These enormous classes began and ended with a spirited chat among people who appeared

DANCING ACROSS THE THRESHOLD

from the names and faces of the regulars in the little Zoom boxes on screen to be a remarkably diverse, international group. With our wonderful teacher at the centre of the conversation, each class ended with a similarly intimate wrap-up, as though the participants were gathering in person in a hallway or locker room to chat.

More surprising still, given the widely reported 'Zoom fatigue' experienced by so many users during the pandemic, none of these people seems in a hurry to log off. In large part this is due to the infectiously joyful and energetic dancing of our teacher – a vibrant, seemingly ageless, Indonesian-born woman (Figure 2.2), even more at home in front of the camera than she was in the gym – who has the uncanny ability to motivate students, regardless of age, body size or talent, to work their way through jazzy dance routines. Known for her varied playlists, creative choreography and infectious energy, Ketty is a dynamo online, where her qualities as natural performer are enhanced by the

FIGURE 2.2 *Multiple computer screens for teaching. Photo: John W. Rosenfeld.*

camera. Another reason why these classes work so well seems to be the very specificity and personalization of the interior in which they are held. We enter a cosy home filled with memorabilia and signs of social gathering, and we stay to dance and chat; we feel better for the experience. In a time of alienating social distancing, widespread isolation and medicalized fear – of droplets, of strangers, of germs – online dancing is a social and spatial anomaly and a welcome relief.

Indeed, something more unlikely than personal charisma and the unfamiliar experience of private space are also clearly at work here. Thanks to the teacher's example and commitment to diversity – a quick Google© search revealed her to be the long-time advisor for international students at a local university in her 'day job' – Ketty and her 'regulars' drew the rest of us into their circle to create an atmosphere of solidarity and shared fellowship that transcended borders and boundaries. Grandchildren and babies were shown off for the camera and sometimes even danced along with the group, birthdays were celebrated and one woman named Betsy from Miami Beach regularly modelled amazing, designer hats from her extensive collection (Figure 2.3). In these 'spotlighted' sessions, we could see her tidy condo bedroom with its white walls, large mirror, rectangular window and simple cast iron bedstead (often with a colourful handbag slung across the pristine white bedspread), yet it was the glamorous hats, the expert posing of the 'model' and the banter that accompanied the performance that made these moments so vivid, intimate, welcoming and often humorous: like some other class participants, Betsy sometimes also laughingly modelled her latest Zumba-themed T-shirts,

FIGURE 2.3 *Participants on one of many Zoom screens. Photo: Alice T. Friedman.*

many printed with Ketty's name in large letters. We were a group, and the shirts simply stated the obvious.

I was an outsider in this group when I first logged on, and remained, for the most part, a 'lurker' hidden behind the wall of my muted microphone and video camera, yet I found myself both cheered by these classes, and motivated to continue the workouts by the commitment of the group. Here, as at in-person fitness classes, the well-documented power of group exercise to encourage ongoing participation and even to reconfigure social and behavioural attitudes clearly came into play (Phillips and Meyer 2021). Yet the peculiar circumstances of Covid-19 isolation further altered the rules: thanks – and I use the word advisedly – to the pandemic, 'normal' spatial and social boundaries have been redrawn, tightened by social distancing and fear of the 'other' in some in-person instances, yet relaxed or done away with altogether in others – like my Zoom Zumba classes in cyberspace. The extensive legal and cultural protections for personal privacy, particularly in the domestic realm, described by Sarah Igo in *The Known Citizen: A History of Privacy in Modern America* (2018) and by generations of scholars around the world, have been redefined here, opening up private homes to strangers. Will these newly redrawn and frequently crossed boundaries continue once the pandemic is finally over?

For those who study interiors and privacy, current Zoom practices present several challenges. Not only can we observe – albeit on a small and often blurry screen – the physical surroundings of other people's homes, looking around in ways we were never invited to do, but we can also sometimes also observe the activities of those who occupy these spaces in real time. As any classroom teacher using Zoom knows very well, the platform facilitates seeing into students' homes in entirely new ways: this unanticipated and often unwanted intimacy is problematic. The debate about keeping cameras on or turning them off is framed as a pedagogical issue, but it is obviously also a question of privacy and social boundaries. Not surprisingly, private rooms give rise to private behaviours: we see students lying in bed, sprawled out across sofas or fast asleep under their duvets, laptops open and broadcasting the sounds of the class to deaf ears. In one well-known case, a Canadian member of parliament forgot to turn off his camera when he changed from his running-kit to his business suit during a government meeting (Singh 2021). More problematic still, especially in the light of new awareness of sexual harassment in person and online, is the case of the well-respected journalist Jeffrey Toobin, who reportedly didn't realize that he was still logged onto another Zoom meeting when he exposed himself to his girlfriend online, resulting in his termination by *The New Yorker* magazine. 'I made an embarrassingly stupid mistake', Toobin was quoted as saying, 'believing I was off camera'. He apologized to his 'wife, family, friends and co-workers', but the damage was done (Robertson 2020).

Like most online students, most participants in real-time Zumba classes keep their cameras on throughout the session (Figure 2.4) to better engage with the teacher and the other members of the group; about a quarter keep their cameras turned off throughout the class, happy to participate in a way that obviates any question of skill or energy level. Screen names are sometimes shortened or changed, but for the most part, they are not. Indeed, many people don't seem at all self-conscious about what others might be looking at: not their bodies, their dance moves or their homes.

Here the familiar challenge of choosing a fictive, waist-up Zoom background has been replaced by the need to position a wide-angle or mid-range view of a living rooms or bedroom big enough to dance in. Yet apart from an almost universal tidiness and an unmistakable Crate and Barrel or Ikea-styled ambience that marks the private spaces of fellow Zumba students as categorically different from the bedrooms or living rooms of online university students (a factor no doubt of maturity, income and middle-class demographic), these interiors don't appear to be staged with the teacher or other students in mind. Moreover, although the Zoom camera literally opens onto these private interior spaces, there really isn't enough time in the class or detail on the screen to look closely. Most people don't seem to care in any case.

This lack of self-consciousness suggests that no one is looking very closely: but unlike university students, most participants in my online fitness classes log on well before the start of the class session and well before the teacher appears, milling around in their living rooms or kitchens, eating breakfast, checking their phones and generally going about their own private business. It's like watching a movie in which nothing really happens, and

FIGURE 2.4 *Modelling a hat after class. Photo: Alice T. Friedman.*

where the 'soundtrack' is silent since the 'host' controls the sound and unmutes participants when the meeting actually begins. The experience of viewing these dream-like live-action scenarios, arranged in a grid of little boxes on the computer screen, is like watching the anodyne footage of surveillance cameras on public streets and in back alleys. The spaces and the people seem anonymous – until they aren't. Yet here the camera's lens is willingly introduced into the domestic space of the home, calling into question fundamental notions of privacy.

For this reason, taking, or watching, these classes can be strangely disconcerting: despite the fact that many of our fellow students appear not to notice, no one is given permission to look at the private interiors of others, private homes about which many people – interior design specialists and historians in particular – are immensely curious. Nevertheless, as with family, the more we get to know the individuals that we see online, the more quickly the queasy feeling of being an unwitting voyeur with a hidden camera dissipates. Online, the banality of the everyday washes over the individuality of people, behaviours, living rooms, kitchens and even bedrooms, but the more familiar people become, the more their homes become places of emotional connection. As I came to know the people in my Zumba classes, the less I wanted to analyse and the more I wanted to connect. Seeing my familiar classmate in their homes was nothing like the academic surveillance in which interiors specialists are trained.

One day last summer, when Ketty unexpectedly told a tiny handful of students who chatted after class that I was writing about cyberspace and interior design, the conversation turned to good-humoured banter about which of the objects or personal mementos in their homes might 'give them away'. At that moment, I immediately unmuted my camera so that others could see me: instead of being 'outed' as an intruder who pruriently studies strangers' houses while they are unaware, I wanted to be seen as a fellow dancer and maybe even a friend. And the others were clearly ready to share: one young woman quickly walked to the back of her living room and retrieved her small statue of 'Garuda', the powerful eagle-like deity familiar as a national symbol in India and Indonesia, known as a protective figure of strength and purity in Hindu culture. Then Ketty went to her shelf and picked up her own 'Garuda' to show the group, mentioning that it had been a good luck charm during her son's military service. These personal mementos, not ordinarily visible on the Zoom screen, were revealed to me and the others in the same spirit of friendship and generosity that filled the virtual space – physical and emotional – that the group had created.

From the wonderful hats and the colourful handbag on the bed, to the stack of folding chairs, to the highchair next to the dining room table in the home of a younger woman whose toddler makes regular appearances, the private things I have seen on screen have become like the personal details one might encounter when visiting friends, their casual appearance a sign of shared intimacy. The anonymity and distance of the researcher have been replaced by the closeness of the neighbour or fellow traveller, one among many in a community struggling to cope with isolation, fear and loneliness by dancing in the living room. Online, we dance across thresholds and are warmly welcomed into other people's homes as we never would have been before the pandemic. It's almost enough to make me think about turning on my camera more often.

References

Erdbrink, Thomas (2017), 'Iran Bans Zumba, and Its Fans Fume', *New York Times*, 17 June, Section A, 12.

Hodge, Rae (2021), 'Zoom Privacy Risks: Here's What Information Others May Be Able to See from Your Video Chats', *Cnet Tech*, 6 June.

Phillips, J. Allison and Jacob Meyer (2021), 'Group Exercise May Be Even Better for You than Solo Workouts: Here's Why', *The Washington Post*, 21 February.

Robertson, Katie (2020), 'Jeffrey Toobin Is Fired by the *New Yorker*', *New York Times*, 11 November, Section B, 7.

Second Life (2022), https://secondlife.com.

Singh, Namita (2021), 'Politician Accidentally Records Himself Naked and Changing Clothes on Parliamentary Zoom', *The Independent*, 15 April.

Turkle, Sherry (2022), https://sherryturkle.mit.edu/

3

Achieving well-being in simple ways

Cosy, comfortable and contented domestic interiors in interwar Vienna

Michelle Jackson-Beckett

During the Covid-19 pandemic, and particularly during lockdowns, when many people are forced to spend most waking hours at home, the question of healthy and happy living and working spaces continues to be an important design question, particularly in small living spaces. Viennese designers and architects took up many of these same issues nearly a century ago. This chapter explores an emphasis on well-being that developed in interwar Viennese interior design and dwelling culture (*Wohnkultur*), especially in smaller apartments; it also touches upon spatial theories that arose from this concern around the issues of comfort, flexibility, modification and adaptability, and bringing nature indoors. Well-being in this context was often defined by an open-mindedness that advocated for individualized taste and comfort over a set of predetermined style principles (Abel 1894; Czuckza 1926, 1934; *Die Wohnungsreform* 1930–1931; Frank 1928; Zimbler 1926).

Health, hygiene and the home

Issues of health and social welfare dominated the thinking behind Vienna's municipal housing programme in the wake of the death and destruction caused by the First World War and the influenza epidemic (1918–19), when many people faced severe economic hardships, widespread tuberculosis, malnutrition and high mortality rates, especially for infants (Weindling 2009: 82). Housing shortages and the woefully inadequate state of housing for working class residents drove demand for modern plumbing, heating and ventilation (Blau 1999; Schrank and Ekici 2016; Sheard and Power 2017; Turda 2015; Weinert 2017). Fear of disease underpinned the new projects for workers' housing, hospitals and sanatoria, as well as exhibitions related to health and hygiene education (Blau 1999; Grabow and Spreckelmeyer 2014; Kisacky 2017; Topp 1997). In 1925, the first large-scale international exhibition to take place in Vienna after the First World War focused on hygiene, including the display of new municipal apartments as models for hygienic housing (Turda 2015). The exhibition was divided between two subjects, the human body and the domestic household. Taking inspiration from German, British and American discourses on rationalization of the modern household and home economics, it also drew from the eugenics and free body culture (*Freikörperkultur*) movements (Turda 2015; Weinert 2017). Health and hygiene manuals for the home were aimed at women as homemakers and provided advice on nutrition, cooking, cleaning and ventilation (Weindling 2009: 82). The well-being of individuals and families through the provision of new homes more conducive to well-being was a primary concern of many architects and designers, and as efficiency apartments (*Kleinwohnungen*) became more common, demand increased for furnishing and interior design advice.

Many designers in 1920s Vienna, some of whom were still under the influence of nineteenth-century ideals, referenced an increasing embrace of the informal and the casual in dwelling culture (Eisler 1936: 9; Abel 1894: 271). In 1894, Lothar Abel, a leading landscape architect and garden designer in Vienna, published *Das gesunde, behagliche und billige Wohnen* (Healthy, Comfortable and Inexpensive Living). An advice manual for better living, it recommended paying attention to improved hygiene, ventilation, lighting, heating and plumbing, as well as access to green spaces. Abel also tackled the slippery question of defining comfort, cosiness and well-being in the home. Rather than focus on any particular style, form or materials, Abel argued that individualized taste and livability (*Wohnlichkeit*) were the primary factors for optimal cosiness. The desire for domestic interiors that were both artful and comfortable was a key topic in fin-de-siècle Vienna, and by the 1920s and 1930s, it was an increasingly significant thread in a varied discourse about modern living. Abel's 'no rules' approach to individualized comfort and living in the 1890s was taken up again in the interwar years by many Viennese designers and architects (Abel 1894: 271; Frank 1928: 126–7).

New theories of spatial psychology and spatial experience appeared in the late 1920s as part of the new housing reform movement (Long 2001, 2016; Mallgrave and Ikonomou 1994; Poppelreuter 2012; Wild 2015). Although advocates of new spatial theories sought to alleviate the burdens of modern life, they did not challenge gender-normative roles within the home. Indeed, gender inequalities were embedded within the new home economics (*Neue Hauswirtschaft*), with practitioners accepting that responsibility for the general well-being and upkeep of a household, including childcare, lies with women (Goeschl 1932; Grossbies 1930; Hainisch 1932; Lazansky 1928; Mandl 1928; Meyer 1929).

Spatial experience, comfort and well-being

The case studies featured here illustrate how the ideals of spatial experience, comfort and well-being were adapted in smaller-scale apartments through modest additions and modifications, such as multi-purpose furnishings, indoor gardening and houseplants. The definition of well-being at home was linked to personal comfort and cosiness, but those ideals were variable in practice, and not universally tied to a particular style. Some of the suggested space-saving solutions echo those given by twenty-first century interior designers and manufacturers. Indeed, demand for flexible furnishings and houseplants increased rapidly during the Covid-19 pandemic, with plants helping to create a calming and relaxing atmosphere within the home, while also helping with air purification (George 2020; Sullivan 2021).

The Viennese architect-designers Oskar Strnad and Josef Frank were among the most influential figures driving Vienna's new culture of interior design and dwelling culture. In 1922, Strnad, who also worked as a sculptor and set designer, called for a new approach to Viennese interior design and dwelling culture that was focused on flexible spatial art (*Raumkunst*). He argued for a full sensory experience of space, commenting, 'You don't just see space, you feel it with your whole body, you hear and smell it' (Strnad 1922: 323). Furthermore, Strnad advocated furniture and furnishings that were lighter and easier to clean than many of those in common use, as well as flexible spaces that could be put to more varied uses.

Josef Frank's emphasis on comfort in the modern home and spatial experience set him apart from many architects and designers working within the broad umbrella of interwar modernism, especially those in Germany,

Switzerland, the Netherlands and France (Long 2001: 103–28). Many modernists considered a focus on comfort old-fashioned, but Frank embraced the notion of the home as a retreat from the harsh world of work. Indeed, in 1928 he went as far as arguing that 'modern man' whose work was becoming increasingly strenuous and stressful, 'needs a home that is a *great deal more* cosy and comfortable than those of former times, so that he can find focused peace as quickly as possible' (Frank 1928: 126–7, emphasis added). For Frank, the home was 'the absolute opposite of the workplace', a place where the 'eye wants to relax, too, which is why it is best to avoid all those things one would find at the factory, office, etc ...' (Frank 1928: 126–7). Frank distanced himself from the notion of *Gesamtkunstwerk* (total work of art) prevalent among many other modernists. He insisted that the home was *not* a work of art, and did not 'have to be stirring ... which would be the opposite of its true purpose'; indeed, in Frank's opinion, uniformity and plainness fostered restlessness, while ornament and variety promoted 'a sense of calm' (Frank 1928: 126–7).

Whose space? Spatial science, gender and class divides

Given that Vienna was the birthplace of modern psychoanalysis, it is not surprising that applications of psychology to interior design were also often featured in the decorative arts press as a site for rejuvenation and relaxation (Gardner and Stevens 1992; Gombrich 1984). In 1930, *InnenDekoration* published a special issue on psychology and dwelling organized by the engineer and architect Franz Löwitsch, who was influenced by contemporary discourses on psychology and empathy theory (*Einfühlungstheorie*) and in 1928 had published a manifesto defining spatial science in Sigmund Freud's journal of psychoanalysis, *Imago* (Löwitsch 1928: 293–321; Mallgrave and Ikonomou 1994; Poppelreuter 2012).

The 1930 special issue offered different psycho-social viewpoints, from gender roles to sensory experiences, rhythm and stasis, elasticity and a proposal for the foundation of a spatial research institute to implement the discipline of spatial science. Löwitsch argued that bodies react differently in different spaces and under different constraints and stimuli. While not the first to connect architecture with sensory experience, he attempted to draw connections between medical studies of muscle tone and interior space (Löwitsch 1931: 169). 'Every person "suffers" space,' he argued, 'experiences it in confinement, in unrest and cramps, or in relaxation, resolution, and freedom: everyone experiences the living room, the festival hall, the cathedral, the great outdoors in a different way' (Löwitsch 1931: 169). Löwitsch believed that a systematic view of what he termed *Raumwert*, or spatial value, could help one understand the varied and multi-layered experiences of space through form and feeling. He defined spatial experience as 'a total phenomenon of the soul, which reaches into the deepest layers of the unconscious, is infinite, and therefore difficult to access by language [...] The increasing interest in deep psychology – psychoanalysis – is parallel to *our growing spatial consciousness*, to the increasing importance of the spatial arts, and to the interest in an emerging spatial science' (Löwitsch 1932: 385). Löwitsch further defined spatial science as the systematic measurement of responses to stimuli in a particular environment, that is, a room's spatial value – the 'sensations of colours, light and dark, warm and cold, airy and dull; narrowness and width, height and depth, openness and closedness ...' (Löwitsch 1932: 385).

The proposal for creating a spatial research institute included consideration of rooms of different sizes, design, proportion and storage, with varied sizes of windows, doors and furnishings, as well as a range of light and colour effects, temperature, ventilation, humidity and acoustics (Löwitsch 1930: 325). The rooms were to be modelled after small-scale apartments, offices, schools and factory spaces to assess the range of emotional responses to different working and living environments (Löwitsch 1930: 325). Proposed studies were to be set up in order to identify feelings of well-being together with attention span and concentration. Measurements would include study of the subject's breathing, pulse and muscle contractions, as well as motor reactions, sense of direction, rhythm and whether the subject felt inhibition or relief in a given space (Löwitsch 1930: 325). This research institute never came to fruition, and Löwitsch's theories remained abstract and idealized.

While Löwitsch's ideas aimed to centre diverse individual experience, rather than an overarching architectural vision, his ideas nevertheless remained disconnected from social roles and biases that influence well-being, particularly the gender divide. Löwitsch's theories passed over the discourse on home economics and household management, as well as the everyday realities of housekeeping and the disproportionate burden of domestic labour placed on women. The double burden of women engaged in labour outside as well as inside the home could become a triple or quadruple burden when considering the frequent need to care for children and family members with disabilities or illnesses. Working-class women employed outside the home struggled to manage both spheres; few could afford the new appliances tantalizingly marketed as labour- and time-saving products (Hagemann 1996: 330). The burn-out situation for women was dire enough that the gynaecologist and sanatorium physician Nelly Stern advised working Viennese women in 1930 that to truly feel refreshed from the stressors of daily life, family care and professional responsibilities, women would need to take longer and longer vacations – 'an ordinary vacation would not be sufficient in most cases' (Stern 1930: 32).

More practical examples of housing and interior design assistance were tied to Red Vienna's social democratic era (1918–34), when the Austrian Association for Housing Reform and Housing Hygiene (founded 1929) organized a non-profit interior design and housing advisory bureau known as BEST (an acronym for the Advice Bureau for Interior Design and Housing Hygiene of the Austrian Association for Housing Reform). Located in the massive Karl-Marx-Hof municipal housing complex, BEST staged free exhibitions of model interiors and furnishings and offered lectures, a library and individual consultations with experts, including Frank and other architect-designers such as Ernst Lichtblau, Liane Zimbler and Walter Sobotka (Jackson-Beckett 2022). Public lecture topics focused on the history of modern dwellings, interior design for older apartments, arranging home furnishings in new municipal housing, the use of textiles for insulation and sound dampening, modern kitchen organization and apartment cleaning techniques (*Die Wohnungsreform* 1930). The journalist and critic Else Hofmann contributed a lecture on the use of old furniture in modern interiors, and artist, designer and pedagogue Friedl Dicker-Brandeis lectured on modern uses of colour in apartment decoration (*Die Wohnungsreform* 1930).

Anecdotes about the design advice provided to anonymous visitors (usually women) often dealt with spatial issues in small apartments, such as suggesting the simple rearrangement of existing furniture to solve quarrels between younger children or noise problems that arose from household sewing machines, cleaning and cooking, and the need for quiet work spaces for children to complete their school work (*Die Wohnungsreform* 1931). The goal of BEST was to support working-class people in finding individualized solutions for efficient, clean and comfortable interior design and furnishings at low or no cost (*Die Wohnungsreform* 1930).

Cultivating well-being in confined spaces

A frequently asked question at BEST was how to organize and furnish a small-scale or single-room apartment to foster a happy and healthy life (*Die Wohnungsreform* 1931). Many Viennese architects and interior designers sought to promote well-being in the home, even in the smallest apartments and single rooms through the flexible use of space, adaptable furniture, larger windows to let in light, along with window boxes, indoor plants and terraria. Access to green space was seen as central to well-being, and an increasing number of designers found ways to incorporate calming features like cleverly placed indoor houseplant walls. Lauded for being an expert in the reconfiguration of small spaces with minimal structural intervention, architect and painter Fritz Gross showed a single-room apartment in the exhibition *Wiener Raumkünstler* (Viennese Spatial Artists, or Viennese Interior Artists, 1929–1930) at the Österreichische Museum für Kunst und Industrie (Austrian Museum of Art and Industry) (Eisler 1930: 78–99; Sonne 1932: 30). Single-room apartments designed by Lichtblau and Gross featured various ways of breaking up space, from privacy curtains and textiles, and fold out-desks and beds to simple shelving used for an in-door plant wall. These modest designs

FIGURE 3.1 *Was in Wien Modern ist? Die wohlangewandte Ecke (What is modern in Vienna. Modern Spatial Art: The Well-Used Corner)*, Wiener Bilder, 7 September 1930. ANNO/ Österreichische Nationalbibliothek. Public domain.

FIGURE 3.2 Fritz Gross, *"Einwohnraum"* (A single multi-use room for living, dining, working and sleeping). InnenDekoration *(January 1929)*. Universitätsbibliothek Heidelberg. Public domain.

were intended to help inhabitants to quickly change the atmosphere and/or expand the functions of a room with minimal effort.

To improve the well-being of city dwellers without access to a private garden or proximity to a public park, Gross incorporated terrarium walls into his designs and advocated houseplants for the inner windowsill space between double-glazed casement windows that were common in older Viennese apartment houses. Similarly, and with a view to keeping costs low, architect-designer Ernst Plischke showed how a window garden could be reconfigured at little cost in a rental apartment (Plischke 1934: 117). Zimbler experimented with low-cost plant walls in order to break up interior space and introduce an element of gardening into small city apartments. Home advice and interior designers at this time, like today, advocated consumers to keep houseplants for purifying the air (Moxon 2012: 50; Sparke 2020: 163–79). A long-running column, 'House and Doctor' in *Das interessante Blatt*, the weekly supplement to the Viennese newspaper *Wiener Bilder*, advised readers to select houseplants like quick-growing vines and creepers for their air-filtering qualities, as well as for the joy of having a green home in the depths of winter (*Das interessante Blatt* 1926). Personal comfort and domestic cosiness were directly connected to a healthy dose of indoor greenery, where the 'frequent spraying of the plants, which is absolutely necessary for them to thrive, also contributes greatly to refreshing the mind and body of the inhabitants of the house' (*Das interessante Blatt* 1926).

Zimbler wrote in 1926 that 'it is not a question of means alone that the dwelling becomes a cosy, comfortable home, corresponding to the personality of its inhabitants. On the contrary, this ideal goal can often be

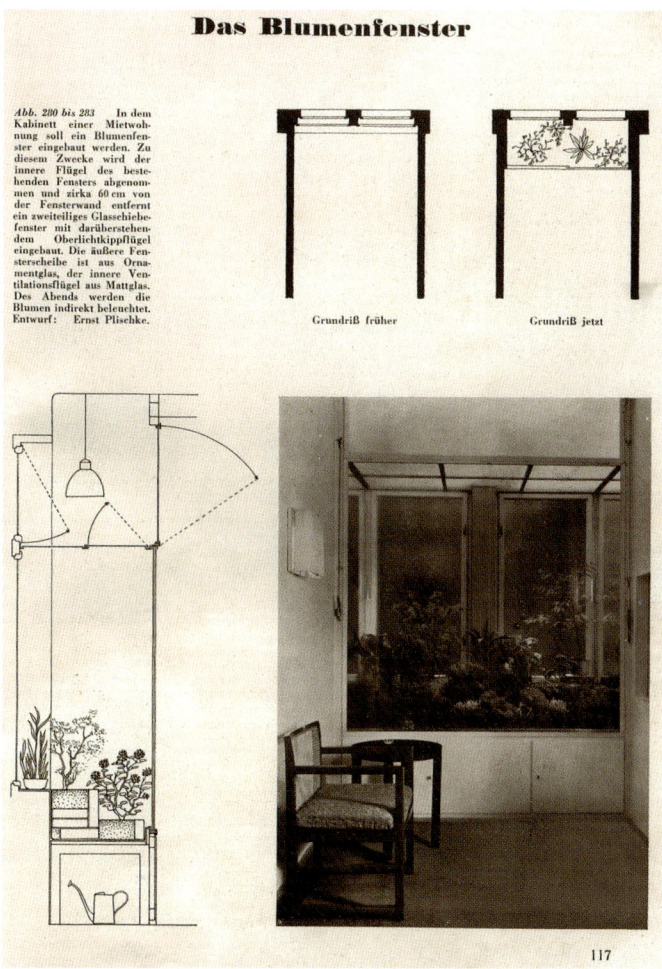

FIGURE 3.3 *Ernst Plischke, "Das Blumenfenster" (design for a windowsill garden), Profil: Monatsschrift für bildende Kunst (April 1934). ANNO/Österreichische Nationalbibliothek. Public domain.*

FIGURE 3.4 *Liane Zimbler, 'Trennungswand in der Diele' (Partition wall in the hallway of an apartment).* InnenDekoration *(August 1931).* Universitätsbibliothek Heidelberg. Public domain.

achieved in simple ways ...' (Zimbler 1926: 41). This emphasis on the simple approach is perhaps the best summation of Viennese ideas about well-being, a comfortable and cosy home and how it could be achieved through modest adaptations, even of rental apartments. Today such ideas ring familiar with many people living in small apartments in cities across the world. As the need to reconsider and reconfigure confined living and working spaces during the Covid-19 pandemic continues, I hope that the Viennese examples presented here provide some useful insights into design for well-being in small homes, both during the pandemic and after.

References

Abel, L. (1894), *Das gesunde, behagliche und billige Wohnen*, Vienna: A. Hartleben.
Blau, E. (1999), *The Architecture of Red Vienna: 1919–1934*, Cambridge, MA: MIT Press.
Bojankin, T, C. Long, and I. Meder, (eds) (2013), *Josef Frank Writings, Vols 1 and 2*, Vienna: Metro.
Czuczka, F. (1926), *Wie richte ich meine Wohnung ein?* Vienna: Steyrermühl.
Czuczka, F. (1934), *Aus alt mach' Neu! Umbau alter Möbel und Umstellen*, Vienna: Steyrermühl.
Die Beratungsstelle für Inneneinrichtung und Wohnungshygiene des Österreichischen Verbandes für Wohnungsreform. (1930), 'Mitteilungen der BEST', *Die Wohnungsreform*, 1(10).
Die Wohnungsreform: Offizielles Organ des österreichischen Verbandes für Wohnungsreform (1930).
Eisler, M. (1930), 'Neue Wiener Innenräume', *Moderne Bauformen*: 78–99.
Eisler, M. (1936), *Oskar Strnad*, Vienna: Gerlach & Wiedling.
Gardner, S. and G. Stevens (1992), *Red Vienna and the Golden Age of Psychology, 1918–1938*, New York: Praeger.
George, C. (2020), 'Why Houseplants Make All the Difference in Self-Isolation', *Vogue Online*, 27 March. https://www.vogue.com/article/caring-for-indoor-houseplants. Accessed 1 September 2021.
Goeschl, A. (1932), *1000 Tricks für den Haushalt*, Vienna: Albrecht-Dürer-Verlag.
Gombrich, E. H. (1984), 'Art History and Psychology in Vienna Fifty Years Ago', *Art Journal*, 44(2): 162–4.
Grabow, S. and K. Spreckelmeyer, (eds) (2014), *The Architecture of Use: Aesthetics and Function in Architectural Design,* London: Routledge.
Grossbies, M. (1930), *Lehrbuch der Haushaltungskunde*, Vienna: Österr. Bundesverlag.
Hagemann, K. (1996), 'Of "Old" and "New" Housewives: Everyday Housework and the Limits of Household Rationalization in the Urban Working-Class Milieu of the Weimar Republic', *International Review of Social History*, 41: 305–30.
Hainisch, M. (1932), *Das Buch des Hauses,* Vienna: Zentraleuropäischen Verlags- und Werbe-Gesellschaft.
Jackson-Beckett, M. (2022), 'Who Knows BEST: Gendered Views of Interwar Design Reform and Wiener Wohnkultur,' in Megan Brandow-Faller and Laura Morowitz (eds), *Erasures and Eradications in Modern Viennese Art, Architecture and Design*, New York: Routledge.
Kisacky, J. (2017), *Rise of the Modern Hospital: An Architectural History of Health and Healing, 1870–1940*, Pittsburgh: Univ. of Pittsburgh Press.
Lazansky, L. (1928), *Der praktische Haushalt*, Vienna: Schwarz-Verlag.
Long, C. (1997), 'Wiener Wohnkultur: Interior Design in Vienna, 1910–1938', *Studies in the Decorative Arts,* 5(1): 29–51.
Long, C. (2001), *Josef Frank: Life and Work*, Chicago: Univ. of Chicago Press.
Long, C. (2016), *The New Space: Movement and Experience in Viennese Modern Architecture,* New Haven/London: Yale Univ. Press.
Löwitsch, F. (1928), 'Raumempfinden und moderne Baukunst', *Imago: Zeitschrift für Anwendung der Psychoanalyse auf die Geisteswissenschaften*, 14(2–3): 293–321.

Löwitsch, F. (1930), 'Beitrag zur Raumwissenschaft (III. Teil)', *InnenDekoration*, 41(8): 325.
Löwitsch, F. (1931), 'Raum und Muskelspannung. Beitrag zur Raum-Wissenschaft', *InnenDekoration*, 42: 169.
Löwitsch, F. (1932), 'Raumwerte und Raumspannung. Ein Beitrag zur Raumwissenschaft', *InnenDekoration*, 43: 385–7.
Mallgrave, H. F. and E. Ikonomou (1994), *Empathy, Form and Space: Problems in German Aesthetics, 1873–93*, New Haven/London: Yale Univ. Press.
Mandl, M. M. (1928), *Das Heim von Heute*, Vienna/Leipzig: Schneider.
Meyer, E. (1929), *Der neue Haushalt*, Stuttgart: Franckh'sche Verlag.
Moxon, S. (2012), *Sustainability in Interior Design*, London: Laurence King.
Plischke, E. (1934), 'Das Blumenfenster', *Profil*, 2(4): 117.
Poppelreuter, T. (2012), '"Sensation of Space and Modern Architecture": A Psychology of Architecture by Franz Löwitsch', *The Journal of Architecture*, 17(2): 251–72.
Schrank, S. and D. Ekici (eds) (2016), *Healing Spaces, Modern Architecture, and the Body*, London: Routledge.
Sheard, S. and H. Power (eds) (2000), *Body and City: Histories of Urban Public Health*, London: Routledge.
Sonne, A. (1932), 'Umgestaltete Mietwohnungen: Neue Arbeiten von Architekt Fritz Gross–Wien', *InnenDekoration*, 43: 235.
Sparke, P. (2020), *Nature Inside: Plants and Flowers in the Modern Interior*, New Haven/London: Yale Univ. Press.
Stern, N. (1930), 'Die berufstätige Frau und die Franzensbader Kur', *Die Frau und Mutter*: 32.
Strnad, O. (1922), 'Neue Wege in der Wohnraum-Einrichtung', *InnenDekoration*, 32: 323–8.
Sullivan, E. (2021), 'Covid Lockdowns Turned Buying Plants into the Next Big Pandemic Trend – For Good', *NBC News*, 30 January. https://www.nbcnews.com/think/opinion/covid-lockdowns-turned-buying-plants-next-big-pandemic-trend-good-ncna1256223. Accessed 1 September 2021.
Thraenhart, s.n. (1926), 'Landluft in unserer Wohnung', *Das interessante Blatt*, 18 March.
Topp, L. (1997), 'An Architecture for Modern Nerves: Josef Hoffmann's Purkersdorf Sanatorium,' *Journal of the Society of Architectural Historians*, 56(4): 414–37.
Turda, M., ed. (2015), *The History of East-Central European Eugenics, 1900–1945: Sources and Commentaries*, London: Bloomsbury.
Weindling, P. (2009), 'A City Regenerated: Eugenics, Race, and Welfare in Interwar Vienna,' in Deborah Holmes and Lisa Silverman (eds), *Interwar Vienna: Culture Between Tradition and Modernity*, Rochester, NY: Boydell & Brewer, 81–113.
Weinert, S. (2017), *Der Körper im Blick: Gesundheitsausstellungen vom späten Kaiserreich bis zum Nationalsozialismus*, Berlin: De Gruyter.
Wild, M. (2015), *Das Umfeld des Menschen: die raumwissenschaftlichen Schriften von Franz Löwitsch*, Saarbrücken: Akademikerverlag.
Zimbler, L. (1926), 'Die moderne Wohnung', *Moderne Welt*, 7(20): 41.

4

The quest for health and well-being in Japanese homes from late nineteenth century to Covid-19

Izumi Kuroishi

The Covid-19 pandemic has caused deep scars in societies across the globe, revealing the extent of many societal problems, including those related to housing, hygiene and well-being. While the official emphasis in Japan has been on the impact of the pandemic on the economy and public health, it has accentuated problems related to Japanese dwellings that, within the urban context at least, largely derive from late nineteenth- and twentieth-century processes of modernization and the increasing focus on consumption related to homes and their interiors since the end of the Second World War. Most people in Japanese cities live in small homes, and space has been at a premium during the pandemic. Faced with housing that has not met their needs during the pandemic, as elsewhere, people have been converting storage areas into workspaces, dividing rooms with furniture or curtains for greater privacy, and even renting workspace outside of the home. In this chapter, I have drawn upon the notion that such acts can be framed as forms of 're-embedding' (to use Anthony Giddens' terminology); the obverse of 'de-embedding', a situation in which people are separated from their local historical and cultural backgrounds and compelled to adapt to standardized living spaces developed according to specialized professional knowledge and broader normative value systems (Giddens 1990: 21–9). I argue that problems with Japan's contemporary housing, as revealed by the pandemic, derive from this 'de-embedding', and that those who try to change their homes and interiors by remodelling their homes are participating in 're-embedding'.

The chapter falls into two parts. In the first I draw upon two studies that I was involved with. They sought to identify and understand problems experienced by particular groups of people in relation to the spaces in which they lived during the pandemic, as part of a wider commentary on issues of health and well-being in the home raised by this period. With these issues in mind, the second part offers a short critical commentary on some key ideas and past practices that I consider either helped or worked against providing healthy, hygienic homes conducive to well-being. I do so in order that readers can better understand these ideas and practices in and of their own right and as pointers to ideas and practices that might, in small or larger ways, re-invigorate discussions about the best types of homes and interiors needed in Japan during periods of pandemic and endemic.

Housing, health and well-being: Japan early 2020–early 2022

Together with twenty-four students at the School of Cultural and Creative Studies at Aoyamagakuin University, I conducted a study based upon participatory fieldwork in residential and neighbourhood spaces around Tokyo from January 2020 to July 2020. We compared the results with those generated by a survey of eight high-school students from Yamagata Prefecture. The method used in the first study was based on the phenomenological surveys conducted by Wajiro Kon and his colleagues after the Great Kanto Earthquake in 1923 (Kon 1986). In addition, from September to December 2020, we issued several questionnaires that involved some sketching to 240 students living in another area of Tokyo, about life experiences during the pandemic. These studies led to my proposing that the Japanese Society of Lifeology (established 1972 to encourage scholarly research among folklorists, sociologists, architects and home economists) establish a research committee on Covid-19. This resulted in a two-month workshop in early 2021 that explored lifestyle and social conditions during the pandemic, the findings of which inform the following commentary on the past two years of pandemic in Japan.

The early months of the pandemic in Japan were marked by public health advice announcements from the national government, especially in relation to infection control. These included track and trace, wearing masks, working from home, floor markings to demarcate space and hand sanitizers. Despite intense pressure on the track and trace system and a serious shortage of hospital beds, the government did not change any laws or introduce mandatory lockdowns on the grounds that it was unfamiliar to the national character. By December 2021, the number of infections and deaths per percentage of population were far fewer than in the United States and the UK, and the mortality rate was also comparatively low (Fujitsu Soken Report 2021) largely due to long-established patterns in Japan of close adherence to governmental instructions and widespread acceptance of face masks and hand washing. Space was a key issue. A 2019 Japanese housing survey, which compared dwelling sizes internationally, demonstrated that the average Japanese home is larger than the average UK home and almost the same as for France and Germany but that Japanese rental homes are much smaller on average than non-rental (Ministry of Land, Infrastructure, Transport and Tourism 2019). Rental housing accounts for more than forty-four per cent of all housing in urban areas, with an average size of 46 square metres compared to 68 square metres in the UK and 70 square metres or more in Germany and France (Ministry of Land, Infrastructure, Transport and Tourism 2019). In short, Japanese rental dwellings are small by international standards. Much of this type of housing was designed for childless, commuting, urban workers. The same survey revealed that the level of satisfaction with housing in Japan was as low as twenty-six per cent (compared to Germany's fifty-four per cent) with insufficient size and facilities, inflexible floor plans and age-related deterioration of housing stock cited as key issues. Thus, before the pandemic began, there were major problems with rented apartments in urban housing complexes, especially in relation to interior spaces.

Uneven hardships and housing

The Society of Lifeology survey revealed that one of the serious issues caused by the pandemic was people unable to pay their rent, because of losing jobs or dependence upon unstable incomes from part-time or temporary jobs. Other spaces usually open for use, such as internet cafes, were closed, leaving many more people sleeping on the streets. Rising homelessness highlighted housing welfare problems and organizations supporting homeless people called for housing to be considered a basic human right. In efforts to help themselves adjust to fewer opportunities for human contact and juggle new working-at-home conditions with family life in cramped domestic spaces, people made efforts to change their interiors, especially when two parents or adults were working online at home. Examples range from greater sharing, especially of quiet spaces, to greater fluidity in terms of 'private' and 'public' space within the home. In a survey, fifty-five per cent of teleworkers reported that lack of appropriate working space and working in living-dining rooms, while forty per cent said that they would like a house with more rooms, and twenty-seven per cent that they would like a larger living room. About the impact of the pandemic on their lifestyle, seventy per cent commented that, having had more time with family than before, they would like to focus more on their private life than career in the future (Ministry of Land, Infrastructure, Transport and Tourism 2020). For those who could afford them, home interior improvements undertaken ranged from sound insulation and air conditioning systems to independent workspaces. A survey of students about their single live/work environments revealed that many were confined to their rooms and that their living centred around their desks. Some claimed that their daytimes and night times came to be reversed (interview with students in my class, October 2021).

The pressures of living in a cramped space for twenty-four hours a day proved too much for some people, and domestic violence cases (mostly against women) increased one point six times over in comparison to pre-pandemic rates (Nihon Keizai 2021). While some people were able to create more private spaces within their homes, it was more difficult in the very small apartments found in Japanese cities. Furthermore, it was also people living in such apartments who missed out most on the well-being effects of connecting with open green spaces and the natural environment. Many elderly people continued to be cared for in family homes but limited access to specialist care facilities meant that, sadly, some were unable to receive appropriate end-of-life care. Lack of school lunches meant that many children were not fed as well, and those in the poorest families often went hungry. Japan was not alone in much of this but the double- and multiple-disadvantaging of the most vulnerable during the pandemic needs to be acknowledged. When the fifth wave of infection spread across Japan in the first half of 2021, lack of sufficient hospital beds and lack of space to isolate infectious people within family homes meant that more than 130,000 people with Covid-19 were nursed at home, thus adding another function to certain rooms in the domestic interior, and resulting in many more people dying than necessary.

Looking back: From well-being and Confucian thought to 'hygienic homes'

Recognition of the serious threat posed to national health by rapidly spreading infectious diseases was a catalyst for change in Japan in the second half of the nineteenth century, as was the broader movement to modernize the nation (Kitazawa 2000). Housing and hygienic living were interlinked thereafter whereas previously healthy housing was regarded as part of a holistic way of life, as in Neo-Confucianist philosopher Kaibara Ekiken's 1716 *Youjou-kun* (*Youjou theory*). Based on Confucian thought, it advocates maintaining physical and mental health by emphasizing the concept of qi (Ki) and aims at living a long and happy life and keeping body and soul in a comfortable state without striving for perfection in everything (Anno 2015; Kaibara 2021). According to Ekiken Kaibara, dwellings should be clean, well ventilated, moderately bright, simple and facing south for peace of mind, while floors should be raised to prevent drafts and avoid moisture because dampness could cause disease (Kaibara 2021).

The extent to which cholera had established itself in Japan before the 'opening up' of the country to the West in 1853 is not clear but it was widespread during the second half of the century. Cholera's heavy death toll was instrumental in the Meiji government establishing the Hygiene Bureau in 1876 to reduce serious disease and publicize the model of the hygienic and efficient modern home, complete with rationally planned interior layouts (Miyazaki and Aoki 1994). In the 1880s, with cholera and smallpox epidemics, and tuberculosis infections rising, official discussions drew heavily from

FIGURE 4.1 *Japanese historical dwelling depicted in 'View of dwelling from garden, Tokio' in Edward S. Morse's* Japanese House and their Surroundings *(1886). Edward S. Morse.*

Western medicine and housing reform practices that included improving location, ventilation, lighting, heating, sleeping quarters, kitchens, toilets and sewers. This is not to say that previous Japanese home were unhygienic. Until then, childbirth and medical treatments were carried out within the home and therefore domestic management advice included hygiene, medical treatments, nursing, childbirth, care of children and the elderly, disease control and methods of reducing humidity and dust, as well as etiquette, and budgeting (Figure 4.1).

In the early twentieth century, however, hygiene education became institutionalized along lines associated with Western ideas of enlightened thought and social reform. In 1916 Sumi Oe, educator and domestic economy specialist, introduced ideas and practices associated with British domestic hygiene reforms related to kitchens and toilets and argued for the systematized teaching of hygiene within the emerging field of domestic science (Susaki 2017). The 1916 cholera epidemic led to the founding of The League for the Improvement of Living and, along with private organizations, the government promoted Western-style housing and lifestyles. Attention to hygiene intensified when the 'Spanish Flu' (1918–19) reached Japan and regular hand washing, curfews and mask wearing were introduced (Kitazawa 2000). This led to the popularization of the 'Cultural Lifestyle' in which tatami rooms were abandoned in favour of chairs which elevated the body from the floor, and kitchens and bathrooms modernized (Nakajima 1974).

An important influence in the 1920s came from architect and environmental engineer Koji Fujii whose books, teaching and practice championed integrating Western and Japanese technologies and tastes. His *The Japanese Dwelling-House* (1928) argued for and illustrated means of achieving dwellings appropriate to local climates, temperatures and humidity levels and designed with hygiene, fresh clean air, abundant light and the reduction of air pollution in mind. Top prize in the 1929 *Healthy House* competition (Fujii was a judge) was a Japanese-style tatami and wooden-floored timber house with garden. Its Western-style interior featured chairs and desks, a family room, as well as separate child's room, dining room, living room and study facing to the south, a veranda, two adjacent multi-purpose Japanese-style tatami-floored rooms, and a garden (Figure 4.2). The kitchen, bath, toilet and entrance are located on the north side of the house, and the space emphasizes effective natural ventilation for each season by utilizing the transoms, veranda and flexible space by the tatami room in line with Japanese traditions of houses being open and easy to clean with decent ventilation, lighting and humidity levels (Osaka Mainichi 1930). Despite such efforts to fuse what Fujii and others considered the best of both worlds, the embrace of Japanese traditions remained strong (Anno 2015).

QUEST FOR HEALTH AND WELL-BEING IN JAPANESE HOMES

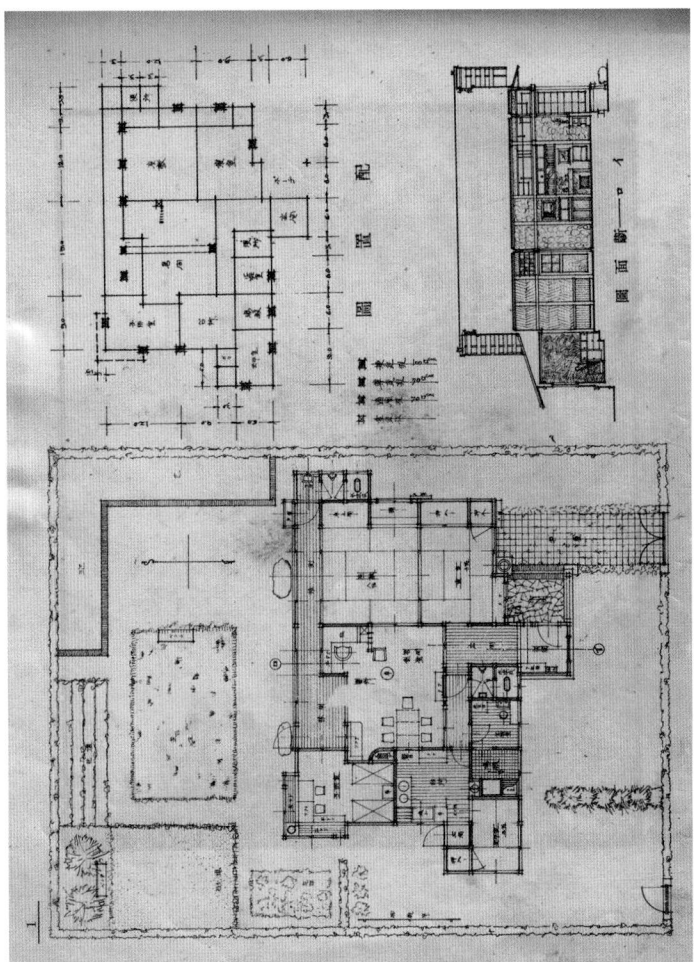

FIGURE 4.2 *Plan of the first prize design, Healthy Housing Competition, organized by Osaka Mainichi Newspaper, 1930. Osaka Mainichi Newspaper.*

Sanitation and public housing planning

In the 1930s, Japan underwent rapid industrial and military expansion, and the Ministry of the Interior's Social Affairs Bureau embarked upon the large-scale provision of public housing for workers. In 1941, in cooperation with the Dojun-kai Foundation, a housing research and design body established after the Great Kanto Earthquake of 1923, and its successor the Nihon Jutaku Eidan, Wajiro Kon, a pioneer researcher into the 'everyday space' of ordinary people in rural areas and advocate of improving low-income housing, led a survey of farming and fishing villages. The resulting report (1941) on housing improvements recommended conventional floor plans that reflected the natural environment, industrial efficiency within the home and a close relationship to the local community (Kuroishi 1998). Uzo Nishiyama, a Japanese architectural engineer and member of Nihon Jutaku Eidan, was a major figure among those who argued that urban workers' tenements should be recognized as the basis for 'people's housing' in the future. Drawing upon the German Alexander Klein's 'functional space theory' that favoured minimal spatial arrangement that closed distances between different parts of the interior, and being

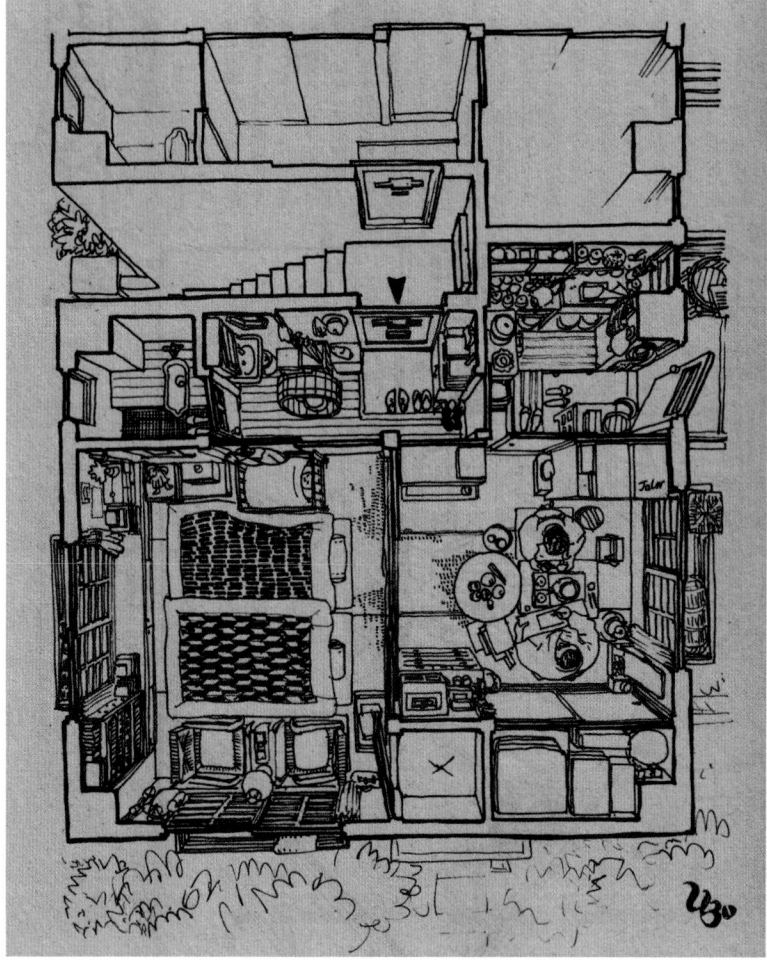

FIGURE 4.3 *Uzo Nishiyama's axonometric sketch of the interior of his small dwelling designed by Dojunkai in the 1930s. Courtesy Nishiyama Bunko Archive.*

based on his own experience, he later proposed a floor plan based on food-sleep separation, which focused on the functions of meals and bedrooms in a 'minimum dwelling' that challenged conventions of private and shared space (Nishiyama 1981) (Figure 4.3). Nishiyama also rejected conventional expectations of interior design, dismissing as unhygienic, wasteful and irrational the main elements of traditional Japanese interiors, from the multi-functional and variable spaces associated with earthen floors and verandas to tatami mats, and sliding partitions. Rooted in ideas of scientific progressivism, frugality and paternalism (Otsuki 2021), this model of densely packed small housing units for urban labourers with nuclear families, cut off from the natural environment and the local community as well as their extended families and hometowns, became the spatial typology for subsequent public housing layouts. Thus, a dwelling, the main purpose of which was a place to eat and sleep at night, rather than a place to live in during the day, has been the norm for public urban housing. This needs to change.

Post-Second World War

The shift to nuclear families accelerated in the post-war years, and the government's policy of encouraging people to acquire their own homes at their own risk led to the construction of large numbers of small houses in urban areas. The 51C model home, which incorporated a US-style dining/kitchen area into the Japanese wartime labourers' housing layout, became the basic spatial typology for such homes. Many people longed to own a home equipped with US-style appliances and equipment, and the 1960s saw the widespread installation of flush toilets. Despite Yotaro Kobayashi and others criticizing architectural studies for not fully recognizing social issues and the spiritual quality of living space (Kobayashi 1973) the 'ideal' for many people remained additional private rooms, modern kitchens and easy-to-clean wood-grained vinyl floor coverings. Living/dining/kitchen-type housing with plural rooms became known as n+LDK housing (Figure 4.4).

Since the 1980s, the expansion of female employment has led to certain household activities, such as the care of children and the elderly, moving outside the home, but, for the most part, architects and housing officials did not consider in any depth the consequences of such changes, nor the loss of social connection between families and neighbourhoods (Funo 1995). Furthermore, responses to high levels of air and noise pollution have led to ventilation systems that make it easy to create airtight homes; indeed, sixty per cent of housing in Japan is now able to transform into 'airtight' bubbles devoid of natural air.

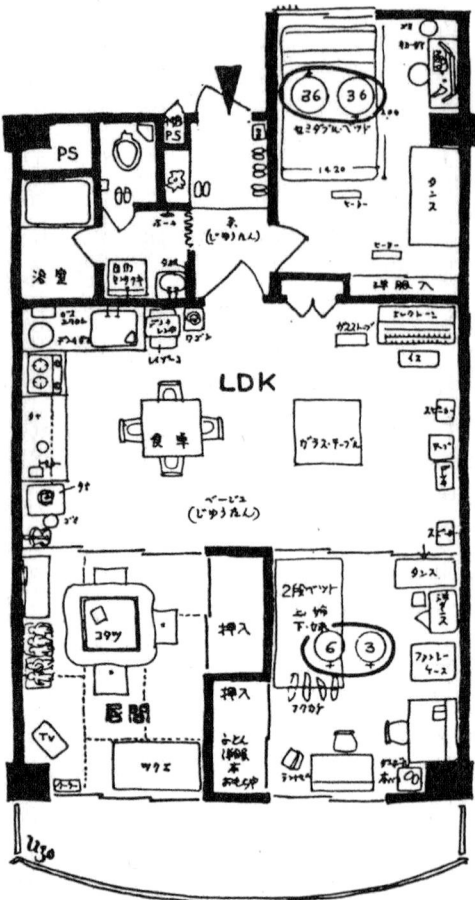

FIGURE 4.4 *Uzo Nishiyama's sketch of a typical n+LDK dwelling in the 1970s. Courtesy of Nishiyama Bunko Archive.*

Past and present issues

As the ideological 'ideal' house type changed from the vernacular Japanese house to the eclectic Japanese/Western house, and from the minimalist house to n+LDK dwellings in housing complexes, the characteristics of Japanese living that emphasized well-being and concern for the common good were increasingly forgotten. The difference between the positives of traditional vernacular design and what I consider our current malaise is marked; today our problems include the ubiquitous simplistic, functional houses with multiple private rooms and technological facilities unrelated to regional characteristics and culturally and socially accumulated living habits. Of the models discussed above, those which offer pointers for the way forward to the gradual connection of rooms as well as natural lighting and ventilation include the examples in the *Healthy House* competition. They offer opportunities to open windows and doors, and to use verandas and other intermediate areas to connect with the immediate natural environs. Relationships between homes, nature and society need readjusting. Indeed, the concept of *Youjou* as advocated by Kaibara was a concept of healing, treating illness, taking care of the bodies and spirits of ordinary people by drawing out and balancing natural healing power within an integrative and holistic perspective.

I would argue therefore that *Youjou* even now offers an effective perspective for countermeasures against infectious diseases; one which emphasizes immunity and calls for healthy living and a lifestyle based on knowledge of basic hygiene. In my opinion there is a continuity between Confucianism and paternalism both of which are behind the idea of *Youjou* and people's responses to national directives during the Covid-19 pandemic when most of the Japanese people wore masks, kept their distance from others and voluntarily stayed at home for the sake of the common good and social stability even without sufficient state support. This suggests that traditional notions of social responsibility endure. It must be acknowledged that the relatively small impact of the pandemic in Japan also relates to the Western-influenced technology-first and paternalistic institutionalization of housing planned with improved sanitation and hygienic in mind, but the pandemic also compels us to confront the limitations of our current system of living environments and of core humanistic values.

For most of this chapter, interiors have been discussed in terms of not only space and rooms – of room size, room type and number of rooms – but also specific features, from earthen to vinyl flooring, sliding partitions, kitchens, toilets and from floor seating on tatami mats to chairs. As discussions about homes of the future takes on additional importance in a period of pandemic and endemic, we need to emphasize interiors in relation to well-being. Indeed, amid the pandemic there has been recognition of the need for 'new lifestyles' (Atarashii Seikatsu Yoshiki) – a slogan raised by Dr Shigeru Omi, chairman of the government's Infectious Disease Control subcommittee; the need to consider the home as medium for social relations, and the basis of well-being in life. Efforts have been made to take hygiene more seriously, remodel homes to create more private spaces, for example, that could be used as isolation spaces if necessary, and to restore and increase contact with the natural environment. I hope that this research has illuminated various pathways to thinking about viable sustainable homes – inside and out – in the face of repeated infections and disease. We need to recognize the limitations of our current understanding related to housing and ways of living and adapt more flexibly to situations that requires us to be sensitive to local knowledge, climate and materials, and consider refurbishing of our interiors with multiple needs and sensitivities in mind and prioritize physical and spiritual well-being while seeking to balance it with functional needs.

References

Anno, A. (2015), 'The Way of Housing in the Books about Yojo-Method Published between the End of Edo and the Early Meiji Period', *Conference Proceeding of Japanese Architectural Academy*, Kanto area, no. 9328, 615–16.

Fujii, K. (1928), *The Japanese Dwelling-House*, Tokyo: Iwanami Shoten.

Fujitsu Soken Report (2021), 'Comparative Study of the Conditions of Covid-19 Occurrence Status', Available from: https://www.fujitsu.com/jp/group/fri/knowledge/opinion/consul/2021/2021-09-02.html (accessed 17 February 2022).

Funo, S. and T. Watanabe (1995), 'Interview with Yamada Hatsue, Matsukawa Junko and Goto Mariko, "Japanese Housing 50 Years After the War,"' *Journal of Architecture*, 110(1371): 16–23.

Giddens, A. (1990), *The Consequences of Modernity*, Redwood City, CA: Stanford University Press.

Kaibara, E. ([1713] 2021), *Youjou-kun*, trans. Michio Matuda, Tokyo: Chuko Bunko.

Kitazawa, K. (2000), *Kenko no Nihonshi* (Japanese history of the idea of health), Tokyo: Heibonsha shinsho.

Kobayashi, Y. (1973), 'Idea of Health and Architectural Environmental Engineering to Protect Healthy Life', *Journal of Architecture*, 1068(1068), July: 739–42.

Kon, W. and K. Yoshida (1986), *Kogengaku (Modernologio)*, Tokyo: Gakuyo shobo.

Kuroishi, Izumi (1988), 'Kon Wajiro: A Quest for the Architecture as a Container of Everyday Life', Ph.D. thesis, University of Pennsylvania (published UMI Database).

Ministry of Land, Infrastructure, Transport and Tourism (2019), 'The Ways People Live', survey. https://tinyurl.com/2p98278z

Ministry of Land, Infrastructure, Transport and Tourism (2020), 'Impact of Covid-19 on Housing Lifestyle, Survey on Housing Condition', (August). https://tinyurl.com/yckp59u4.

Miyazaki, N. and M. Aoki (1994), 'Experiment of Revising the Sanitary Function of our Housing in Meiji 10th: Historical Examination of House Planning from Sanitary Function no.1', *Journal of Architectural Planning*, Architectural Institute of Japan, 458(458): 43–52.

Nakajima, K. (1974), 'Life Improvement Movement in Taiso Period (Taisho kiniokeru Seikatsukaizen undo)', *Journal of Historical Studies. Shisō*, 15(15): 54–83.

Nihon, K. (2021), 'Domestic Violence Rescue Call Increased 1.6 Times by the Impact of Covid-19, Influenced by Staying Home', 24 May.

Nishiyama, U. (1981), *House Planning*, 1, Tokyo: Nishiyama Uzo collection of writing, Keiso shobo.

Omi, S.'s public recommendation reported on Mainichi (1 May 2020), 'The Professional Committee Claimed a Need to Prepare for a Long-Term Battle with Covid-19 by Settling "New Lifestyle"'. https://mainichi.jp/articles/20200501/k00/00m/010/272000c

Osaka Mainichi (1930), *Drawings of the Competition of Healthy Housing*, Osaka: Okura shoten.

Otsuki, T. (2021), 'Examination of the Transformation of Housing in the Last One Year', *Sumai ron*, Jusouken, 109: 4–6.

Susaki (2017), 'Housing Sanitation which Oe Sumi Learned in England; Education and Texts of Sanitation in the Bedford College', Japan Lifeology Annual Meeting.

5

A space of their own

A case study advocating appropriation of the domestic interior for well-being

Eliza Sweeney and Sebastian Messer

Introduction

This chapter discusses how scenographic (Hann 2019, 2021) and design practices coupled with narrative concepts offered a means of 'voyaging' beyond the confines of living spaces during the Covid-19 pandemic. It does so through a French case study, which is conceptualized using the Embodiment–Projection–Role (EPR) model of dramatherapy (Jennings 1998), and draws parallels with literary precedents. Employed in a programme of telehealth workshops, EPR was used to reconceive the domestic interior, supporting the mental health and well-being of children in precarious socio-economic circumstances. Telehealth refers to all uses of telecommunication technologies to increase equality of access to healthcare (Collie and Ćubranić 1999). Since the onset of the Covid-19 pandemic, use of tele-therapy has become commonplace as doctors and therapists turned to digital spaces to support patients and clients during periods of legally imposed 'Stay-at-Home' orders and curfews. Online interactions change the relational dynamics between therapist and client. Participants engage differently with the digital format and the content of the session or workshop; for example, asynchronous (pre-recorded) content enables them to progress at their own pace and convenience.

Children often play in special spaces chosen for their reassuring qualities, on the borders of their world and the world around them: a tree house, cupboard, attic, cardboard box or under a table. Through the appropriation of space, part of the psychic self is projected into reality, which demonstrates aspects of identity to others, symbolized in and by that space. In creating imaginary worlds, the physical space is transcended, becoming a psycho-social and emotional place. Fiction for both children and adults often features confinement or separation, sometimes both. In C.S Lewis' allegorical fantasy *The Lion, the Witch and the Wardrobe*, Lucy, the youngest of four siblings, finds the eponymous wardrobe in the spare room, which defines a liminal space. It is a portal from a world filled with adult uncertainty and the terror of helplessness, to another world besieged by magic but allowing the children to exercise agency. Lewis' readers follow the fictional children's triumph over adversity, embodied in the defeat of the adult-like figure of the White Witch. Their adventures create a bridge between childhood and adulthood (Turner 1967, 1982; Van Gennep 1960). In dramatherapy, tales provide a liminal space between reality and imagination, where potential change can happen. We conclude with Sweeney's proposition for '*psychoscenography*', a neologism that denotes the 'understanding of the effect of scenography on the psychology and behaviour of individuals and groups' (Sweeney 2021, after Debord 1955), and speculate this might be developed further to re-imagine living spaces benefiting families in overcrowded and precarious environmental conditions.

Safe as houses?

Gaston Bachelard proposed the twin notions of imagination (representation) and reverie (daydreaming) as tools for the poetic re-reading of home (1958). Choosing a broadly positive interpretation of the symbolic value and meanings of interior spaces, he reassures the reader that any darker associations can be transmuted, just as telling ghost stories safely rehearse and diffuse fears. For Bachelard, 'home' represents a refuge; '[the] house shelters daydreaming, the house protects the dreamer, the house allows one to dream in peace' (Bachelard 1958: 28). Yet corners, cupboards and 'nests' are not always secure places for reverie in the lived reality of many adults and children, they 'lose [their] protective function' (Nemet Pier 2006: 222). As John Fletcher sardonically noted in the seventeenth century, 'Charity and beating begins at home' (Fletcher 1639).

Interviewed for television, Christophe Robert, general delegate of the Abbé Pierre Foundation in France, recalled testimonies of children doing their homework in stairwells, toilets or the back of a car. True of pre-pandemic times, it became more evident during the confinement of a 'lockdown' (Mansour 2020). Physical isolation from friends and teachers makes children especially vulnerable to hidden domestic abuse and increases susceptibility to mental health conditions. Living in overcrowded housing offers little opportunity for privacy, exacerbating intra-familial tensions between parent and child, siblings or adults in a household, leading to heightened states of emotional behaviours: irritability; acting out; aggressiveness; violence; or alienation, depression and anxiety. The National Institute for Statistics and Economic Studies in France document overcrowded accommodation affects only 2.3 per cent of households in towns and districts with less than 10,000 inhabitants (Bernard et al. 2020). This rises to 13.7 per cent in the conurbation of Paris. Household composition also strongly influences instances of domestic over-occupation: 9.9 per cent of couples with one or more child under the age of ten live in overcrowded housing, increasing to 25 per cent for single-parent families with one or more child in that age group. Precarious living environments, combined with confinement, illness, stress, unemployment and loss of social support (e.g. school closures), can make life especially difficult for children with pre-existing psychological, behavioural, emotional or learning difficulties.

As Covid-19 spread throughout Europe in March 2020, across France, schools, workplaces and extra-curricular activities, including therapeutic programmes and support groups, closed overnight. Families found themselves juggling work or unemployment with homeschooling. Being unable to withdraw to a separate space can create or amplify tensions where intrusion can be psychologically, as well as physically, invasive. Psychoanalyst and clinical psychologist, Lyliane Nemet Pier, recalls a client's observations:

> It was my room, but it wasn't protected. Anyone could enter it at any time. It was not a well-defined territory. It was a corner of mine, but fragile, a jar made even smaller by the furniture that encumbered it. I was not allowed to put things on the wall so as not to mark the wallpaper.
>
> (2006: 215)

Case study

Early in 2019, Sweeney was leading an arts-for-wellness programme in a lower socio-economic quarter of Paris, in partnership with child protection and social services. Children between five and seven were invited to join the programme due to a precarious domestic situation, their social environment and case histories, coupled with presenting developmental, behavioural, emotional and/or mental health needs. The programme was designed to boost self-esteem, strengthen communication and relational skills, promote individual potential for creativity and emotional expression, and to reinforce resilience, as well as offer a safe space to express, master and transform their emotions.

In-person sessions were halted abruptly with the first lockdown. Countering the loss of routine and the sudden absence of the face-to-face, arts-for-wellness workshops, Sweeney proposed a telehealth programme to address the children's anxieties arising from the national response to the pandemic, including fears of a novel virus, wearing face-coverings, isolation, and from the loss of relationships and social bonds. Utilizing the concept of scenographics (Hann 2019, 2021) – defined as the crafting of objects, the creation of atmospheres and the qualities of place orientation within a specific space – Sweeney responded to the needs critical for the well-being of these children and their families in adjusting to domestic confinement and Covid-related limitations.

The three objectives for participants were to

1 *Create* a sustainable safe space, an appropriated territory of their own, away from the gaze of other members of the household, where they could safely explore fears and anxieties
2 *Explore* the affordances offered by their physical environment, imaginatively 'going out to play' without actually leaving the domestic space
3 *Reduce* fear and anxieties related to the virus (masks, illness and isolation)

We elaborate each of these objectives below.

Methods

A sequence of twenty-minute videos, titled *Exploration in Space*, were pre-recorded, affording households the flexibility to access the programme via the internet at convenient times. The video files were kept small so they could be played on any electronic device. The frequency of the sessions was accelerated (from weekly when face-to-face, to a new video link sent to families every four days) to encourage motivation and commitment to the therapeutic process.

The programme's content was framed with reference to the EPR model of dramatherapy (Jennings 1998). EPR is based on empirical observations

Table 5.1 EPR framing of the *Exploration in Space* programme

Developmental stage	General descriptor	Application in programme
E/embodiment	Movement and sensory experience	Awareness of physical movement and controlled breathing
P/projection	Engage with the world beyond the boundaries of one's own body	Creative writing, self-portraiture, costume-making and 'set' design
R/role	Identifies with relationships to and with others	Inhabiting the astronaut's character within the narrative

which Jennings asserts are 'value free' (see Table 5.1, middle column). The three stages can be integrated with any therapeutic or educational model, and methods applying EPR demonstrate their relevance with participants of any age. Sweeney proposes engaging first in P/projection can help to ease participants' transition into the therapeutic process. As this facilitates a slight psychological distancing at first, participants are more willing to respond creatively, rather than react defensively, before entering into E/embodiment. As the scenario becomes more familiar and participants are more comfortable in the therapeutic setting, EPR provides the opportunity for clients to enter their estranged world of imagination and symbolism, through dramatic play. The *Exploration in Space* programme centred on the archetype of an astronaut and the metaphor of their journey framed by EPR (see Table 5.1, right-hand column). The stages of EPR play were modulated throughout the videos and imaginative improvisations repeated during the period of domestic confinement.

Create

Implicitly, networks of relationships traverse and unfold in space, in which the subject is caught, and which also constitutes the self (Sweeney 2014). Nemet Pier proposes the family dynamic is defined by the (re)arrangement of space, through the processes of appropriation, visibility and limits. Spatial relationships are a non-verbal means of communication used by a family or couple, which must be decrypted and understood (2006: 223). Living in domestic situations where not every person is able to assert their individual personality can be a cause for increased tensions and conflicts. It becomes a matter of urgency to propose solutions to domestic spaces that will encourage living well together.

Literary works present these familial and domestic dynamics through the metaphor of space where we can grasp, symbolically if not literally, the ways in which our environment shapes and informs relationships, thoughts and feelings, social conventions and politics, and mental and physical health. The leitmotifs, 'five hundred [pounds] a year and a room of one's own', in Virginia Woolf's influential 1929 essay act as symbols for the autonomy and self-determination historically denied to women by societal conventions, economic circumstances and in law: 'The lock on the door means the power to think for oneself', she asserts (2002 [1929]). Lack of privacy can be emotionally difficult for everyone, where the gaze and the incursion into the private space can be felt as invasive. Nemet Pier notes, 'the impossibility of being able to appropriate a space is often experienced as an abuse of power, a domination, or a negation of oneself from which the subject suffers' (2006: 218).

Exploration in Space was designed to encourage dramatic play within the child's domestic space responding to the complexities of finding a 'room of one's own' during confinement. Invited to create a 'spaceship' – a scenographic environment – the children appropriated a domestic space using whatever materials could be readily sourced: dining room tables covered in tablecloths, bunk beds and bed sheets, toilet cubicles decorated with cushions, chairs

FIGURE 5.1 *A scenographic spaceship: A table with recycled materials and personal belongings. Drawing by Sebastian Messer.*

in a square formation with a picnic blanket thrown over them, under desks, in a giant cardboard box, and even a bath were all used (Figure 5.1). The children were encouraged to kit out their spaces with personal items including drawings, objects, toys, blankets, cushions and anything else that made their spaceship feel safe, fun, homely and comfortable to be in. Thus, for the children participating in the telehealth programme, the appropriation enabled an act of personalization exercised consensually in a communal family space.

The scenographic place becomes the portal: a liminal space between the domestic, inside space and the world of possibilities and adventure outside of the everyday. In their imaginations, the spaceship takes the children 'out of the world', without them ever leaving their living room, by mediating between their psychic and real environment. The children also made space helmets, using materials recycled from around the home (Figure 5.2). Putting on the helmet provided a threshold for the child to transform into their astronaut persona. The helmets represented safety for the astronaut and signified their

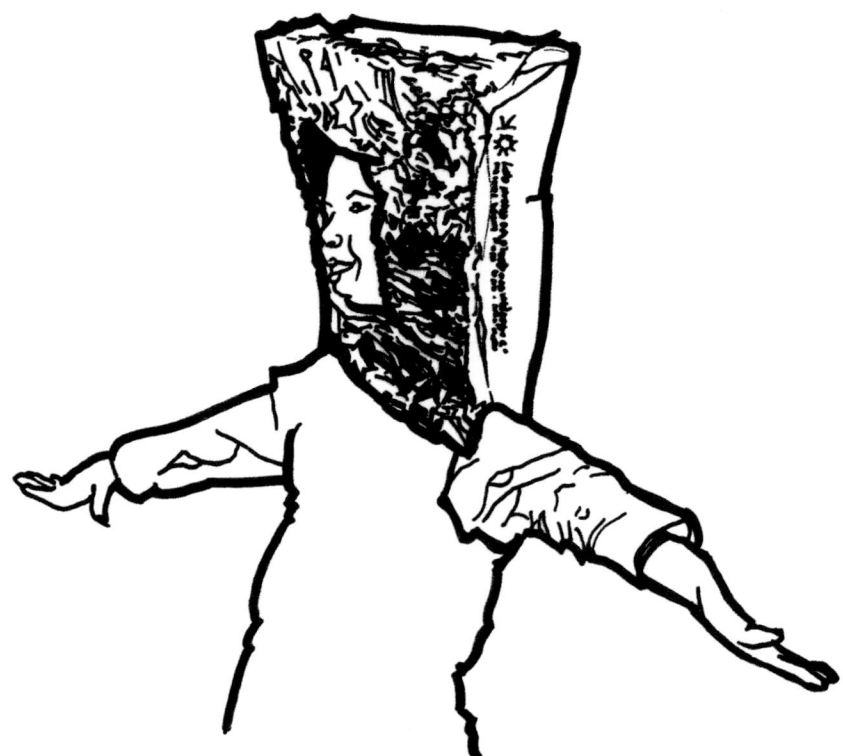

FIGURE 5.2 *A space helmet: paper grocery bag, aluminium foil, coloured card stars. Drawing by Sebastian Messer.*

character's bravery. Symbolically they took the place of the surgical masks worn by the children in public spaces to protect them and others from passing on the virus. The creation of the astronaut's costume allowed children to identify the wearing of a mask as ludic, adventurous, imaginative. Each helmet was imbued with the identity of the individual and worn with pride. Parents reported in post-workshop reflections that, following the creation of the helmets, the children's anxieties around wearing surgical masks outside of the home had diminished.

Explore

In many children's fictional narratives, the protagonists are transported beyond their bedrooms via their imaginative transformation of domestic spaces into a 'wilderness', best exemplified by Maurice Sendak's illustrations for *Where the Wild Things Are*, '[that] very night in Max's room a forest grew and grew – and grew until his ceiling hung with vines and the walls became the world all around' (Sendak 1963). Thus, in *The Lion, the Witch and the Wardrobe* (1950) the Pevensie children enter Narnia through a wardrobe, and in *Peter Pan and Wendy* (1911) the Darling children fly out of their bedroom window to Neverland. In *Where the Wild Things Are*, Max re-enacts his familial dynamics in first encouraging the wild rumpus and then sending the Wild Things to bed without their supper, mirroring his own misbehaviour and punishment. In the process, he intuits something of the loss of spontaneity and loneliness in assuming adult authority, before also experiencing the solace of unconditional love and forgiveness: after sailing through night and day, in and out of weeks, and for almost a year, he finds his supper awaits him … 'and it was still hot' (Sendak 1963: no page numbers).

Sweeney introduced the scenario of *Exploration in Space* through storytelling. Drawing on tropes of Joseph Campbell's archetypal, hero's journey structure, the narrative describes an astronaut preparing to go into space, putting on their spacesuit and helmet, saying goodbyes to family and friends, launching the rocket, exploring unknown planets, overcoming a challenge, returning to Earth and reuniting with loved ones. The story was a prompt for exploring the validating qualities of astronauts: bravery, health, intelligence, strength and innovation. The children were encouraged to think of other qualities which had not been mentioned; to enact these physically, vocally and emotionally in play; and therefore, reinforce an identification with these qualities in themselves. The video sessions developed through creating their spaceships (P/projection), to the children beginning to E/embody the astronaut in readiness for R/role play. The children drew and wrote narrative texts and followed this with movement exercises. Walking as 'lightly' as astronauts in zero gravity increased awareness of their body in relation to space around their home. Consciously varying their breathing, which accompanies the slower movement, decreases heart rate and regulates anxiety, providing a playful form of relaxation.

The final stage of the programme was to incorporate all the elements into a long improvisation:

> Settling into the scenographic spaceship, helmets on, preparing for the big adventure, the children engaged with my video, one spaceship to another (I was also under my table/ in my spaceship on the video recording). We counted down to zero and lifted off into outer space ... Upon landing, the astronauts bravely stepped out into the unknown wilderness of the 'new planet' to explore every room, space, corner, and piece of furniture. Reimagining each anew, these domestic spaces and objects were transformed into a 'wilderness'. One child visited Neptune, formerly their kitchen, where a battle ensued between the heroic astronaut and the terrible refrigerator demon (recounted by a parent). Another traversed their couch, which became like sinking sand (as told by the child in debrief). The control panel was once again engaged, and the astronauts all returned safely home. This ended the play.

Reduce

Processing difficult emotions through the archetypal narrative of the hero's journey, positively reaffirmed in the children the magical-imaginative belief that they were as brave as astronauts. The spaceship and the helmet metaphorically embody protective functions, allowing a sense of agency to be asserted over fears arising from the virus itself and the inexplicable losses of routine, social and relationships bonds. They also function practically, by enabling the child to experience time away from the gaze of other family members. Instrumentalizing the spatial 'othering' re-enchants their home environment.

Pyschoscenography

Theatre is a heightened and immersive space where anything can happen, reverie and nightmares come alive to be rehearsed emotionally, yet are contained within the duration of the performance. Therapeutic space typically is defined by familiarity, regularity and order. Often a neutral place, freed from the normal progression of time and external influences or judgement, it is a container trustworthy and resilient enough to withstand whatever emotional storms arise within. Both spaces are predicated on 'scenographics'.

From empirical, phenomenological observations of 'theatre-therapy space' (Sweeney 2014) and practising 'therapeutic scenography', Sweeney proposed the neologism 'psychoscenography' to describe an emerging understanding of the implicit role that spatial appropriation and place-making, through scenographic practices, plays in human development and well-being. Beyond simply observing, 'visualizing' or 'thinking about' spaces, psychoscenography engages participants in an embodied experience of space and of practices making place, for 'communicating' and 'transforming' feelings which might not be easily articulated through words. Psychoscenography invites participants to touch, smell, see, hear and even taste fabrics and materials to create environments which project their interior, mental spaces into the material world. This encourages us to think beyond the programme detailed here, about ways our multidisciplinary knowledge in design, architecture, scenography and therapy could facilitate individuals and communities in re-imagining their lived spaces. Domestically, this might contribute to promoting health for families living in overcrowded and precarious environmental conditions. Collectively, this can encourage a communal agency in their built environment.

Conclusion

In times of crisis, harnessing available resources is key to survival. This chapter presents a case study where domestic space became that resource for wellness needs. The perspectives developed above offer a unique insight and new methods for addressing the intersectional issues highlighted by the Covid-19 crisis. Through the metaphorical narrative of space exploration, the implementation of a telehealth programme offered a liminal space between the interior of the participants' dwellings and the psychic-emotional place they created of and within it.

Teachers noted an increase in attention span during online homeschooling amongst those students who participated in the programme. One parent noted her son's anxiety had decreased when leaving the house for his daily, mandated hour of outdoors exercise. The children reported finding it easier to concentrate, and expressed increased agency over their circumstances, which enabled them to feel better while unable to see their friends. They identified with the astronaut's characteristics and experiences – remaining isolated with the same people for many months in a spaceship – mirroring their confinement and social separation during the pandemic. The families voiced the benefit of imagining their home in different ways, thus allowing them to find wellness solutions in rearranging, appropriating (Nemet Pier 2006) and rethinking domestic spaces in ways they had previously not, and offering each child the opportunity to mark their territory, to have a space of their own.

References

Bachelard, G. (1958), *The Poetics of Space*, trans. Maria Jolas. Reprint, Boston, MA: Beacon Press, 1994.

Barrie, J. M. (1911), *Peter Pan and Wendy*. Reprint, London: Penguin Classics, 2005.

Bernard, V., G. Gallic, O. Léon and C. Sourd (2020), 'Logements suroccupés, personnes âgées isolées …: des conditions de confinement diverses selon les territoires', *INSEE Focus*, 189, 21 April [Online]. https://www.insee.fr/fr/statistiques/4478728?sommaire=4476925#titre-bloc-5. August 2021.

Collie, K. and D. Ćubranić (1999), 'An Art Therapy Solution to a Telehealth Problem', *Art Therapy: The Journal of the American Art Therapy Association*, 16(4): 186–93.

Debord, G. (1955), 'Introduction to a Critical Geography', in Ken Knabb (trans.), *Les Lèvres Nues #6,* ed. (1981) *Situationist International Anthology,* 5–8, Berkley, CA: Bureau of Public Secrets.

Fletcher, J. (2004 [1639]), *Wit without Money: A Comedy,* [online]. https://www.gutenberg.org/files/13425/13425-h/13425-h.htm

Jennings, S. E. (1998), *Embodiment-Projection-Role (EPR)*, [online]. http://www.suejennings.com/epr.html

Hann, R. (2019), *Beyond Scenography*, Abingdon, Oxon: Routledge.

Hann, R. (2021), 'Painting Scenographics', in S. Otto-Knapp and Solveig Øvstebø (eds), *Silke Otto-Knapp: In the Waiting Room*, 73–9, Chicago: The Renaissance Society at the University of Chicago.

Lewis, C. S. (1950), *The Lion, the Witch, and the Wardrobe*. Reprint, Glasgow: HarperCollins Children's Books, 2009.

Mansour, L. A. (2020), 'Coronavirus: Mal-logés et confinés, la double peine', *20 minutes société.* https://www.20minutes.fr/societe/2758675-20200410-confinement-calvaire-personnes-mal-logees

Nemet Pier, L. (2006), 'Investissement et aménagement de l'espace dans la dynamique familiale', *Imaginaire & Inconscient*, 2(18): 215–24.

Sendak, M. (1963), *Where the Wild Things Are,* London: The Bodley Head.

Sweeney, E. (2014), 'Une étude de l'espace théâtro-thérapeutique', Unpublished Master's thesis, University Paris Descartes.

Sweeney, E. (2021), *Ecopoiesis: A New Perspective for The Expressive and Creative Arts Therapies in the 21st Century.* In Press, London: Jessica Kingsley Publishers.

Turner, V. (1967), *The Forest of Symbols*, New York: Cornell University Press.
Turner, V. (1982), *From Ritual to Theatre: The Human Seriousness of Play*, New York: PAJ Publications.
Van Gennep, A. (1960), *The Rites of Passage*, Chicago: University of Chicago Press.
Woolf, V. (2002 [1929]), *A Room of One's Own*, [online]. https://gutenberg.net.au/ebooks02/0200791h.html

SECTION TWO

The unstable home

6

The re-materialization of everyday life

New aesthetic experiences of staying at home in Sweden during the Covid-19 pandemic

Maja Willén

Introduction

In this chapter I focus on the material changes that take place when people stay at home because of pandemic restrictions. I discuss how they make room for work, school activities or a new family life by re-furnishing, using existing objects in new ways, or investing in new interior decorations and functions. The focus is on how new uses and combinations of objects originating from different arenas create innovative aesthetic experiences and ideals within the home.

This chapter derives from a larger research study in which I am analysing different aspects of how the staying-at-home situation is reorganizing our homes, socially, materially and spatially. In this chapter, I present my first reflections on and findings from this project. The research material has been collected within a Swedish context and is based partly on interviews with people who are staying at home for various reasons, and partly on visual mediations of the staying-at-home situation. In Sweden, the pandemic has been managed somewhat differently from the ways in which many other Western countries have handled it. Here we have experienced no forced quarantine or lockdown of society, but instead have received strong recommendations to work from home, to stay at home when feeling ill and to quarantine when diagnosed with Covid-19. The recommendations have also been to stay at home during weekends and holidays and to avoid physical social contact with people outside one's family (Folkhälsomyndigheten: 1 2021). Up to September 2021 around 1.1 million people (10 per cent of the population) had been officially infected with Covid-19 and were therefore forced to quarantine at home (Folkhälsomyndigheten: 2 2021). Almost 40 per cent of the workforce were working from home, at least part of the time, in January 2021 (Statistiska centralbyrån 2021). And according to mobile data statistics, people, to a large extent, stayed at home during the first year of the pandemic (Trafikanalys 2021).

I have chosen to take an ethnological approach in this project in order to make visible the everyday, personal experiences of staying at home and to highlight the shifting uses and functions of home. This is a work still in progress, and I have so far conducted eleven interviews out of the planned twenty. The interviews have been conducted digitally via Zoom, and I have used a semi-structured method to enable my informants to speak as freely as possible (Fägerborg 1999: 59). The interviews have been recorded with both sound and image and then transcribed. The project also uses different visualizations of the staying-at-home situation in order to highlight the mediation of the aesthetic ideals of the phenomenon. In this chapter my examples are two advertising photographs by IKEA and two documentary photographs by the Swedish photographer Daniel Nilsson.

The chapter focuses on the reorganization of home in a material sense. In line with Kim Dovey (1999) I regard housing as an architectural frame that constructs and reproduces power and identity relations of, for example, gender, class, ethnicity and familial relationships. Dovey argues that architectural design frames everyday life, both in a material sense and discursively (Dovey 1999: 1–2). I consider the objects of everyday domestic life to work in a similar way, orchestrating or choreographing life according to social, political and economic conditions (Hand and Shove 2004: 3). Choreographing is in this project understood as 'the existence of rules of daily life, correspondingly to those of dance', as formulated by Mika Pantzar (Pantzar 1989: 27). The ethnologists Billy Ehn, Orvar Löfgren and Richard Wilk elaborate this idea and argue that all daily routines, including the handling of objects, bodily movements and social behaviours, are executed in a particular manner, and constantly repeated (Ehn et al. 2016: 6). This perspective implies a focus on how the material organization of the home directs the social and bodily practices of inhabiting it, and how, when the materiality changes, our relationship with, and experience of, everyday life changes too.

Practising a new home aesthetics

The material changes of the home particularly interest me. While interviewing my informants I asked them questions about how they had been using their furniture during their time at home; the changes they made to the organization of the interior; and their dreams about new objects and functions. All of them said they have made material adjustments to their interiors in response to the staying-at-home situation. Below, I focus on three different examples of this material reorganization, namely the addition of non-traditional home interior objects, the reuse of already existing objects and the consumption of new interior objects.

The first theme of material reorganization that I address is the clash between the ideals of a traditional home interior and those of a more public space. The most notable story is told by Petra, a single woman in her sixties living in a two-bedroom apartment in Linköping, a town in southern Sweden. Petra has been working mostly from home since the autumn of 2020 and has also spent most of her leisure time at home. She tells me that she hasn't made any significant material changes while working from home, apart from one thing, that is, the positioning of an office chair by the kitchen table where she has been working (Petra, 24 May 2021). By introducing this change, she has turned this everyday private environment into a semi-public space and at the same time altered the use, look and experience of her kitchen. When she is working, she sits on her office chair, and when she is having her meals, she moves to one of her dining chairs.

Another variant of what could be called the arrival of 'semi-private aesthetics' in the home is described by Inga, a seventy-year-old retired woman who lives by herself in a detached house in the small town of Mjölby. Since the arrival of the pandemic, she has spent almost all her time at home and has adapted her use of her house to the new conditions. The most drastic change is that she has turned one spare bedroom into a work-out space where she exercises every day in front of the TV to the programme *Gympa med Sofia* (workout with Sofia). This very popular Swedish TV show was introduced in spring 2020 with the purpose of enabling people to work out from home (SVT 2021). Inga has placed some training equipment in her work-out room, changing its function from that of a strictly private space to that of semi-private one in which different aesthetic ideals and functions are brought together (Inga, 7 June 2021).

The phenomenon of mixing different aesthetic practices in the home can also be observed in the wider visual culture of the pandemic society. Some of the most striking examples come from IKEA, the Swedish furniture company known for its ability to pick up new trends from everyday life, turning them into efficient marketing tools (Kristoffersson 2014: 117). I have chosen two pictures from the IKEA brochure of 2021 showing two different living rooms which are characterized by a mixture of functions and furniture. The first picture (Figure 6.1) illustrates a newly launched laptop table placed in front of a sofa, combining probably the most traditional item of domestic furniture with a new kind of domestic object adapted to staying-at-home situations

FIGURE 6.1 *Laptop table, illustration from IKEA catalogue, 2021. Courtesy of IKEA.*

including working and watching films. The second picture (Figure 6.2) shows a large table placed behind a sofa. A mixture of chairs has been placed around the table, among them a typical office chair. Above the table are some shelves containing books and what can be defined as working material of some kind, for example, notebooks and papers files. Under the shelf a traditional office lamp is found. In these pictures IKEA is playing with the aesthetic norms of the home, combining traditions from two different environments, the home and the office.

The second theme in my account of a changed materiality concerns the new use of objects. Anneli, a woman in her forties, lives with her husband and son in a three-bedroom apartment on the outskirts of Stockholm. She tells me that she and her husband have been working from home since the start of the pandemic and that they have been homeschooling their son from time to time. Anneli uses the combined guestroom and home office for her work, while her husband uses their bedroom, standing while working on his laptop which is positioned on a chest of drawers. He has to stand up as there is no room for a proper desk in that space (Anneli, 28 April 2021). A similar story is told by 35-year-old Nils. During the first year of the pandemic, he and his girlfriend were living in a small, one-bedroom apartment in which they

FIGURE 6.2 *A living room working space, illustration from IKEA catalogue, 2021. Courtesy of IKEA.*

both worked. While his girlfriend used the living room as her home office, he worked in the kitchen, often standing by the kitchen counter to enable a more ergonomic position (Nils, 25 May 2021). Catharina, sixty years old, uses her living room sofa as her home office during the day, so that it has a double function (Catharina, 21 April 2021). In these examples, traditionally privately coded home objects are given new and shifting identities. During the daytime they are used for work, and in the evenings or the weekends their original function returns.

One highly illustrative visual representation of this phenomenon is the documentary photo project *Hemmakontor* (home offices) by the Swedish

FIGURE 6.3 *Women working from home, photo from* Hemmakontor *by Daniel Nilsson, 2021. Photo: Daniel Nilsson.*

FIGURE 6.4 *Couple working from home, photo from* Hemmakontor *by Daniel Nilsson, 2021. Photo: Daniel Nilsson.*

photographer Daniel Nilsson, published as a book in September 2021. In this project Nilsson photographed people working from home during the spring of 2020. His photographs illustrate the first, acute phase of the transition to working from home. The images show people working from the most unusual spaces and furniture within their homes. One example depicts a woman working at her dining table on which she has placed a garden table, with some books placed underneath her laptop in order to obtain a proper height for working in a standing position (Figure 6.3). The second example shows a couple using their children's room as their home office. The woman is working, standing by a climbing tree for cats, while her husband is sitting in an armchair using a plastic chair with a wooden box on top as his office table (Figure 6.4). These people are clearly using existing objects in new ways, adding new functions while simultaneously negotiating the meanings of those objects.

A third theme of the material reorganization of home is the addition of new objects. Malin is a fifty-year-old woman living in a two-bedroom apartment with her adult son who is a university student. She has spent a lot of time at home owing to unemployment. In order to remain occupied during this time she started to buy and sell home objects through Facebook's marketplace. Her home is now in a constant state of aesthetic change (Malin, 27 April 2021). Other informants are making more permanent changes in their homes due to the staying-at-home situation. Felicia and Anders, a married couple in their mid-thirties, live with their young daughter in a small, detached house in the southern part of Stockholm. They have both been working from home since March 2020 and have also spent their weekends and holidays at home rather than travelling around as they would normally do. At first, they had their working equipment in the open plan kitchen and living room, but, when the situation became more permanent after summer 2020, they decided to create two office spaces in the basement of their house. They now have two fully equipped offices clearly separated from the living spaces in the house (Anders & Felicia, 28 April 2021). Similar stories are told by others, for example, by Tobias who tells me that he has turned one of his children's rooms into a home office making room for both him and his wife to work from home (Tobias, 27 May 2021). For these informants, the pandemic has changed the way in which their home interiors are used, from the first temporary solutions discussed above, to the more permanent material changes mentioned in this section.

Ideas of new home aesthetics

My informants all mention some form of re-materialization in the everyday use of their homes. Whether large or small, incrementally achieved naturally or consciously carried out, they all affect the function of home in some way. Some of the re-materializations are permanent, some more temporary. Some are welcomed, some less so. But how could these material changes be understood theoretically?

During the staying-at-home situation the traditional boundaries between private and public have been challenged in many ways, spatially as well as socially – spatially when activities that are normally accomplished outside the home in a public or semi-public environment start to be executed within the physical boundaries of home; and socially when people working from home adopt their professional personae in a normally private setting. Many even invite their work colleagues into the intimate environments of their homes. Traditionally, though, the boundaries between the private and the public spheres are not only drawn by social or spatial means. Materiality also plays a part. The form and function of interior decoration and design are historically adapted to the defined needs of a specific environment and manifested aesthetically (see e.g. Gejvall 1954, Wikström 1994 and Nylander 2013). The most striking example of this phenomenon is, perhaps, the aesthetic division between the home and the office. While early offices looked rather like homes from home, by the early twentieth century they had become more overtly functional and mechanistic in appearance. Simultaneously the home became aligned more closely with intimacy, femininity and safety, which was expressed aesthetically by its, often elaborate, decoration (see e.g. Sparke 2008, Massey 1994, Heynen and Baydar 2005).

Even though the boundaries between the public and the private spheres have been blurred and contested for many reasons during the past hundred years, there is still an essential difference between the design of public and private spheres expressed by, for example, furniture and home decorations (see e.g. Colomina 1994 and Sparke 2008 or Strannegård 2009 and Ulver-Sneistrup 2008). Most importantly, home is often defined by its material artefacts, which contain specific memories relating to ourselves and our history (Cieraad 1999: 92). These objects play an important role in how we relate to our homes, emotionally and aesthetically. In the situation of staying at home, the materiality of the home is changing according to new needs, leading to new negotiations between private and the public ideals. The aesthetic function of home objects is being contested.

In the introduction to this chapter, I referred to Dovey and to Hand and Shove to underline how both housing itself and the objects we fill our homes with are part of the orchestration of our homes. The things we use choreograph everyday domestic life, both mentally and spatially (Dovey 1999: 1–2; Hand and Shove 2004: 3). When my informants Anders and Felicia added two office spaces in their basement; when Malin is constantly changing the experience of home by buying and selling new object; or when Inga transforms the function of a whole space with the addition of new functions and practices; they are changing both the way they move within the home and the way they relate aesthetically to it. A *rechoreographing* of the everyday domestic life is occurring.

This rechoreographing process of home can also be observed in the ways in which home environments are changing through the combination of different aesthetic practices. This is done either by relating professionally to already existing home objects or by adding new non-domestic objects to the home environment. My interviewee Petra, for example, places an office chair at her kitchen table, changing the whole aesthetic experience of her kitchen. In the IKEA advertising photographs this new mixed aesthetic is visualized in an explicit way. The mixing of aesthetic expressions is not a new phenomenon at IKEA but has been clearly emphasized during the pandemic period. In *Interior Design and Identity* (2004), Penny Sparke calls this kind of mixed aesthetic environments, combining ideals from both the traditional home environments and public arenas, 'hybrid interiors' (Sparke 2004: 7). There have been many examples in recent years of 'hybrid interiors' when public environments such as hotels or offices are made more homely (Strannegård 2009). In my examples it is the home that has been made into this 'hybrid', contesting traditional divisions of public and private aesthetic ideals.

The Danish philosopher Henrik Kaare Nielsen describes the aesthetic experiences of everyday life as a kind of social practice in which we relate to artefacts 'from the perspective of an aesthetic-expressive rationality of action' (Kaare Nielsen 2005: 62). Our behaviours towards everyday objects are inscribed both in the objects and in ourselves. This aesthetic or social practice depends, in turn, on inherited traditions or meanings within objects, which are historically specific (Dovey, 62–3). He explains that our expectations about objects are based on certain conventions and that we relate to objects in specific ways according to our own biographical histories (Dovey, 63). We react sensitively to, or handle, specific objects in certain determined ways. When objects or behaviours change, so does the aesthetic experience of everyday life along with the social relations emerging from, and within, the home. Both Nils and Anneli's husband, for example, use nonwork-connoted furniture to create an ergonomic working environment, and, in the photos from the project *Hemmakontor* by Daniel Nilsson, people are seen using domestic objects in new and often very creative ways. In these cases, we can see how the inherited use of objects is contested by new habits, changing the aesthetic practice of everyday life. And, as Kaare Nilsen argues, aesthetic practice is a sub-category of social practice, meaning that our changing relation to certain objects in our homes will also affect the way we relate socially to, and understand, both our everyday domestic life and ourselves. And if home is partly defined by the feelings invested in the things inhabiting it, as argued by Irene Cieraad, new things, and new relationships with already existing things, might change the actual idea of home. Home is becoming something different, maybe permanently, maybe only temporarily.

Conclusion

The conclusion of this chapter is that the staying-at-home situation has changed the way everyday objects are used within the home and, as a consequence, an introduction of both a new choreography of the everyday domestic life as well as new aesthetic experience of dwelling. I suggest that this is a change in the long run that might affect both the way we define home and ourselves. But who are included in this change?

During the first years of the pandemic the housing market has flourished in Sweden along with the market of home improvement and home-related consumption. The possibility to remake your home and take control over the staying-at-home situation seem endless for those who can afford it. But not all can or want to. The changing materiality of home is, as always, a question of resources, economic, social and cultural. The inequality of dwelling has seldom been so clear as during the years of the Corona pandemic.

My ambition with the project is to include a wide range of Swedish people, which means people staying at home for various reasons including illness, loss of work, working for home or just avoiding going out to stay healthy. I intend to take a broad approach on what home is when the rules of leaving it are changing. Despite this ambition, many of my interviewees so far are staying at home for similar reasons and with similar experiences. If I want to say more about the eventual long-term changes of what home is or can be, I will need to include an even wider range of people and staying-at-home situations. I will also need to study the change over time. My hope is therefore that I will be able to follow the shifting phases of the staying-at-home situation for a longer period, discussing the premises of dwelling not only for the home-working middle classes but also for all (or at least most) people.

References

Cieraad, I. (1999), *At Home. An Anthropology of Domestic Space*, Syracuse: Syracuse University Press.

Colomina, B. (1994), *Privacy and Publicity: Modern Architecture as Mass Media*, Cambridge, MA: MIT Press, cop.

Dovey, K. ([1999] 2008), *Framing Places. Mediating Power in Built Form*, London: Routledge.

Ehn, B., O. Löfgren and R. Wilk (2016), *Exploring Everyday Life: Strategies for Ethnography and Cultural Analysis*, Lanham, MD: Rowman & Littlefield.

Folkhälsomyndigheten: 1 (2021), https://www.folkhalsomyndigheten.se/contentassets/0ac7c7d33c124428baa198728f813151/hslf-fs-2021-55u.pdf (4 October).

Folkhälsomyndigheten: 2 (2021), https://experience.arcgis.com/experience/09f821667ce64bf7be6f9f87457ed9aa (4 October).

Fägerborg, E. (1999), ´Intervjuer´, in L. Kaijser and M. Öhlander (eds), *Etnologiskt fältarbete*, Lund: Studentlitteratur, pp. 55–72.

Gejvall, B. ([1954]1988), *1800-talets Stockholmsbostad: en studie över den borgerliga bostadens planlösning i hyreshusen*, Stockholm: Komm. för Stockholmsforskning.

Hand, M. and Shove, E. (2004), 'Orchestrating Concepts: Kitchen Dynamics and Regime Change in *Good Housekeeping* and *Ideal Home 1922–2002*', *Home cultures*, 3: 1–22.

Heynen, H. and G. Baydar, eds (2005), *Negotiating Domesticity: Spatial Productions of Gender in Modern Architecture*, New York: Routledge.

Kaare Nielsen, H. (2005), 'Totalizing Aesthetics? Aesthetic Theory and the Aestheticizing of Everyday Life', *The Nordic Journal of Aesthetics*, 17(32): 60–75.

Kristoffersson, S. (2014), *Design by Ikea. A Cultural History*, London: Bloomsbury.

Massey, D. (1994), *Space, Place and Gender*, Minneapolis: University of Minnesota Press.

Nylander, O. (2013), *Svensk bostad 1850–2000*, Lund: Studentlitteratur.

Pantzar, M. (1989), 'The Choreography of Everyday Life – a Missing Brick in the General Evolution Theory', *The Journal of New Paradigm Research*, 27(2–4): 207–26.

Sparke, P. (2004), ´Introduction´, in S. McKellar and P. Sparke (eds), *Interior Design and Identity*, Manchester: Manchester University Press, pp. 1–9.

Sparke, P. (2008), *The Modern Interior*, London: Reaktion.

Statistiska centralbyrån (2021), https://www.scb.se/pressmeddelande/allt-fler-arbetar-hemifran/ (4 October).

Strannegård, M. (2009), *Hotell Speciell. Livsstilskonsumtion på känslornas marknad*, Mölnlycke: Elanders.

Sveriges television (SVT) (2021), https://kontakt.svt.se/guide/hemmagympa-med-sofia (15 October).

Trafikanalys (2021), https://www.trafa.se/globalassets/rapporter/2020/rapport202013-resmonster-under-coronapandemins-forstahalvar.pdf (4 October).

Ulver-Sneistrup, S. (2008), *Status Spotting: A Consumer Cultural Exploration into Ordinary Status Consumption of 'Home' and Home Aesthetics*, Lund: Lund Business Press.

Wikström, T. (1994), *Mellan hemmet och världen: om rum och möten i 40- och 50-talens hyreshus*, Stockholm: Symposion graduale.

Interviews

Anders and Felicia, 28 April 2021.
Petra, 24 May 2021.
Catharina, 21 April 2021.
Anneli, 28 April 2021.
Malin, 27 April 2021.
Nils, 25 May 2021.
Tobias, 27 May 2021.
Petra, 24 May 2021.
Inga, 7 June 2021.

7

Room for independence: Home-based women workers and their interiors

Fiona Del Puppo and Paule Perron

Introduction

During the Covid-19 era, the popular media have often encouraged women to deal with their stress by transforming their interiors. This illustrates the continuation of the prescribed and perceived role of women as carers (Molinier 2021: 30) and homemakers. Combining paid work with the other responsibilities assigned to them, they are expected to find fulfilment in these tasks. This observation encouraged us to renew our interest in the interior, the privileged space not only of invisible labour and inequalities, but also of an essentialist vision of feminine independence. From Virginia Woolf's *A Room of One's Own* (Woolf 1929: 4) to Mona Chollet's *Chez-soi* (Chollet 2015: 9), feminist writers through the years have highlighted the emancipatory power of a familiar enclosed and controlled environment. The lockdowns and transformation of the rhythms of daily life that accompanied the Covid-19 era highlight the domestic sphere as both a space of independence and of resistance to gender-domination patterns *and* as a space that perpetuates and enhances these gender inequalities. This chapter is based on the experiences of seven female home-workers, collected through semi-directed interviews.[1] Long before the Covid-19 situation, they had been seduced by the opportunities offered by new technologies to become independent home-based workers.

As our built environment – including home interiors – is produced by a patriarchal society, we suggest that it directly contributes to gender inequalities

(Dadour 2018: 15). We aim to interrogate this relationship in the context of the home and to understand the material strategies implemented to cope with these domination dynamics before and during the Covid-19 lockdown. We focus on the situations of mainly white Northern European women, working in independent jobs from home (most of our interviewees are highly educated and in intellectual or creative professions) and living in heterosexual households. In this chapter we aim to define the concept of independence and to reflect on the material tools that home-based women have developed in order to negotiate their experiences of working domesticity. We will focus on the part space plays in this organization and interrogate the possibility of independence in confined spaces.

Home-based and independent

The *Oxford Dictionary* defines 'independence' as 'the freedom to organise your own life, make your own decisions, etc. without needing help from other people'. It has long been promoted as a virtuous concept, containing the emancipatory power required to question the social reproduction that perpetuates injustice. This was especially the case in the 1970s feminist movement which made women's independence the central tool with which to achieve equality (Appay 2012: 2).

Since 1990, neoliberalism has influenced a shift in work organization from external supervision towards autonomy, self-control and self-evaluation (Jouan 2012: 3). Yet, by questioning a vertical hierarchy model, this management ideology also imposes on individuals a responsibility for constant adaptation and availability (Perilleux 2001: 35). It promotes access to independence at the price of stability. Indeed, both working hours and employment status become less stable with the increase of independent work and temporary and short-term contracts (Bergström and Storrie 2003: 2).

Many coaching discourses promote individual development and fulfilment through autonomy at work. Instead of embracing freedom from all structures, they encourage strong boundaries between private and professional life and advocate a spatial and temporal 'territory hygiene' (Salman 2014: 48). This gives a rigid structure to the instability of everyday life. Aimed primarily at women, who experience an overlap between the different spheres of existence (Zimmermann 2011: 91), this encourages a new ideal of feminine self-realization. Like many pieces in women's lifestyle magazine mentioning Covid-19 and home-offices, an online article from *Journal des femmes* suggests 'Create a house zoning; Ease the access to toys; Don't let the mess accumulate; Tidy the food supplies; Clearly separate the working space;

Establish a planning for house chores' (Hebrard 2020: online). It illustrates the imperative for women to be in charge of the spatial and material dimensions of the home. They are more likely than men to turn to independent work as a coping strategy to achieve this balance (Marlow 1997: 3). When questioned about why she chose self-employment, Laura – a 31-year-old independent artist and entrepreneur who sells her art mainly on Esty and lives with her partner (a PhD student) in a two-bedroom rented apartment in Geneva – enlightened us on these multi-layered considerations, 'I always knew that you know childcare is a massive thing' she explained. 'If you are self-employed that eases that up quite a lot. I'm also really bad at being told what to do. I'm not a good employee at all' (Laura 2020:6).

The women discussed in this chapter were encouraged to embrace the flexibility offered by independent work, enabled by new technologies, which promised a work/life balance. Independent women workers are also more likely than men to locate their workplace within the home rather than establish separate business premises or workshops (Ehlers et Main 1998: 6). They deliberately place themselves in the middle of domestic agitation instead of seeking shelter from it. The independent inhabitant of Woolf's room, who needed a space to compose away from agitation, has been transformed into a neoliberal, flexible independent subject (Fraser 2013: online) who struggles with both patriarchal and capitalist pressures within her domestic space.

The domestication of independence

The current flexibility of the professional sphere encourages workers, and especially women, to aim for independence. Within the context of the domestic economy, Virginia Woolf, in 1929, had already addressed the financial independence of women. She stated that, in order to access freedom to write, women needed money to support themselves (Woolf 1929: 20). One might suppose that being self-employed is indeed a way for women, usually disadvantaged in most work organizations, to achieve financial independence. Because of the instability of their incomes, many of our interviewees, such as Laura, suggested the opposite dynamic, 'I'd say you are probably more independent because you have guaranteed income coming in, whereas I am reliant at the moment on my partner. […] I wouldn't say it [online small business ownership] is a way to empower women to have independence' (Laura 2020: 14).

Besides providing unstable remuneration, independent work, especially when it is home-based, also needs to blend in with other time-consuming and unpaid activities. Feminist writers have already challenged the traditional division of paid work performed outside and domestic activities happening inside the home by defining the concept of the 'domestication of work' (Martín Palomo 2009: 2). Not only does this concept highlight domestic activities as legitimate work, it also acknowledges the evolution of paid labour towards an activity that can take place at home. Its organization increasingly values adaptability, versatility and availability, and imposes an unstable and elastic time schedule, much like domestic work. Through the experiences of the women interviewed, we propose the notion of the 'domestication of independence' through which to study the flexibility of both domestic and independent work blended within the home.

From the domestication of independence to autonomy

In *A Room of One's Own* (Woolf 1929: 88), Woolf associates the privatization of space with the freedom to organize her time freely within that space, the protection from distraction or domestic obligations, and the constant reassessment of its ownership. The enclosed room she describes is a non-negotiable space, free from all social constraints. She refers to an autonomy that relies strongly on the capacity to escape any social and normative rules, to compose your own temporality and to create a distance from the social world in order to be able to be part of it (Pattaroni 2007: 13). In this chapter we refer to autonomy as emancipatory. Alexandra, an independent artist, describes it through the experience of isolation, 'In my opinion you need to have a haven. Like a layer. Somewhere you don't let anyone in. […] but that's basically what an artist needs. You need to be alone. You and the universe' (Alexandra 2020: 3).

Yet independent work relies on social constraints, including the neoliberal version of independence that pressures individuals into the need for self-realization. Therefore, inside the spatial qualities of the necessary separation from the social world reside the negotiating tools to achieve a domestic experience that is more or less free from both professional and domestic requirements. The enactment, defined as the entanglement of actors (the inhabitants), acts (the situations the interviewees described to us) and the architecture (the material conditions of the household observed and transcribed by us) of home (Bonnevier 2007: 16), helps us to identify the spatial strategies that the interviewees use to negotiate their domesticated independence. This leads us to study the possibilities of autonomy offered by this domestication of independence.

The possibility of a boundary

In Woolf's writings, architectural features (a wall, a door and a flight of stairs) are ways of distancing gendered hierarchical behaviours. The physical separations they create enable her to develop transgressive discourses, without them being directly submitted to, or silenced by, a patriarchal audience (Bonnevier 2007: 389). Space acts as both a setting and a condition to tackle what she identifies as the social and domestic pressures directed at women. Ahead of second-wave feminism Woolf upheld the development of women's independence through material and spatial culture.

Most of our interviewees (five out of seven women) confirmed that Woolf's closable room was essential to deal with the incorporation of their professional, independent activities within the home. However, their experiences deeply differed from Woolf's. Laura, for example, explained that the closable room helps to contain professional pressures within it and protect the rest of the domestic sphere from them, 'The simple act of being able to shut the door ….is huge. I will not go into the studio and … my workroom unless I am working. […] That room is only for working. And that really helps' (Laura 2020: 7) (Figure 7.1).

In the nineteenth century, the incorporation of hallways within the home produced a spatial compartmentalization of activities and space ownership (Evans 1978: 62). It reinforced the gendered specification of spaces, such as the feminine *boudoir* or the masculine study (Logoz 2021: 18). In the beginning of the twentieth century, the normative nuclear household established the standard European home that still shapes housing production today. Master

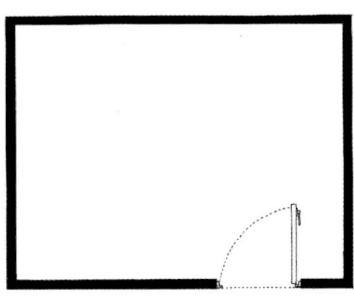 

FIGURE 7.1 *Interpretative sketch of Virginia Woolf's and Laura's workrooms, 2022. Drawing by Paule Perron and Fiona Del Puppo.*

bedrooms, bedrooms and living rooms are hierarchized (by size and position) living units, while kitchens, bathrooms and toilets are smaller functional rooms positioned to perpetuate the patriarchal household structure (Evans 1997: 54).

Woolf's room – the habitation unit – has been, in the past hundred years, the financial core of Western architectural production. The struggling incorporation of the interviewed women's neoliberal borderless professional activities within such a home architecture challenges the contemporary relevance of a rigid material boundary (Woolf's walls and doors). Partly because of the emergence of digital objects (phones, computers) along with calls and emails (from within her workroom, Laura mentioned dealing with pressures related to social media, the time it consumes and the pressure of overachieving that it creates), this rigid boundary of the working area fails to prevent non-domestic pressures related to work flexibility and domestic ones from colliding with each other.

Unstable boundaries

In the shared space of a home, the privatization of a room for individual purposes and the creation of an unequal distribution of spatial resources are under constant negotiation (de Singly 2000: 231). This produces inevitable frustrations and frictions (Evans 1978: 85) and instils instability in the boundaries between different inhabited spaces. The act of inhabitation itself, through settling into and arranging a space, creates a familiar environment in which furniture and personal belongings testify to individual space appropriation (Breviglieri et al. 2003: 92). The observed overlapping of different activities or space ownership intertwines the notion of domesticated independence with the notion of cohabitation. To understand the spatial arrangements related to sharing a private space, we need to pay attention to the unstable boundaries it produces, the temporality of their variations and the potential for the inhabited space to absorb it.

Pia, a 39-year-old nutrition coach, lives in a rented apartment with her husband and child in a three-bedroom rented apartment in Geneva. The room dedicated to her professional activities also acts as a storage room for clothing and miscellaneous accumulated things. This part of her office acts as the backstage to the domestic scene. What is left of it for her working space relies on the amount of non-essential elements stored to protect her child and husband's domestic experiences in the rest of the house. As it happened gradually, this growing storage encroaching on to her workspace didn't trigger any tensions. She describes it as the 'junkyard', and she acknowledges the uncomfortable messy impression it gives and the typical feeling of losing control of her own space (Breviglieri et al. 2003: 112). As Pia explains, 'This is an old drum, [...] it's not at all decorative in my office, we don't know where to put it ... To the office! So, there is a lot of stuff like this, it burdens me a lot but ... I cannot handle it' (Pia 2021: 9). Hidden behind the opaque wall, this burden doesn't affect the other members of the household, but it manifests in Pia's workspace as an additional domestic pressure.

In Laura's case, what she defines as 'her' workroom is shared with her boyfriend who sometimes works at home. He placed a desk there and arranged his belongings around it, thereby extending his familiar environment into Laura's privatized workroom. This created an area of tension between different kinds of space appropriation (Breviglieri 2009: 21). Even though nothing prevents Laura from using the whole room when her partner is absent, his familiar environment is inconsistent with a setting where her work activity would naturally find ease and comfort. His ownership of this part of the room acts as a very real limitation on the space she uses. Within the room there are also limits on the space she can control (e.g. by setting a sound environment she enjoys for work). These fluctuate depending on her partner's schedule.

The limitations of the workspace which rely on the rhythms of the other members of the household appear daily in the home of Dalila, a 37-year-old Tunisian who lives with her husband and their three children in a rented three-bedroom apartment in Geneva. She dedicates the night-time to work once she has completed all the housework and the others have finished their days. When her husband is asleep, she uses the desk she installed in their bedroom to work on. The obscurity of the night-time offers a thin atmospheric boundary that isolates her, but which is fragile. Its qualities depend on others, and on her own ability to de-synchronize herself from social temporalities (work during the day, rest during the night). This immateriality prevents her from acting on it and the hierarchical organization of her social life from being challenged (Figure 7.2).

  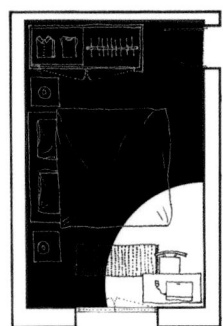

FIGURE 7.2 *Interpretative sketch of Pia's, Dalila's and Laura's workrooms, 2022. Drawing by Paule Perron and Fiona Del Puppo.*

The instability of the non-material limits of Laura's sound environment and Dalila's lighting atmosphere compromises the existence of a controlled workspace. However, it also ensures the possibility of its negotiation. Although, for them to be able to react to these frictions, to build demarcations to protect both their working space and their autonomy, they need their separation to exist materially (Debray 2013: 36). Just as the linear wall forbids passage, the thick border, on the contrary, regulates it. In the intertwined thickness and instability of this boundary lies a politically active territory, a 'space-of-variation' (Manning 2019: 2).

The thick boundary

Alexandra found in the 300 metres separation between her domestic sphere and her rented workshop the material answer to an 'out-of-time' experience (Barbey 1990: 101), which she needed to be able to negotiate her autonomy. However, this thick, but stable, separation doesn't protect her from domestic pressures. As she explains, 'I only spend … 3 half days of the week there. So otherwise, I have to come back and do something at home' (Alexandra 2020: 5).

The separation doesn't allow both entities to exist concurrently but tries to force the impossible disappearance of one or the other for a short period of time. There is no room for negotiation. Two of our interviewees found answers in the articulation of border-objects (Star and Griesemer 1989: 393), malleable enough to absorb the material and variable existences of the two spheres it separates. Alice, a 26-year-old video game streamer who lives alone in a one-bedroom rented apartment near Paris, has installed a thick shelf which separates her professional space from her personal space. She had to cope with her apartment being visible through her webcam, 'Actually, my apartment is well divided […] I've put the [shelf] to split. […] it's really extremely separated' (Alice 2020: 4).

Professional interactions are spatially restrained between her screen and her shelf. By arranging each side of this shelf differently, she controls the image she wants to give on camera and preserves the display of her privacy on the other side, 'There is the part facing me being 100 % video game and stuff. And the other side is more lifestyle, like my jewellery …' (Alice 2020: 4). Her ability to arrange space and to control the boundary between her different spheres of activities created the possibility of autonomy.

Sophie, a 41-year-old architect, who lives with her partner in his large family house, has materialized a personal protected space with an 'armchair'

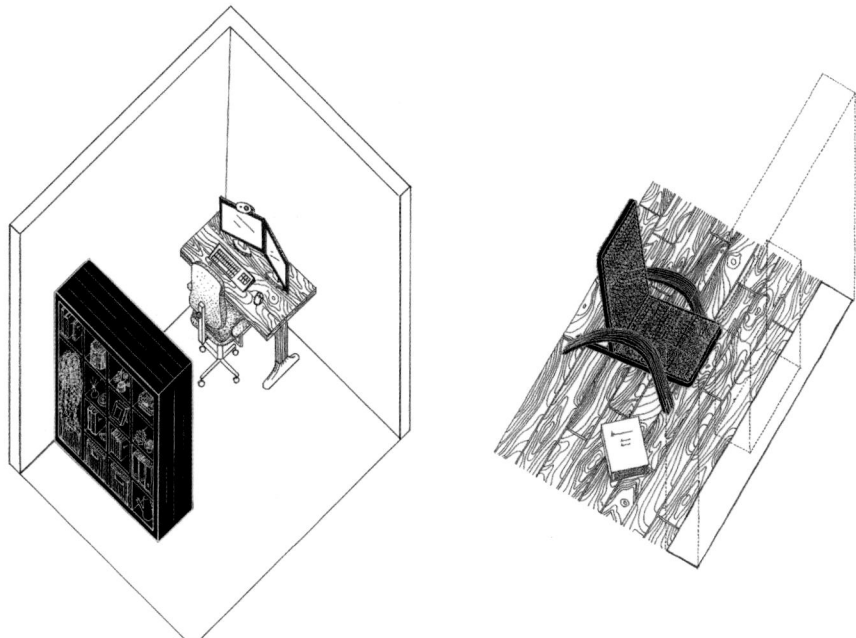

FIGURE 7.3 *Interpretative sketch of Alice's and Sophie's border-objects, 2022. Drawing by Paule Perron and Fiona Del Puppo.*

and 'books'. She explains that 'It's a corner where I can […] be sheltered, I mean, from the world, kinda. It would be my books, a good armchair' (Sophie 2021: 29). In addition to the major architectural structure of the unit-based habitation, inhabited object borders (Alice's shelf, Sophie's armchair) act as minor architectures (Stoner 2012: 2) which perform the spatial work that is needed for the inhabitants (Figure 7.3).

Sylvie, a 44-year-old seamstress (and former nurse) who lives with her husband and three children in a four-bedroom rented apartment in Geneva, has installed her practice in the main hall in her apartment which separates the intended collective areas from the bedrooms and bathrooms. Choosing to place herself in 'the centre of the agitation' can be understood as a result of her assigned role as caregiver in the family. Nevertheless, by putting her desks and working furniture in the hall, she controls the movement of people during the day. Through her own agency (Butler 1990: 128) and by inhabiting the thickness of this protective boundary, she determines when the common rooms act as collective spaces and produces a domesticated independence, the rhythm of which she controls (Figure 7.4).

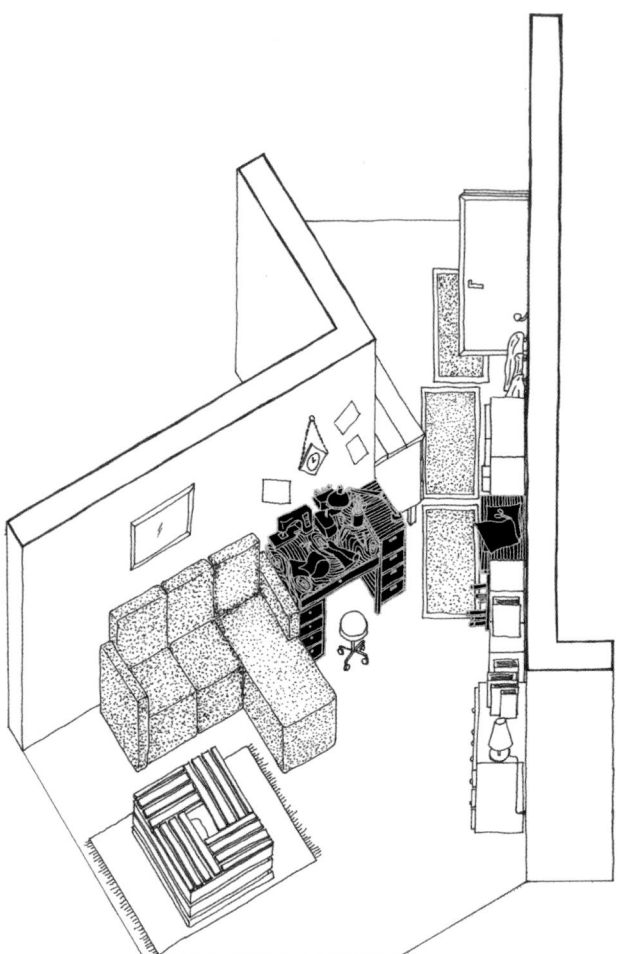

FIGURE 7.4 *Interpretative sketch of Sylvie's inhabited hallway, 2022. Drawing by Paule Perron and Fiona Del Puppo.*

Conclusion

Conceptualizing the domestication of independence led us to study the spatial strategies implemented by home-working women to integrate the neoliberal ideal independent subject within a patriarchal matrix: the architectural structures of homes. Through the daily reproduction of minor gestures, the professionally and domestically inhabiting body interiorises and perpetuates social and hierarchical norms (Froidevaux Metterie 2021: 100). However, it also provides an opportunity for its subversion, for the body experience to be transformed into its own expression (Manning 2019: 7). Through their own agencies, and when given the spatial opportunity, the seven women we studied are controlling the boundaries of their spaces. Within the thickness of these limits (which depend on material qualities but also on the social interactions they articulate) and through their instability, the gestures of their inhabiting bodies enable negotiation and make room for autonomy. The enactment of these seven domestic spaces provides a glimpse of a built environment that gives bodies the opportunity to push back.

Note

1   These case studies are part of a wider body of work that is part of the research project 'Domotopy: At home in a world in motion' led by Luca Pattaroni (Urban Sociology Laboratory, École Polytechnique Fédérale de Lausanne) financed by the Swiss National Science Foundation (n° 192831). This project started in September 2020 and involved a multidisciplinary team of sociologists, architects, engineers and geographers. It is partnered with HEAD - Genève and Line Fontana's interior design workshop. The whole body of work consists of thirty-four semi-directed interviews, with thirty-eight interviewees, including twenty-two women and sixteen men between twenty-four and seventy years of age. The interviewees mainly live in Switzerland, mostly in the Geneva area, one of them in France (Paris area). The interviews mainly took place at the interviewees' home, but eight of them were conducted via Zoom (considering the sanitary restrictions at the time). Most were led in teams of two, by either Dr Garance Clément, sociologist, or Paule Perron and Fiona Del Puppo, architects. They were all recorded. Photography and architectural drawing were used as a complementary ethnography method in order to describe the spatial and material qualities of the interviewees' places.

References

Appay, B. (2012), 'De l'autonomie émancipatrice à l'injonction d'autonomie', *Vie sociale,* 1(1): 29. https://doi.org/10.3917/vsoc.121.0029 (accessed 14 January 2021).
Barbey, G. (1990), *L'évasion domestique: Essai sur les relations d'affectivité au logis*, Lausanne: Presses polytechniques et universitaires romandes.
Bergström, O. and D. W. Storrie (2003), *Contingent Employment in Europe and the United States*, Cheltenham: Edward Elgar Publishing.
Bonnevier, K. (2007), *Behind Straight Curtains: Towards a Queer Feminist Theory of Architecture*, Stockholm: Axl Books.
Breviglieri, M., C. Lafaye, and D. Economica, eds (2009), 'L'insupportable. L'excès de Proximité, l'atteinte à l'autonomie et Le Sentiment de Violation Du Privé',

Competences Critiques et Sens de La Justice. https://hal.archives-ouvertes.fr/hal-01533280 (accessed 14 January 2021).

Breviglieri, M., B. Conein, P. Garcia, L. Pattaroni and J. Stavo-Debauge (2003), *Tenir Ensemble et Vivre Avec. Explorations Sociologiques de l'inclination à Cohabiter*, Rapport de l'action Financée Par Le Programme Habitat et Vie Urbaine (PUCA), Paris: EHESS, Groupe de Sociologie Politique et Morale.

Chollet, M. (2015), *Chez soi, une odyssée de l'espace domestique*, Paris: Zones.

Dadour, S. (2020), 'Introduction: architecture et féminisme: De la théorie critique à l'action – Qu'entend-on par "architecture féministe"? Une manière inclusive et critique d'approcher le projet et non une "sensibilité" spécifique', in S. Dadour (dir.) *Des féminismes en architecture, Revue Malaquais*, 6, 9–23, Paris: Beaux Arts de Paris éditions.

Debray, R. (2013), *Éloge des frontières*, Paris: Folio.

De Singly, F. (2000), *Libres ensemble: l'individualisme dans la vie commune*, Paris: Cle International.

Ehlers, T. B. and K. Main (1998), 'Women and the False Promise of Microenterprise', *Gender & Society*, 12(4): 424–40, https://doi.org/10.1177/089124398012004004 (accessed 14 January 2021).

Evans, R. (1997), 'Figures, Doors and Passages', in R. Evans (ed.), *Translations from Drawing to Building and Other Essays*, 54–91, Cambridge, Mass: MIT Press.

Froidevaux-Metterie, C. (2021), *Un corps à soi*, Paris: Seuil.

Hebrard, J. (2020), '6 pieces of advice for a Better Home Organisation during Lockdown', *Journal des femmes*, November 2020. (Quotes translated from French by the authors). Available online: https://deco.journaldesfemmes.fr/tendances-deco/2626377-conseils-pour-mieux-organiser-la-maison-pendant-le-confinement/ (accessed 12 January 2021).

Hughes, K. D. (2003), 'Pushed or Pulled? Women's Entry into Self-Employment and Small Business Ownership', *Gender, Work & Organization*, 10(4): 433–54. https://doi.org/10.1111/1468-0432.00205 (accessed 14 January 2021).

Jouan, M. (2012), 'L'autonomie, entre aspiration et injonction: un idéal ?' *Vie sociale* 1 (1): 41. https://doi.org/10.3917/vsoc.121.0041 (accessed 14 January 2021).

Judith, B. (1990), *Gender Trouble: Feminism and the Subversion of Identity*, London and New York: Routledge editions.

Logoz, C. A. (2021), *Scénographie du genre*, Master thesis, EPFL scientific publications.

Manning, E. (2016), *The Minor Gesture*, Durham and London: Duke University Press.

Manyka, J. and et al. (2016), *Independent Work: Choice, Necessity, and the Gig Economy*, San Francisco: McKinsey Global Institute.

Marlow, S. (1997), 'Self–Employed Women – New Opportunities, Old Challenges?' *Entrepreneurship & Regional Development*, 9(3): 199–210. https://doi.org/10.1080/08985629700000011 (accessed 14 January 2021).

Marlow, S. (2002), 'Women and Self-Employment: A Part of or Apart from Theoretical Construct?', *The International Journal of Entrepreneurship and Innovation*, 3(2): 83–91. https://doi.org/10.5367/000000002101299088 (accessed 14 January 2021).

Martín P. and M. Teresa (2009), 'Domestiquer le travail', *Multitudes*, 37–8(2): 90. https://doi.org/10.3917/mult.037.0090 (accessed 14 January 2021).

Molinier, P. (2021), *Le travail du care*, Paris: La Dispute.
Nacy, F. (2013), 'How Feminism Became Capitalism's Handmaiden – And How to Reclaim It', *The Guardian*, [online]. https://www.theguardian.com/commentisfree/2013/oct/14/feminism-capitalist-handmaiden-neoliberal (accessed 14 January 2021).
Pattaroni, L. (2007), 'Le Sujet En l'individu: La Promesse d'autonomie Du Travail Social Au Risque d'une Colonisation Par Le Proche', in F. Cantelli and J. L. Genard (eds), *Action Publique et Subjectivité, Droit et Société*, 46, 203–18, Paris: LGDJ Editions.
Perilleux, T. (2001), *Les tensions de la flexibilité*, Paris: DDB.
Salman, S. (2014), 'Un coach pour battre la mesure ?', *Revue d'anthropologie des connaissances*, 8(1). https://journals.openedition.org/rac/3965#tocto2n4 (accessed 14 January 2021).
Star, S. L. and J. Griesemer (1989), 'Institutionnal ecology, "Translations", and Boundary Objects: Amateurs and Professionals on Berkeley's Museum of Vertrebate Zoologie', *Social Studies of Science*, 19(3): 387–420.
Stoner, J. (2012), *Toward a Minor Architecture*, Cambridge: MIT Press.
Woolf, V. (1989 [1929]), *A Room of One's Own*, San Diego: Mariner Books.
Zimmermann, B. (2011), *Ce que travailler veut dire: une sociologie des capacités et des parcours professionnels*, Paris: Economica.

Interviews

Alexandra, 2020.
Alice, 2020.
Dalila, 2020.
Laura, 2020.
Pia, 2021.
Sophie, 2020.
Sylvie, 2021.

8

Working at home: Architects during the pandemic in China

Ye Xu, Katharina Borsi and Jonathan Hale

Introduction

Since the Covid-19 outbreaks in late 2019, some of the most important matters relating to individual bodies and health have increasingly moved out of the familiar and relatively intimate setting of the home and into the public setting where healthcare is dispensed, and digital tracking occurs. At the same time, digital technology and communication allow the 'managed intrusion' (Mahmood 2007: 77–100) of the workplace into the domestic space, and shopping, education and other services further moved from the public sphere to the spaces of the home. Simultaneously, the connection between people operating in virtual space – for work, communication and leisure – is accelerating rapidly, reshaping our experiences of living and working. This study seeks to expand the existing research on home-based working and explore how the relationships between the public and the private, the urban and the domestic, are constructed in our homes. Only in this way can we improve the design regulation of the built environment better to support new types of live/work combinations, at both the individual building and the urban scale.

Studies undertaken to date about the architecture of home-based work have been approached from two main angles. One has focused on the rise of the bifurcation between living and working and the corresponding construction of the idea 'domesticity' in the nineteenth century (Benjamin 1999; Borsi 2009: 132–52; Evans 1978: 267–78; Hayden 1982; Heynen and Baydar eds. 2005; Rybczynski 1986). In the modern tight domestic unit, the relationships between public and private, and selves and others, are different from those in the medieval multi-functional households. Other writings explore the dual use building type that combines dwelling and workplace primarily through case studies. *Beyond Live/Work: The Architecture of Home-Based Work* (Holliss 2015) traces the architectural history of the work-home. It analyses the lives and premises of eighty-six contemporary home-based workers and has generated a series of typologies and design considerations for the work-home. *Living Over the Store: Architecture and Local Urban Life* (Davis 2012) argued that the architecture and living type of the shop/home is an important component of the liveable city, one that facilitates walkability, face-to-face interactions and a vibrant street scene. *House as a Mirror of Self: Exploring the Deeper Meaning of Home* (Marcus 2006) suggested that spatial, visual and aural separation is critical when we work at home.

Topics within this theme also include urban research that analyses mixed-use planning strategies (Zenkteler et al. 2019); the investigation into architecture/interior design to better accommodate home-based work (Dolan 2012; Holliss 2017); the feminist research focusing on the relationship between women's social production and domestic reproduction (Giudici 2018: 1203–29; Tattara and Aureli 2018: 194–202); and smart homes and teleworking in the context of information technologies (Gurstein 2001). Much of this research stems from a period prior to the pandemic and foregrounds existing or new typologies able to accommodate multiple scenarios of occupation. The ongoing shift and generalization of flexible working provides a new urgency for an analysis of the ambiguity and diversity of live/work scenarios in standard dwellings, which has so far not received much attention.

This chapter is positioned within the growing discourse about the interior that disconnects the idea of home territory from a static and private place, presenting the former as a more open, permeable, social and mobile concept (Bachelard 1969; Deleuze and Guattari 1987; Mallett 2004: 62–89; Massey 1994; Rice 2006; Smitheram and Woodcock 2009; Wise 2000: 295–310). The initial investigation was conducted in 2020 during the pandemic and a total of ten architects from five major cities in China were interviewed. The two cases studies selected for this chapter represent ambiguous and complex modes of domesticity and are representative of Chinese architects' ways of homeworking and cultures of inhabitation during the pandemic. The primary aim of this chapter is to conceptualize different ways of shaping and mobilizing home territories in the context of working at home. The second aim is to contribute to discussions about the potential of drawings as both illustrative forms and analytic methods for observing and representing the interior and domesticity. Finally, it argues that the home can be seen as a constantly changing territorial network, thus pointing to the shifting conceptions of the public and private in domestic space.

Figure 8.1 shows the minimal dormitory room of a young male architecture student who lives alone in the student accommodation on the campus of Tongji University in Shanghai. The generic space is static, dull and cold. But when lived in (encountered, manipulated, touched, voiced, glanced at, practised) it radiates a field of force, a shape of space (Wise 2000: 297). The drawing shows the architect's body movements as well as the room, furniture and objects, in order to reveal the fluid socio-spatial relationships in temporal and scalar dimensions. Although living in a collective housing unit, the occupant kept quite a secluded, atomized lifestyle and did not interact with the other residents. His typical day involved several hours sitting at his desk, clicking the mouse to draw architectural plans and communicating with colleagues via email and zoom; browsing through a restaurant take-out application and ordering food delivery from nearby, eating at the same desk and, sometimes before the meal, taking a food picture and posting it on Instagram. The regular repetition of his bodily and mental actions blends with the living space he moves through, establishing his everyday life and thus a layer of the home territory.

Although some actions are routine and repeated, they are also unpredictable, impermanent, non-linear and grounded in the evanescent reality of movement. Some fleeting behaviours also indicate certain spatial boundaries of his home which can quickly change, e.g. body positions, or the

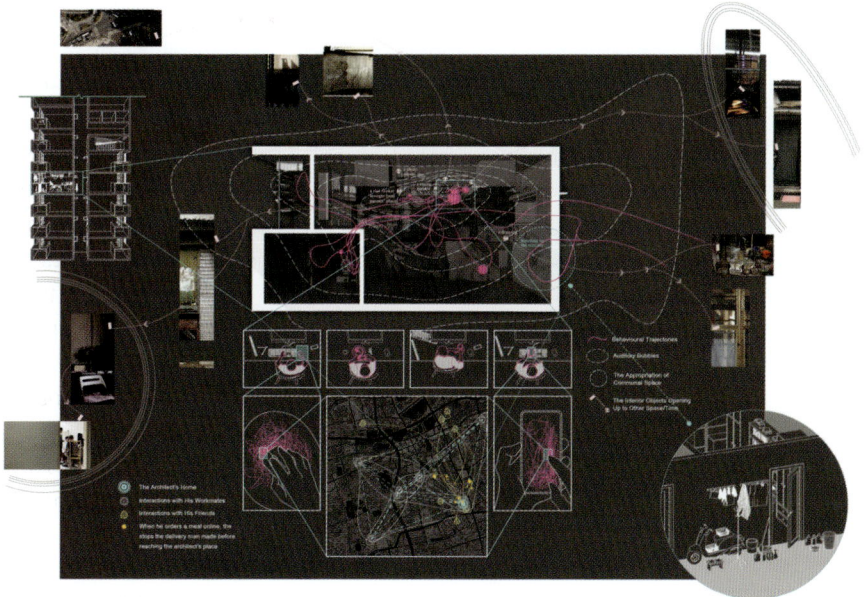

FIGURE 8.1 *A minimal home of one's own. Drawn by Ye Xu.*

sound of laughter. 'During the lockdown there were no other occupants in my building', said the architect, 'so I was free to play music louder than usual and make a more heavy-smelling meal of curry.' The territorial bubbles of sound, smell, light and smoke extend beyond his minimal dwelling. The extension of domestic space also includes more permanent scenarios. For instance, the appropriation of communal space shows a material way of expanding the home territory beyond the interior. During the pandemic, the architect occupied the shared corridor space as a semi-contaminated zone, leaving there worn masks, trash can, shoes and coats, as well as cleaning supplies – from disinfectant to a small vacuum cleaner – and entering his room only after being fully cleaned and disinfected.

The opening up of home starts from the communal space and moves on to the expanded spaces of the urban and the global. The trajectories of the architect's fingers moving the mouse or sliding across the phone screen show the relationship between interactions in virtual space and circulations in physical space, and a continuity between interior and exterior, public and private.

For the purposes of virtual meetings, the architect redecorated his home in order to set the partial interior suitable for public display, using bookshelves, decorative paintings and plants as the background setting, and the behaviour was shared by several other interviewees. Here parts of the domestic space were transformed into a de-individualized space. The photos, travel souvenirs and dozens of project drawings on his desk and the bookshelf above helped to project different territories, linked to different partial identities. The interior objects glowed with memories or imaginations of experience, of history, of people, that were distant in space and/or time. It is these connections with, and openness to, other space/time that in part construct the home, one that is always permeable and social. As Doreen Massey put it, 'a large component of the identity of that place called home derived precisely from the fact that it had always in one way or another been open; constructed out of movement, communication, social relations which always stretched beyond it' (Massey 1994: 170–1).

A growing home

The second case study is the home of an architect couple (Li Han & Hu Yan, the founders of *Drawing Architecture Studio*) who lived in a typical urban apartment with two bedrooms in Beijing. Like many successful architectural practices, their working space evolved from the bedrooms and kitchen table to a separate studio. However, they didn't rent a standardized office but bought an apartment of two bedrooms in the same neighbourhood and changed it into a workspace/studio (Figures 8.2 and 8.3). When they first moved into it, they would still go home for lunch every day. But later they just cooked and ate there. The stove, used to boil water and make coffee, gradually became a real kitchen, rendering the inhabitation of the office more ambiguous and complex. One of the partners said, 'The boundaries get blurred, especially when you don't think of it as a rented office but as a part of your home … My work has become more and more intrusive into my domestic life, and you could even say that it fills up my entire life. My work is my life, and my life is my work.' Their home grew from one place to two and constantly split like a cell. Each

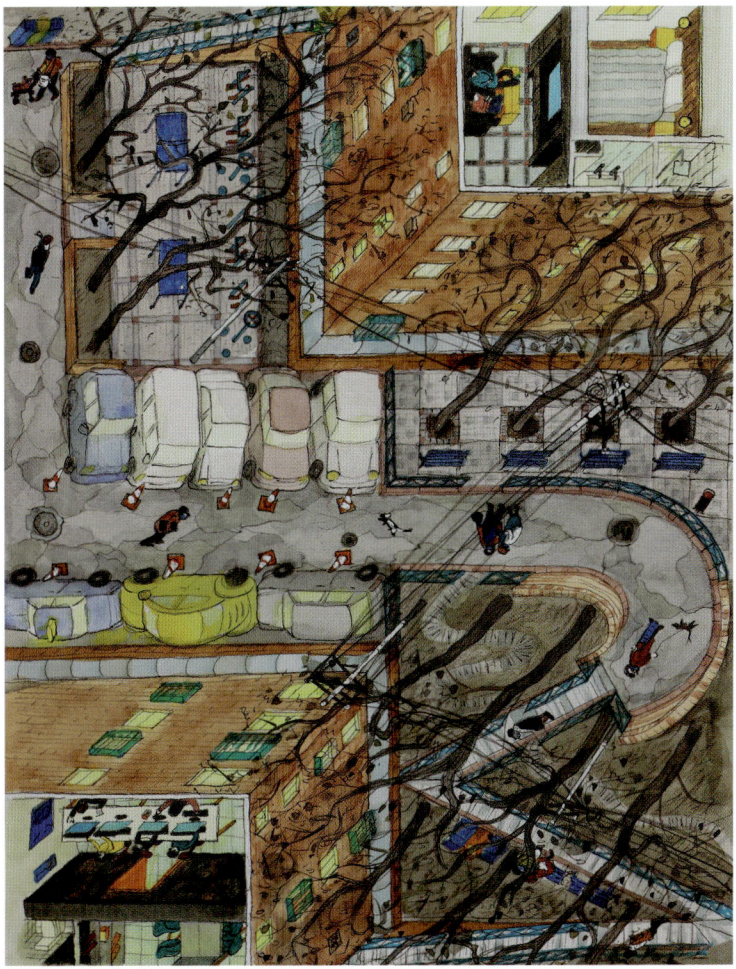

FIGURE 8.2 *Drawing architecture studio office. Drawn by Drawing Architecture Studio.*

FIGURE 8.3 *A tale of two apartments. Drawn by Drawing Architecture Studio.*

cell, however, contains information about the whole and is not divided up according to its function. The home territory is no longer centred around the apartment or a particular interior but is multi-centred and constantly changing as our lives unfold. An office can be one node within the network of one's personal realm, so can a private car, a café, an art gallery or a library.

The behavioural trajectories and space occupied by each household member within the two dwelling unit are also completely overlapping. As they said: 'We don't need (physical) personal space or privacy between us, except occasionally when we both have online meetings, and the sound could be a

WORKING AT HOME

FIGURE 8.4 *Living by interface. Drawn by Feng Lu.*

bit interfering. The rest of the time we prefer sitting face-to-face and burying in our own work, or leaning together on the couch, socialising or entertaining'. This is not an isolated case. Architect Feng Lu, who lived with his wife and son in an apartment of a gated community in Shanghai, also offered his opinion on personal space in his home during our interview:

> When we talk about privacy or the personal sphere in our home, it's usually about the physical space. However, the floor area of a typical Chinese home is around 100 square meters, or less. The limited space has to include functional spaces such as the kitchen and the bathroom, leaving even less space for activities. So how can we discuss privacy in such a limited space? In my opinion, the privacy in physical space of our home might be meaningless. On the one hand, it is impossible to establish one's own territory in such a small space. On the other hand, I don't need a physical territory. One's privacy is gradually being instrumentalized by technology, for example the setting of a smart phone. The moment when you sit down

on the couch and take out your phone to socialize, you're in your own world, and have nothing to do with the person sitting just next to you. To a certain extent, today the way a person maintains privacy and constructs his/her own subjectivity is no longer by having an intimate space, or the space is no longer a physical space, but more of a virtual space, an information space, for example, your Facebook, WeChat, or Twitter. They construct your individuality.

(Figure 8.4)

The observations and interviews from this research suggested that the juxtaposition, combination and leap between physical and virtual privacy are key scenarios of contemporary everyday life. They not only set us free from the limit of real space and time, but also render different spatial scales and different lengths of time equivalent, forming a seamless continuum. It shapes our perception in a particular way and can generate a sense of humility and insignificance, as well as one of hubris and omnipotence through our belief in the compensatory power of technology.

Conclusion: Drawing domesticity

We applied drawing as an exploratory and critical visual practice in this research, trying to reveal a process of thinking or forming questions, rather than presenting a singular conclusion. The drawings, including both the architects' sketches and the authors' diagrams, speak of how home territories are formed and appropriated by inhabitants, objects and activities. Based on the case studies, we applied the architectural drawing conventions to everyday space/objects/practices, emphasizing their importance as sites of spatial studies. The specificity of the drawings, and the character, density of traces of inhabitation, overlaid over the typically standard domestic floor plan, aerial views or axonometric, yields an understanding of the territorializing process and a shift in the way our homes are conceived. Different modes of inhabitation suggest how private and social life came to be configured to respond to economic relations, and how the architectural work – the design of the external world – comes from an interior condition. When the domestic and social practices, as well as the cultures of inhabitation, encapsulated simultaneously in the drawings of the rooms, furniture, objects and activities, we perceive them and their interactions all at once, instead of seeing them unfolding sequentially, i.e. first entering a room; second, perceiving objects in it; and third, attaching cultural significance to them, as language makes us do.

Drawing inhabitation – tracing patterns of inhabitation and movement in real and virtual realms – calls for following individual routines, habits and modes across the spaces of working desk, to the neighbourhood and the city. By allowing the overlay, juxtaposition and collapse of different scales and domains into one perceptual realm, varied relations are activated, and more possibilities are explored. The drawing, as Robin Evans (1986: 3–18) insisted, is not so much a projection of an idea, it creates a particular reality of its own. The drawing of 'A minimal home of one's own' in the first case study maps the habitual pattern of eating, working and socializing in a fixed position at the table and shows how the frantic close circles of the mouse inscribing in the virtual world project into the real world. In the second case study, the axonometric views of the interiors show not so much 'home' and 'work', apart from the presence of a bed. Instead, the architects' drawings underscore the richness of their lived experience stemming from communication and intellectual pursuit. Figures 8.2 and 8.3, depict a culture of communication and intellectual exchange, architectural production and display.

Informed by the study of architects' work-homes during the pandemic, we suggest that home-working practices can be understood as a dynamic process of territorialization. In this context, home territories are constantly produced and represented, in different ways and across scales. We have identified here two of the many different forms of territorial production that we are likely to find in domestic spaces. The first is the material traces left by previous behaviours, which cannot be easily erased or changed within a certain period, such as decoration, collections or the appropriation of communal space by objects. The territories constructed are usually the result of long-term negotiations and are relatively stable. The second is routinely repeated behaviours that mark or indicate existing space boundaries in the home, such as habitual actions. These forms of territorial production are not planned or intentionally established but are, rather, consequences of regular or occasional practices. These practices may be the effects of rational and planned decisions but are not made with the explicit intent of producing a home territory (Kärrholm 2007: 441). For example, the decoration of the interior or regular housekeeping activities is carried out after careful home-making considerations, but without any thought about marking or delimiting a territory. What is produced through those territorial process are not static and dichotomous home territories, but rather the dynamic spatial/social relations, including private/public, individual/collective, indoor/outdoor relationships which together constitute our homes.

The drawings in this research yield the home territory as a multi-centred, constantly changing network composed of both physical and virtual spaces, domestic and urban spaces. In some instances, the home took on most of the roles of the traditional public sphere, i.e. performs as a mediator that both keeps people apart and brings them together. The trend has been accelerated by the pandemic. This is both an architectural prototype and a new field for architecture to confront.

References

Bachelard, G. (1969), *The Poetics of Space*, trans. Maria Jolas, Boston, MA: Beacon Press.

Benjamin, W. (1999), *The Arcades Project*, Cambridge, MA: Harvard University Press.

Borsi, K. (2009), 'Drawing and Dispute: The Strategies of the Berlin Block', in V. Di Palma, D. Periton and M. Lathouri (eds), *Intimate Metropolis: Urban Subjects in the Modern City*, 132–52, London: Routledge.

Davis, H. (2012), *Living over the Store: Architecture and Local Urban Life*, London: Routledge.

Deleuze, G. and F. Guattari (1987), *A Thousand Plateaus: Capitalism and Schizophrenia*, trans. B. Massumi, Minneapolis: University of Minnesota Press, 311–15.

Dolan, T. (2012), *Live-Work Planning and Design: Zero-Commute Housing*, Hoboken, NJ: John Wiley & Sons.

Evans, R. (1978), 'Figures, Doors and Passages', *Architectural Design*, 48: 267–78.

Evans, R. (1986), 'Translations from Drawing to Building', *AA Files*, 12: 3–18.

Giudici, M. S. (2018), 'Counter-Planning from the Kitchen: For a Feminist Critique of Type', *The Journal of Architecture*, 23(7–8): 1203–29.

Gurstein, P. (2001), *Wired to the World, Chained to the Home: Telework in Daily Life*, Vancouver: UBC Press.

Hayden, D. (1982), *The Grand Domestic Revolution: A History of Feminist Designs for American Homes, Neighborhoods, and Cities*, Cambridge: MIT Press.

Heynen, H. and G. Baydar, eds (2005), *Negotiating Domesticity: Spatial Productions of Gender in Modern Architecture*, Oxon: Routledge.

Holliss, F. (2015), *Beyond Live/Work: The Architecture of Home-based Work*, London: Routledge.

Holliss, F. (2017), 'Designing for Home-Based Work–Lessons from Two English Villages', *Architecture and Culture*, 5(1): 21–39.

Kärrholm, M. (2007), 'The Materiality of Territorial Production: A Conceptual Discussion of Territoriality, Materiality, and the Everyday Life of Public Space', *Space and Culture*, 10(4): 437–53.

Mahmood, A. N. (2007), 'Work and Home Boundaries: Socio-spatial Analysis of Women's Live-work Environments', *Housing and Society*, 34(1): 77–100.

Mallett, S. (2004), 'Understanding Home: A Critical Review of the Literature', *The Sociological Review*, 52(1): 62–89.

Marcus, C. C. (2006), *House as a Mirror of Self: Exploring the Deeper Meaning of Home*, Florida: Nicolas-Hays.

Massey, D. (1994), *Space, Place, and Gender*, Minneapolis: University of Minnesota Press.
Rice, C. (2006), *The Emergence of the Interior: Architecture, Modernity, Domesticity*, Oxon: Routledge.
Rybczynski, W. (1986), *Home: A Short History of an Idea*, 10, New York: Penguin.
Smitheram, J. and I. Woodcock (2009), 'Affective Territories', *IDEA Journal*, 9(1): 8–19.
Tattara, M. and P. V. Aureli (2018), 'The Home at Work: A Genealogy of Housing for the Laboring Classes', *Harvard Design Magazine*, 46: 194–202.
Wise, J. M. (2000), 'Home: Territory and Identity', *Cultural Studies*, 14(2): 295–310.
Zenkteler, M. et al. (2019), 'Home-Based Work in Cities: In Search of an Appropriate Urban Planning Response', *Futures*, 135(2022): 102494.

9

From *Caseta* to *Cuarto*: The spaces of restorative and transitional justice in Colombia before and during the Covid-19 pandemic

Cynthia Imogen Hammond, Greg Labrosse, Vanessa Sicotte and Marcela Torres Molano

Introduction

In 2016 the government of Colombia set up a nationwide Truth Commission in order to deal with five decades of violence that had shattered social bonds across the nation. Architecture has played a significant role in the Truth Commission's activities. Retro-fitted office buildings have served as sites where survivors' testimonies have been gathered, while purpose-built museums have hosted exhibitions and events that bring these testimonies into the public realm. In more rural areas, many communities have used informal spaces such as the *caseta*, or kiosk, for the purpose of bearing witness to their lived experiences. A flexible, open structure with a concrete floor and roof, the *caseta* is well established within Colombian vernacular traditions, and – unlike the more formal architecture of Truth Commission offices – makes no clear distinction between its 'exterior' and its 'interior'.

After the outbreak of Covid-19 in 2019–20, the Truth Commission's activities moved into the private spaces of caseworkers' homes. This shift had a major impact on caseworkers' abilities to gather testimonies, and on their experiences of doing so. We interviewed Colombian architects, case workers and other individuals involved with the Truth Commission to better understand the spatial aspects of their work, both pre- and post-pandemic. This chapter explores our findings, with particular emphasis on the spatial story of one Truth Commission case worker, Alejandra Gutiérrez Gómez. In the spring of 2020, like millions of other people around the world, Gutiérrez Gómez began working from home after the start of the Covid-19 pandemic, transforming her bedroom, or *cuarto*, into a place of work. Through Gutiérrez Gómez's descriptions, photographs and drawings of her new 'office', we explain how this caseworker perceived the emotional, spatial and gendered implications of working from home. The last is significant; many testimonies that Gutiérrez Gómez gathered in her bedroom were stories of sexual violence.

This chapter contributes to the broader understanding of the move to working from home during an unprecedented global health crisis, and the spotlight that this shift has thrown upon the capacities of the domestic interior to contain all that individuals, families and societies require (Adams 2020; Chayka 2020). We shed light on the intimate nexus between testimony, witnessing and interior space that distinguishes the work of restorative and transitional justice. Throughout the chapter, the figure of the *caseta* remains an imperfect but wholly flexible space that resonates with survivors because, as Gutiérrez Gómez put it, people 'feel free to leave anytime they want to' (Gutiérrez Gómez 2021). So long as the pandemic contains both survivor and witness indoors and online, this freedom remains elusive, however, raising the question of how truth and reconciliation processes unfold in conditions of spatial constraint.

Restorative and transitional justice

In Colombia, as in South Africa, Australia and Canada, the model for truth and reconciliation has been 'restorative justice'. The values of 'truth, accountability, reparation, reconciliation, conflict resolution and democratic participation' (O'Mahony and Doak 2012: 305) are key for restorative justice, which aims to promote reparation in the wake of war, colonialism and violent conflict. The main strategy is to engage survivors and perpetrators in an intimate, shared journey of understanding by bringing to light all sides of a conflict and making space for the ways in which perpetrators themselves (such as child soldiers) were often also victims (Walklate 2007: 273–85). Indigenous traditions have provided the inspiration for restorative justice (Blagg and Anthony 2019: 133–52; Jung 2009; Omale 2006: 33–63; Seeger 2005: 75–84) and offer an alternative to mainstream or 'adversarial' justice (Toews 2018: 209), which is characterized by authoritative and hierarchical structures and dehumanizing spatial interiors (Wener 2012: 243–79).

Restorative justice tends to undertake its small-scale reparation work with a focus on the future, while transitional justice is employed as a means to reckon with widespread, past trauma at the scale of the community or the nation (Uprimny and Saffon 2006: 6). When restorative techniques are adapted to deal with a nationwide conflict, as they have been in Colombia, the process is a hybrid between restorative and transitional justice. In this country, six decades of internal conflict between paramilitary forces and the government claimed more than 220,000 lives and caused the displacement of over six million people. Social inequality and labour informality continue, as does ongoing territorial strife. In this context, the Truth Commission aims to collect 20,000 interviews with survivors. These testimonies, it is hoped, will create an enhanced awareness of human rights violations committed across the country.

The architecture of truth in Colombia

Sometimes existing buildings have been recycled, such as the main Truth Commission offices in Bogotá, which previously served as the country's Ministry of Justice, and, later, the Office of the Comptroller General (Comisión de la Verdad 2020). This ten-storey, stone-clad building features a double-height atrium, where many public initiatives and hearings take place, while the upper floors follow a traditional spatial distribution pattern for offices. Rooms for collecting individuals' testimonies are small and neutral, whereas areas where employees analyse and process data are distinguished by bright colours and an open plan. Figure 9.1 shows an interior where Gutiérrez Gómez would have spent much of her day when not collecting testimonies in rural areas. The room is institutional but calm, its banality offset by natural light and natural materials such as that of the wooden floors and tables (Figure 9.1).

Beyond urban centres, the Truth Commission's activities have overlapped with grassroots efforts at truthtelling that predate the Peace Accord. In the rural Montes de María region of Colombia, an itinerant museum called *El Mochuelo* is the outcome of the work of Línea 21, a collective founded in 1994 in support of local communities affected by the conflict. The museum, designed in 2008 by architects Carlos Puerta and Verónica Ortiz, is a partially open wooden structure that can be disassembled and moved (Castellar et al. 2013: 159–74) (Figure 9.2). The vertical slats and open roof allow the passage of air, while the flexible interior can be used for participatory events,

FIGURE 9.1 *Interview room, Truth Commission office, Bogotà, Colombia, 2018. Design by DUCON Disenos y espacios productivos. Reproduced with permission of DUCON Disenos y espacios productivos.*

performances and installations, thus echoing the fluid boundary between exterior and interior that is found in the *caseta*. A different example of Truth Commission architecture can be found in twenty-two 'houses of truth' that are spread across Colombia. These came from the desire to create spaces for communities that were removed from the more bureaucratic character of the Truth Commission's urban offices. For this purpose, the Truth Commission purposefully adopted a home environment where, it was hoped, people would feel safe enough to share their stories. Murals and symbols of hope, peace and forgiveness often animate the design or decoration of such spaces (Castellar and Samudio Reyes 2021; Casas de la verdad 2019) (Figure 9.2).

Annette Pearson de González, a Truth and Reconciliation consultant, believes that the success of such interior spaces derives from the capacity of their users 'to make these spaces their own, even if it's something as small as [adding] a candle' (Pearson de González 2021). Our interviewees also noted the importance of implementing a non-hierarchical spatial organization anywhere that difficult memories would be shared, even if that simply meant rearranging the furniture in an otherwise inflexible space or putting up a curtain to provide a symbolic barrier between survivors and perpetrators (Jimenez 2021). Justice architect Ana Lopez further observed that the time frame

FIGURE 9.2 El Mochuelo, *Itinerant Museum of Memory and Identity of Montes de María, Colombia (2008)*. *Photograph by Sergio Gómez. Reproduced with permission of Sergio Gómez.*

of architecture, which is usually geared towards completion, is not always the time of reconciliation. Speaking about a purpose-built project that was originally intended to be a house of memory, Lopez explained,

> The reconciliation process was longer than the actual architectural project. [So the design team] left certain spaces that were needed in the community and [which] became activation devices that could eventually become spaces for memory. In the meantime, they provide spaces for the hope of the future generations and allow the healing of those who have suffered extremely painful situations.
>
> (Lopez 2021)

Lopez pointed out that the flexibility of the built project was its major attribute. Only once the community was ready to fill the space with their memories would the walls be finished. Until that time the structure would be open, like a *caseta*. The emotional significance of such spaces within local communities cannot be underestimated. Lopez recalled one alternative justice space that was so important that the local residents referred to it as a person, with its own identity, integrity, fragility and social relationships (Lopez 2021).

The shift to working from home

Alejandra Gutiérrez Gómez is a 28-year-old Colombian anthropologist who started working for the Truth Commission in 2019. She was hired to collect testimonies in different regions of Colombia, and then to file the interviews on the government's database. Her space within the Truth Commission offices in Bogotá, shared with thirty other caseworkers, occupied half of one floor of the building. Each analyst's personal workstation in the larger shared workspace had windows and access to a cafeteria, amenities that gave respite from the emotional strain of gathering testimonies. The seating arrangement made it easy for staff to communicate with one other and share the psychological challenges of their work. Gutiérrez Gómez described the office as a quiet environment that allowed for deep conversations and mutual care (2021) (Figure 9.3).

After the countrywide lockdown, all Truth Commission workers were obliged to relocate their workstations to their own homes, and all in-person interactions with survivors ceased. The shift from Gutiérrez Gómez's communal office environment to working from home placed unprecedented demands on her domestic space. Once Gutiérrez Gómez accepted that she

FIGURE 9.3 *The* cuarto *of Alejandra Gutiérrez Gómez in Bogotà, Colombia (2021). Original photograph by Alejandra Gutiérrez Gómez, rendering by Marcela Torres Molano. Reproduced with permission of Alejandra Gutiérrez Gómez.*

would be spending nearly the entire day in her bedroom – a compact room that strains to accommodate her double bed – she set up a small workstation. To help us understand her spatial decisions, Gutiérrez Gómez shared with us a photograph of her bedroom (Figure 9.3). In placing her desk in a carefully selected corner of the bedroom, Gutiérrez Gómez prevented accidental captures of the home's other residents on her computer's camera, assuring the privacy of the online encounter. This corner also gave Gutiérrez Gómez a work location that was adjacent to the room's only window, which frames sunset views of Bogotá. For it to be visible to her interviewees, Gutiérrez Gómez hung a favourite poster about cycling, one of her passions, on the wall behind her work chair. The poster, with its fuchsia, orange and turquoise palette, is one of the brightest spots in the room and a reminder of activities outside the home. Through these small acts of 'spatial agency' (Awan et al. 2011: 29), Gutiérrez Gómez modified the physical elements of her bedroom, and thus mediated the image of this interior in an effort to compensate for the lack of physical co-presence.

The folding of the public interior into the private room

Working from home had consequences for Gutiérrez Gómez's mental health. Video conferencing is especially draining when the work is emotional or foregrounds human connection because it is not a genuine substitute for physical spaces of intimacy. Rather, as Adam Lerner explains, virtual meeting spaces were designed to be 'transactional spaces' (2020). At the same time, the home is discursively associated with women, privacy and femininity, while also being a key site for the production of gender and the gendered production of space (Heynen 2005: 10–1, 23–5). Gutiérrez Gómez's effort to be an empathetic interlocutor during many hours of listening to difficult testimony each day, and doing so within a transactional virtual space that actually inhibits personal connection, was difficult enough. In addition, Gutiérrez Gómez mourned the loss of her formerly private bedroom, which became a more intensely gendered environment as a result of the accounts of violence that were part of her job (Gutiérrez Gómez 2021). Gutiérrez Gómez's bedroom thus became a very uneasy environment in which to carry out her Truth Commission work.

Once Gutiérrez Gómez's working day came to end, her next challenge was to make a separation between the difficult knowledge in which she had been immersed and an interior that now had to accommodate her private life. 'Many times, I wanted to talk with someone who did the same work as me. This was something I could do at the office. A possibility I no longer had when I started working from home' (Gutiérrez Gómez 2021). During the pandemic, Gutiérrez Gómez's work began to have an impact on her dreams and personal relations. 'Working from home,' she told us 'changes your way of behaving around people, because you feel no one understands the amount of pain we have to deal with; pain you wish to explain to everyone, but it wouldn't be ethical or right, and also people wouldn't understand it' (Gutiérrez Gómez 2021).

Gutiérrez Gómez's case study brings to mind recent literature that explores what Penny Sparke calls 'the public interior' and the consequences of 'the erosion of the boundaries between public and private interiors' (Sparke 2020: 236, 238). Gutiérrez Gómez's shift to working from home underscores how interiors, despite their long conflation with privacy and domesticity, have close ties to sites of labour and production and are places that are shared with the wider world through the flow of media, such as photography, television and social platforms (Sparke 2008: 200–1, 206–8; see also Colomina 1994: 141–200). These ideas resonate with what we learned from our interview with Gutiérrez Gómez about the compressed nature of Gutiérrez Gómez's makeshift workspace in her *cuarto*, entirely mediated by online communication platforms, and fraught with the emotional demands of gathering testimony from survivors of atrocious violence.

The gendered space of alternative justice

Prior to the Covid-19 pandemic, Gutiérrez Gómez was collecting in-person testimonies along the Caribbean coast, primarily working with Afro-Colombian women who had survived sexual violence. When describing these interviews Gutiérrez Gómez highlighted the benefit that her physical presence had brought to these encounters. 'Being there in person allowed me to listen with profound empathy', she recalled. 'My body language could show the other person how important they are, and they could feel that' (Gutiérrez Gómez 2021). Gutiérrez Gómez also stressed the importance of physical proximity in establishing a sense of trust, such as 'sitting close to the person, holding their hand as they recall difficult events, getting up to offer them a glass of water'. Gutiérrez Gómez noted that she would frequently cry with her participants as they shared their stories. Sharing the physical space of the interview was essential for Gutiérrez Gómez; in doing so she could 'actively listen' and 'engage empathetically' with a participant in the moment of receiving her testimony (Gutiérrez Gómez 2021).

Gutiérrez Gómez was keenly aware of how spatial and emotional considerations were entwined in her pre-pandemic interviews. 'I myself looked for spaces that were not inside the home or the neighbourhood,' she told us 'a non-familiar space for the women that I was interviewing, because many of them have emotional conflicts when talking about these situations around their families, children and spouses' (Gutiérrez Gómez 2021). For such women, the *caseta* was preferred because it is neither domestic, public nor wholly an interior. 'A *caseta* is a structure with one part built with a concrete roof and floor, and another part can have a soil floor, with palm-leaf roofing. It is open and it is used for meetings and parties' (Gutiérrez Gómez 2021). *Casetas*, Gutiérrez Gómez explained, are inherently associated with freedom of movement. '*Casetas* are spaces that people use day to day. They are spaces where people are used to coming and going' (Gutiérrez Gómez 2021). Unlike a bedroom, or *cuarto*, which is often located deep within the home, far from any egress, the *caseta* and its associations with freedom and informality helped to ease the burden of both sharing and receiving difficult recollections of gendered violence during the conflict (Figure 9.4).

After giving us the photograph of her bedroom, Gutiérrez Gómez decided to create another document to help us better understand her workspace: a hand-drawn sketch (Figure 9.4). The drawing shows how Gutiérrez

FIGURE 9.4 *The* cuarto *of Alejandra Gutiérrez Gómez (2021). Hand drawing by Alejandra Gutiérrez Gómez. Reproduced with permission of Alejandra Gutiérrez Gómez.*

Gómez rearranged this interior and added key objects to personalize the virtual interaction and make it more welcoming and intimate. But the drawing represents Gutiérrez Gómez's room from a different angle than her photograph. Rather, it is Gutiérrez Gómez's own view of her *cuarto* that we see, from her perspective as creator and user. Unlike the photograph, which shows a cramped room where various aspects of Gutiérrez Gómez's life are competing for space, the drawing depicts a harmonious environment where everything has its place. A closed door to the left is an index of privacy and clear boundaries, while on an uncluttered dresser sit a key and a box of tissues: small indicators that, in the drawn version of Gutiérrez Gómez's world, there may be tears but there is also the capacity to securely close the door. The bed is a serene volume that, in contrast to her photograph, does not dominate the space but instead provides a nesting place for a sleeping animal, Gutiérrez Gómez's beloved dog. We can see a cup of something warm steaming comfortably on Gutiérrez Gómez's desk, where an open laptop shows an unnamed interlocutor. To the right of the image is a spectacular sunset: the golden yellow sky, brilliant red sun and saturated green trees speak decisively about the richness of the natural world beyond this room. As much of the drawing is rendered in dark lines on light paper, Gutiérrez Gómez's additions of colour are notable. They occur only where she feels a connection to something living, or life-giving. In addition to the luminous window scene, the onscreen figure wears a vivid green sweater, linking her to the trees outside, while the books seen in the mirror's reflection are a mix of greens and blues, as are the artworks above and to the right of the door. The softest colour in the drawing is reserved for what is most precious: the little dog is rendered in a warm, light brown. On this bed, it is safe, and one can sleep peacefully.

Conclusion, or the spatial tools of reconciliation

During the global pandemic, the spatial tools of reconciliation changed dramatically as Truth Commission workers shifted to working at home and online. Our case study of Alejandra's Gutiérrez Gómez's bedroom interior illustrates Karin Tehve's observation that the most radical lesson that interiors offer, and what distinguishes interiors from architecture, is that the former exist both inside and outside of the domain of design (Tehve 2020: 5). Much like *casetas*, with their fluid flow from inside to outside and their embrace of community, the interior spaces of restorative and transitional justice are not simply architectural problems to be solved. The unexpected emphasis and pressures placed upon domestic interiors since early 2020, when the effects of the Covid-19 pandemic began to be felt, have only underscored this fact. Our investigation of the spatial experiences of one Truth Commission case worker echoes Lirio Gutiérrez Rivera's argument that women's relationship to housing in Colombia 'acquires a political dimension as it becomes a space of negotiation ... between grassroots movements, civil servants, and state urban practitioners' (Gutiérrez Rivera 2020: 3). Since the onset of the pandemic, we would add to this list the survivors of decades of extreme violence who have become the virtual co-occupants of case workers' private spaces.

Alejandra Gutiérrez Gómez did not conduct all her interviews in *casetas* prior to the pandemic, but the contrast between the experience of collecting testimony within this flexible spatial typology and the more constrained experience of collecting testimony remotely and online was acute. 'To be able to hold a hand, to feel physically close, allows an empathy that can't reach the person on the other side of a screen', she asserted. Her experience of working at home during the pandemic prompted Gutiérrez Gómez to recognize that 'conducting virtual interviews requires us to be much more explicit in what we express to each other' (Gutiérrez Gómez 2021). In Gutiérrez Gómez's case, she extended this expression to the look and organization of the physical space of her *cuarto*, or bedroom, where she had to conduct difficult interviews largely about sexual violence. Despite limited resources, Gutiérrez Gómez succeeded in configuring an interior that would communicate her empathy, virtually, to her interlocutors. In the process of sharing the details of this new hybrid and shared space, one that had previously been hers alone, Gutiérrez Gómez produced a drawing that is a clear representation of the balance of hope, empathy for others and care for herself that is surely the ideal for any restorative or transitional justice initiative. In so doing, Alejandra Gutiérrez Gómez made an interior for herself in the ongoing global project of reparation and justice.

Acknowledgements

The Social Sciences and Humanities Research Council of Canada (SSHRC) supported the larger research project to which this chapter is connected: 'The Spaces of Restorative and Transitional Justice' has to date collected forty-five interviews and thirty-five case studies of purpose-built and adapted architecture for alternative justice practices, mostly in Canada, Colombia, Australia and the United States. We would like to thank all our interviewees, especially Alejandra Gutiérrez Gómez and the designers and photographers who provided us with images.

References

Adams, A. (2020), 'No Place Like Home: Changing Relationships of Private and Public Space during COVID-19', Learning from COVID Perspectives on Health and Social Policy – COVID and Beyond (blog), *Institute for Health and Social Policy*, Montréal: McGill University, 23 July. https://blogs.mcgill.ca/learning-from-covid/2020/07/23/no-place-like-home-the-changing-relationships-of-private-and-public-space-during-covid-19/ (accessed 1 March 2021).

Awan, N., T. Schneider and J. Till (2011), *Spatial Agency: Other Ways of Doing Architecture*, London: Routledge.

Blagg, H. and T. Anthony (2019), 'Restorative Justice or Indigenous Justice?', in Blagg, T. and T. Anthony (eds), *Decolonising Criminology: Imagining Justice in a Postcolonial World*, 133–52, London: Palgrave Macmillan.

Casas de la verdad (2019), 'Valledupar tiene un Jardín para contar la Verdad', *Comisión de la Verdad*. https://comisiondelaverdad.co/actualidad/noticias/valledupar-tiene-un-jardin-para-contar-la-verdad

Castellar, S. B. (pedagogical coordinator for the Línea 21 collective) and I. Samudio Reyes (anthropologist and research coordinator for the *El Mochuelo* museum), interviewed by Greg Labrosse, 17 April 2021, trans. Greg Labrosse. https://listeningacts.org/spaces/interviews/

Castellar, S. B., I. Samudio Reyes and G. Castro (2013), 'Museo itinerante de la memoria y la identidad de los Montes de María: tejiendo memorias y relatos para la reparación simbólica, la vida y la convivencia', *Ciudad Paz-ando*, 6(1): 159–74.

Chayka, K. (2020), 'How the Coronavirus Will Reshape Architecture: What Kinds of Space Are We Willing to Live and Work in Now?' *The New Yorker*, 17 June. https://www.newyorker.com/culture/dept-of-design/how-the-coronavirus-will-reshape-architecture

Colomina, B. (1994), *Privacy and Publicity: Modern Architecture as Mass Media*, Cambridge, MA: MIT Press.

Comisión, de la Verdad (2020), '¿Cómo Puedo Aportar al Esclarecimiento de la Verdad?' *Comisión de la Verdad*. https://comisiondelaverdad.co/la-comision/como-puedo-aportar-al-esclarecimiento-de-la-verdad

Gutiérrez Gómez, A. (2021), (Colombian Truth Commission case worker), interviewed by Marcela Torres Molano and Greg Labrosse, 12 February, trans. Marcela Torres Molano and Greg Labrosse. https://listeningacts.org/spaces/interviews/

Gutiérrez Rivera, L. (2020), 'A Safer Housing Agenda for Women: Local Urban Planning Knowledge and Women's Grassroots Movements in Medellín, Colombia', *International Journal of Urban and Regional Research*, 44(July): 1–9.

Heynen, H. (2005), 'Modernity and Domesticity: Tensions and Contradictions', in H. Heynen and G. Baydar (eds), *Negotiating Domesticity: Spatial Productions of Gender in Modern Architecture*, 1–30, London and New York: Routledge.

Jimenez, J. (2021), (coordinator for Tuscany; Italian node of the Colombian Truth commission), interviewed by Marcela Torres Molano, 5 March, trans. Marcela Torres Molano. https://listeningacts.org/spaces/interviews/

Jung, C. (2009), 'Transitional Justice for Indigenous People in a Non-transitional Society', *Research Brief for the International Centre for Transitional Justice*, 2009. https://www.ictj.org/sites/default/files/ICTJ-Identities-NonTransitionalSocieties-ResearchBrief-2009-English.pdf

Lerner, A. (2020), 'Humanizing the Spaces of Video Conferences (Zoom et al): Part I, No Space at All', *Medium*, 24 April. https://medium.com/@adamler/part-one-humanizing-the-spaces-of-video-conferences-zoom-et-al-d44057f6fae

Lopez, A. (architect, geographer and cofounder of *Arquitectura Expandida*, a community-facing architectural collective), interviewed by Marcela Torres Molano, 9 April 2021, trans. Marcela Torres Molano. https://listeningacts.org/spaces/interviews/

O'Mahony, D. and J. Doak (2012), 'Transitional Justice and Restorative Justice', *International Criminal Law Review*, 12(3): 305–12.

Omale, D. J. (2006), 'Justice in History: An Examination of "African Restorative Traditions" and the Emerging "Restorative Justice" Paradigm', *African Journal of Criminology and Justice Studies*, 2(2): 33–63.

Pearson de González, A. (Truth and Reconciliation Consultant), interviewed by Greg Labrosse, 13 July 2021, trans. Greg Labrosse. https://listeningacts.org/spaces/interviews/

Seeger, A. (2005), 'Who Got Left out of the Property Grab Again: Oral Traditions, Indigenous Rights, and Valuable Old Knowledge', in R. Ghosh (ed.), *CODE: Collaborative Ownership and the Digital Economy*, 75–84, Cambridge, MA: MIT Press.

Sparke, P. (2008), *The Modern Interior*, London: Reaktion.

Sparke, P. (2020), 'Interior Provocations: A Conclusion', in Anca I. Lasc et al. (eds), *Interior Provocations: History, Theory, and Practice of Autonomous Interiors*, 233–42, New York: Routledge.

Tehve, K. (2020), 'Introduction', in Anca I. Lasc et al. (eds), *Interior Provocations: History, Theory, and Practice of Autonomous Interiors*, 1–7, New York: Routledge.

Toews, B. (2018), '"It's a Dead Place": A Qualitative Exploration of Violence Survivors' Perceptions of Justice Architecture', *Contemporary Justice Review*, 21(2): 208–22.

Uprimny, R. and M. Saffon (2006), *Transitional Justice, Restorative Justice and Reconciliation: Some Insights from the Colombian Case*, Madison, WI: University of Wisconsin Press.

Walklate, S. (2007), 'Changing Boundaries of the "Victim" in Restorative Justice: So Who Is the Victim Now?' in G. Johnstone and D. Van Ness (eds), *Handbook of Restorative Justice: A Global Perspective*, 273–85, Cullompton: Willan Publishing.

Wener, R. (2012), *The Environmental Psychology of Prisons and Jail: Creating Humane Spaces in Secure Settings*, New York: Cambridge University Press.

10

Games without frontiers – Covid living in refugee camps

Mark Taylor and Iris Levin

Introduction

Refugee camps house displaced people for whom notions of home, security, stability and safety no longer apply, or are difficult to realize. They are one group that seems to lie outside Gaston Bachelard's poetic reimaging of the home as 'our corner of the world' and 'our first universe' (Bachelard 1958: 4). Such nostalgic prose does not apply to those sheltering in place due to a migrant crisis or a pandemic, particularly when in an unfamiliar location controlled by government departments, aid agencies and security forces. The insecurity of migrant living in camps, or under temporary protection orders, often marks out difference and reinforces notions of alienation. Under such conditions, and within the enclosed camp where homes are closely packed together and privacy is at a premium, spatial boundaries are often transgressed by both outside agents, like aid workers and camp residents.

This highlights the fragility of boundaries between the private and the public realms. An examination of both scientific and grey literature indicates that many researchers and writers focus on broader public issues of displacement, alienation, health, children and gender issues. But within these texts are fragments of interviews and observations that disclose private lived practice inside refugees' shelters. That is, they provide glimpses into the interior spaces and how they are constructed, used and contribute to emotional fears.

This chapter examines the effects of Covid-19 on living in refugee and migrant camps. It begins by tracing living conditions effected by previous pandemics on dispersed communities in unfamiliar situations, such as the 1918 influenza pandemic. This is followed by more recent examples that include the overcrowded Cox's Bazar in Bangladesh, the Moria and Mavrovouni refugee camps in Lesbos, Greece, and in an Australian context, the Flemington and North Melbourne public housing towers lockdown in Melbourne. Although the public housing towers are not a refugee camp, they house many displaced persons. The way lockdown was handled, the effect on living conditions and the threat of cultural alienation make them relevant to this discussion.

Background

The Spanish flu pandemic of 1918–19 spread widely across the world and is thought to have accounted for the deaths of fifty to a hundred million people (Johnson and Mueller 2002: 105). Named after Spain, a neutral country in the Second World War that first disclosed the epidemic, it is thought to have occurred among frontline soldiers but was not reported for fear of them seeming weakened by the enemy. Crowding almost certainly assisted the spread of the disease (Aligne 2016: 642). Civilians mostly 'wrestled with the disease in familiar places, surrounded by family and familiar institutions' whereas migrant refugees and displaced persons 'sought to regain their health and cope with their mortality among strangers' (Kraut 2010: 124) (Figure 10.1).

FIGURE 10.1 *A Jewish woman and her two children outside a makeshift hut, Poland, 1920. Courtesy of American Jewish Distribution Committee Archives.*

Many of those migrant groups, already marginalized by society, were mistreated and blamed for the spread of disease. Returning home from France to Spain, Spanish workers were treated, but Portuguese workers were ushered through without any assistance, in a process that was aimed at 'protecting the insiders and excluding the outsiders' (Dionne and Turkmen 2020: E217). This practice of regarding 'outsiders' with suspicion is common during outbreaks of communicable diseases.

Across many pandemics from the Spanish Flu to the 2009 H1N1 swine flu epidemic, marginalized groups were more impacted based on predisposed conditions relating to poverty levels, inadequate working and living arrangements, and higher levels of chronic illness and comorbidities (Ali et al. 2020: 416). Thus, when faced with a pandemic, Covid-19, rapidly raging around the world in early 2020 it was clear that refugees and migrants were potentially more at risk because of overcrowded conditions without adequate access to basic sanitation (Kluge et al. 2020: 1238). The ability to access the healthcare services in humanitarian settings is usually compromised, and this is further exacerbated by shortages in medicine and lack of health facilities. Moreover, refugees typically face administrative, financial, legal and language barriers to access the health system. Below we discuss the insecure and physically unstable aspects of the domestic and public refugee spaces through examples from two main refugee camp locations, namely Bangladesh and the Greek Islands, and a lockdown situation in Melbourne.

Everyday life in refugee camps during Covid-19

Overcrowded refugee camps or similar settings do not provide adequate help to keep inhabitants safe during pandemics. The lack of basic amenities, such as clear running water and soap, and lack of good quality medical care and poor access to health information pose major challenges (Kluge et al. 2020: 1238). Public health measures, such as social distancing, personal hygiene and self-isolation, are very difficult to maintain in camps and camp-like settings, as people often share communal lavatories and cooking facilities, or have to wait for hours in long queues for food (Kluge et al. 2020: 1238).

Life under such unsettling conditions is marked by insecurity and instability. Homes constructed from makeshift materials and located in close proximity offer only the most limited forms of privacy and security. Common acts usually taken to be provided inside the home shelter now occur in communal spaces of kitchens, washrooms, toilets and so on. The spatial boundaries of individual or shared dwellings are flimsy at best inside and overlap and intersect outside.

Negotiating such boundaries is difficult, whether due to camp structures intersecting with varied cultural practices, or institutional enforcement of containment lines by militaristic presences.

Cox's Bazar, Bangladesh

The world's largest refugee settlement near the city of Cox's Bazar, Bangladesh, is home to around one million Rohingya refugees who, since 2017, have fled violent persecution in Myanmar and are currently living in thirty-two unregistered and two registered camps (Guglielmi et al. 2020: 1; Kolstad 2018). These overcrowded camps with poor sanitation and lack of water experienced infectious outbreaks before the pandemic, putting extreme pressure on insufficient health resources (Raju and Ayeb-Karlsson 2020: 515). At the start of the pandemic, projections in Cox's Bazar suggested that a Covid-19 outbreak could exhaust medical resources and overwhelm camp hospitals within fifty-eight days (Alemi et al. 2020: 510). Fortunately, it seems the camps escaped the worst and by March 2021, a little over a year after the start of the pandemic, only 406 people in the camps had tested positive, although there is the suggestion that people were reluctant to seek tests, so this number is definitely lower than it should be (Kotowski 2021). Fear of being isolated in quarantines and separated from loved ones, or even because rumours spread that they would be killed in order to slow down the pandemic, can explain why aid workers in Rohingya camps reported low testing amongst residents with Covid-19 symptoms (Alemi et al. 2020; Raju and Ayeb-Karlsson 2020: 515).

While governments and agencies have done much to support and improve conditions, living in these camps remains perilous. Oxfam International observes that in some camps it is virtually impossible to have social distancing, particularly when a single water tap can be shared among 250 people. At the same time, lack of earnings engenders insufficient food and economic stress, placing families further at risk (Kotowski 2021). For single mothers their flimsy shelters might be safer than being outside where they are subject to violence, sexual harassment, kidnapping and rape, but being inside these homes is also not safe. In March 2021, a fire ripped through the camp affecting about 48,000 refugees, destroying 'health centres, women friendly spaces, learning centres, food distribution points, markets and offices' (Chiriac 2021). Makeshift shelters built of bamboo, plastic sheet and tarpaulin burned to the ground. For many refugees, this physical instability and destruction led to another loss of home and identity – the first in Myanmar, the second in Bangladesh. Refugees who had already fled homes that were destroyed by outside agencies, such as military or civilian mobs, faced a second loss within the camp.

In one of the camps, Camp-22, the closely packed shelters are within stepping distance of each other, making navigation between homes difficult and often leading to territorial intrusions. This means boundaries are crossed, social distancing is nearly impossible and the prospect of natural cross-ventilation, vital to inhibit airborne transmission, is reduced. Each family, regardless of size, has a few square metres of land surrounded by makeshift walls as their private space, their 'home'. Within the 'privacy' of the bamboo and plastic walls, 'curtains of silk or plastic sheets divide the interior creating the false illusion of living in separate rooms' (Barua and Karia 2020: 1). In such situations, boundaries between spaces are fragile. There is little sense of home, comfort or place, since such structures are argued as being 'not a home, it is only a box made out of bamboo and tarp' (Rahman 2019: 885).

Moria and Mavrovouni, Lesbos

Since the spring of 2015, the number of refugee arrivals to Europe rapidly increased with most arriving at the Greek Islands of Lesbos, Chios, Samos and Kos (Franck 2018). On the island of Lesbos, the notoriously overcrowded Moria camp was destroyed in a fire in September 2020 that is alleged to have been started by refugees who were distressed by the precarious living situation and the physical instability in the camp that had been exacerbated by Covid-19 infections (Figure 10.2). More than 12,000 people were left without shelter after the fire, but eventually the inhabitants were moved into new accommodation, where over 200 of the migrants tested positive for Covid-19 (ABC News 2020). Some were moved to other locations, such as mainland Europe, but thousands were moved to the hastily built tent camp Mavrovouni, adjacent to the more established Kara Tepe camp. The temporary Mavrovouni camp has been criticized for having no fresh water supply or running electricity (Oberti 2021) and was under lockdown for long periods to prevent the spread of the virus (Bathke 2021). In Mavrovouni, eight women live in one of eighteen small basic rooms under a large tent, nicknamed 'the women's camp'. Their 'room' is littered with mattresses and cooking pots. Thé Kongé, a woman from the Democratic Republic of Congo, said, highlighting the fragility of boundaries between private and public:

> We sleep in the middle of the plates and next to the hot pot, there is no way to move, we have no room. [...] The toilets we use are so dirty that we are afraid of catching infections. So we relieve ourselves in a bucket, behind the tent, sometimes in front of men passing by. [...] Also, there is no supervision and we are sometimes tormented by men who come in here. [...] It's as if we are being mentally tortured.

(Oberti 2021)

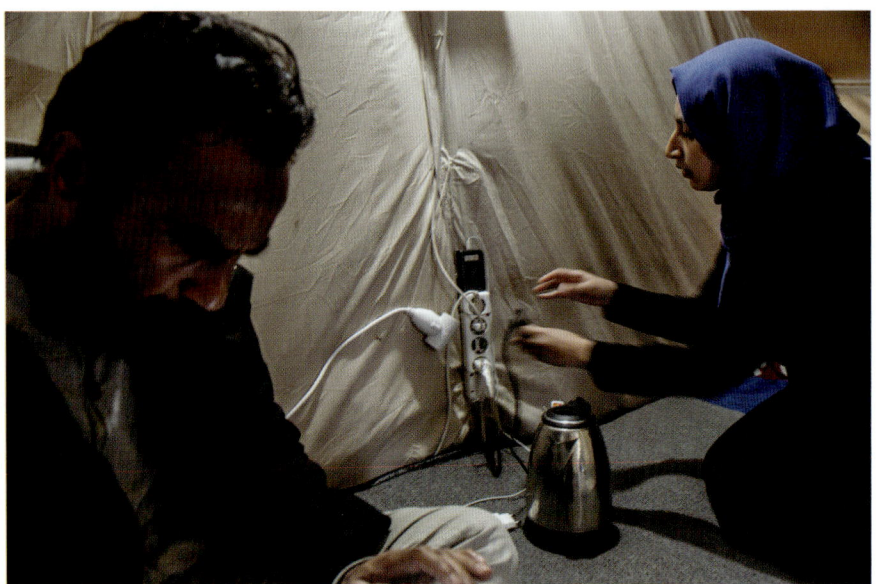

FIGURE 10.2 *Moria Camp Refugees fear possible Coronavirus outbreak, Lesbos, Greece, March 2020, 2020. Courtesy of Getty Images Europe, © Guy Smallman / Contributor.*

The fragility of boundaries between private and public adds to the sense of insecurity and instability of this 'home'. Women in particular feel threatened and live constantly in fear due to the lack of privacy in their 'room'.

The Covid-19 restrictions have been detrimental to the mental health of the Mavrovouni camp inhabitants, with self-harm shown to have increased 66 per cent since the start of the pandemic, thus, highlighting the dangers of lockdowns to the mental well-being of already stressed refugees (Rielly 2021). Lockdown measures dictated that camp residents can only leave once a week, meaning that there is no longer any temporary reprieve from the camp. There are no activities and no school for children. The camp is governed by a large police presence that enforces the strict lockdown (Rielly 2021). When interiors are so constrained and the boundaries between private and public are fragile, public space would offer relief during normal times. But the pandemic has resulted in restrictions being put on public space and the use of the outdoors, which further restricts camp residents (Figure 10.3).

In Mavrovouni, many refugees have reported that 'they have bigger concerns than Covid-19' (MacGregor 2021) in the camp, with very poor living arrangements in tents exposed to rough weather and often without electricity. Some complain they do not have enough food as well as poor hygiene facilities. During summer the searing heat can reach forty-seven degree Celsius in a camp

FIGURE 10.3 *Refugee camp on Lesbos, Greece – stock photo, 2020. Courtesy of Getty Images Europe, © Joel Carillet.*

with no trees and little shade. The tents and Isoboxes (prefabricated containers) are the only places to get shade, though they heat up and become what one refugee described as 'sweltering greenhouses' (Geiger and Andersen 2021). Cooling is only possible with showers, buckets of water or in the case of one Syrian refugee, having two fans pointing directly at her sleeping one-year old. But while they move the warm air, they offer nothing cold (Geiger and Andersen 2021). Waiting for asylum status decisions under these conditions often leads to tensions, depression and other mental health issues. Despite a vaccination campaign announced for migrants on Lesbos, as of May 2021 many of the inhabitants, mostly Africans, are refusing to be vaccinated. The majority are under forty years old and, if they are sick, they display only mild or no symptoms at all, so they 'see no reason to get vaccinated' (MacGregor 2021).

These examples of refugee camps in Bangladesh and the Greek Islands show how such settlements offer unsafe, unstable and controlled living conditions. They separate the inhabitants from the rest of the country's population, control their movement and maintain an ongoing surveillance over them. During the Covid-19 pandemic, this surveillance has intensified to prevent the residents from spreading the virus inside and outside the camps, leading to local fear and alienation of the camp residents. By intensifying control measures during the pandemic, camp dwellers have been made to feel that, like the Chinese migrants who were scapegoated for the 1870s smallpox outbreaks in North American cities, they are the carriers of the disease. These practices have enhanced the feeling of residential alienation, of camp residents 'not feeling at home' in the place that is there to protect them (Madden and Marcuse 2016: 55). When the home is unsafe because spatial boundaries are easily transgressed; when it is unstable because it can be dismantled at any moment and its inhabitants sent away to unknown locations; and when movement is controlled by external agents, a feature intensified during the pandemic, feelings of alienation and resistance to authorities exhibited by camp residents come as no surprise.

During a series of interviews with Rohingya women in the Bangladesh camps, gender researcher Farhana Rahman discusses an interview with one woman, Ismat Ara, about life in the camp. Ismat states 'we don't have any opportunities and nothing to do here in the camp. When I sit here [in the tent] I feel depressed – there is no comfort in this place. This is not a home, it is only a box made out of bamboo and tarp' (Rahman 2019: 885). But visits to the *taleem*, a religious space for Muslim women, offer an opportunity to engage culture in a women-only space. Rahman argues that this gendering of place relates to feeling at home, whereas the physical shelter of bamboo and tarp 'does not so much provide a sense of "home", but rather it is through the "personal dimension" that gives meaning to it that is affected by experience and culture' (Rahman 2019: 885).

Flemington and North Melbourne Towers, Melbourne

On 4 July 2020, a local outbreak of Covid-19 in Australia led to a rushed lockdown of nine public housing high-rise towers in Melbourne's inner-city suburbs of North Melbourne and Flemington. Following a state government order, police were deployed to contain residents because of the outbreak, at the time when the broader community of the city was not in lockdown (Om 2020). In total, about 3,000 people were confined to their public housing apartments for up to two weeks and placed under police guard (Covid 2020). After five days the lockdown was lifted in all but one tower where residents had to complete fourteen days of hard lockdown because 'some 11 per cent of whom by now had tested positive' (Victorian Ombudsman 2020).

According to the ABC News, some residents were allowed to exercise but only in enclosed fenced areas. Some residents were locked out of the towers and had to sleep in their cars or pay for hotel accommodation, while others were left without food and medical supplies, including chronic mental health medications (Om 2020). Community spaces on the ground floors were locked, creating a situation that isolated the community and impeded any organization. Here the boundary between the private and public realms was kept impenetrable.

As local government implemented the lockdown, they warned that the virus had the potential to spread within these public housing towers because facilities such as lifts (which are sometimes broken), corridors, laundry rooms and rubbish areas were shared spaces. Other factors, such as poor airflow and ventilation, coupled with the lack of hand sanitizers on each floor also had the potential to contribute to the spread of infection (Weedon 2020). The government argued its immediate response was health-related, but its focus shifted to tenants' 'wraparound support' including medical care and mental health support (Murray-Atfield 2020).

The immediacy of the response, heavy police presence and lack of care and compassion (food, medicine, etc.), is in some ways reminiscent of the conditions described in Cox's Bazar and Mavrovouni. This is all the more relevant since, after the late 1930s and early 1940s, public housing in Australia has provided home for countless refugees who have settled in the country, first from war-torn Europe, and then from Asia and the Middle East (Refugee Council of Australia 2019). More recently, Australia has welcomed refugees from African countries, including South Sudan, Eritrea and the Horn of Africa (Somalia, Ethiopia and Kenya). Refugees who settle in Australia are in acute need of affordable housing (Ziersch et al. 2017), and many refugee communities therefore live in the public housing towers in Melbourne.

The Covid-19 lockdown in the towers 'left the community feeling anxious, fearful and as if they were being "treated like criminals"' (Om 2020) (Figure 10.4).

FIGURE 10.4 *Melbourne in lockdown as Victoria works to contain Covid-19 Spread, 2020. Courtesy of Getty Images AsiaPac, © Darrian Traynor/Stringer.*

According to Inner Melbourne Community Legal, '[t]he extreme police presence was re-traumatising for residents with lived experiences of war or persecution and stoked racist community sentiment that further stigmatised already marginalised people' (Om 2020). This experience must have been similar to living in the camps of Bangladesh and the Greek Islands where controlled conditions were used to prevent the virus from spreading. The report recommended that the government apologize for its treatment of public housing residents and acknowledge the severe impact of its strategies. The government, however, has refused to apologize 'for saving people's lives'.

Conclusion

The Covid-19 pandemic has reinforced a range of issues to do with migrant groups and their containment within controlled arenas, from health centres, adequate living conditions and freedom of movement to food security. As with earlier viral epidemics, migrant groups were often made scapegoats for outbreaks or assumed to carry the disease. This stigmatizing of people and their lifestyles that were different was evident in the Melbourne situation where the government had assumed the towers were 'a hotbed of criminality and non-compliance and that the people could not be trusted, if warning was given, not to escape the lockdown'. In reality, the opposite was true (Simmons 2021).

Covid-19 has accelerated the alienation of migrants from the general host society. In addition to the existing perilous housing conditions in the camps, public health measures have been near impossible to maintain, and camp dwellers have been further exposed to the threat from the pandemic. The physical instability of the living conditions and the fragility of the boundaries between public and the private spaces experienced by residents in the camps, both before the pandemic and even more since then, have led to feelings of frustration and despair. In the case studies discussed here, the refugees living in both camps and public housing have been treated as scapegoats who need to be quarantined and separated from the general public to protect it from the spreading virus, further exacerbating feeling of alienation and homelessness.

References

ABC News (2020), 'About 9,000 Migrants on Greece's Lesbos Move into Tent Camp after Fire', *ABC News*, 20 September. https://www.abc.net.au/news/2020-09-20/about-9,000-migrants-on-greeces-lesbos-move-into-new-tent-camp/12683048

Alemi, Q., C. Stempel, H. Siddiq and E. Kim (2020), 'Refugees and COVID-19: Achieving a Comprehensive Public Health Response', *Bulletin of the World Health Organization*, 98(8): 510–510A.

Ali, S., M. Asaria and S. Stranges (2020), 'COVID-19 and Inequality: Are We All in This Together?', *Canadian Journal of Public Health*, 111(3): 415–16.

Aligne, C. A. (2016), 'Overcrowding and Mortality during the Influenza Pandemic of 1918', *American Journal of Public Health*, 106(4): 642–4.

Bachelard, G. (1958), *The Poetics of Space*, trans. Maria Jolas, Boston: Beacon Press.

Barua, A. and R. H. Karia (2020), 'Challenges Faced by Rohingya Refugees in the COVID-19 Pandemic', *Ann Glob Health*, 86(1): 129.

Bathke, B. (2021), '9 Months after Moria Fire, Work on New Lesbos Migrant Camp Still Hasn't Begun', *InfoMigrants*, 10 June. https://www.infomigrants.net/en/post/32850/9-months-after-moria-fire-work-on-new-lesbos-migrant-camp-still-hasnt-begun

Chiriac, M. (2021), 'Rohingya Refugee Camps in Cox's Bazar Rise from the Ashes', *European Commission*, 31 March. https://ec.europa.eu/echo/blog/rohingya-refugee-camps-cox-s-bazar-rise-ashes_en

Covid: Melbourne Towers Lockdown Breached Human Rights (2020), *BBC News*, 17 December. https://www.bbc.com/news/world-australia-55342990

Dionne, K. Y. and F. F. Turkmen (2020), 'The Politics of Pandemic Othering: Putting COVID-19 in Global and Historical Context', *International Organization*, 74(S1): E213–E230.

Franck, A. K. (2018), 'The Lesvos Refugee Crisis as Disaster Capitalism', *Peace Review*, 30(2): 199–205.

Geiger, G. and S. S. Andersen (2021), '"I Can't Take it Anymore": Refugees Struggle to Cope in Extreme Heat', *Vice World News*, 9 August. https://www.vice.com/en/article/5db4y3/i-cant-take-it-anymore-refugees-struggle-to-cope-in-extreme-heat

Guglielmi, S., J. Seager, K. Mitu, S. Baird and N. Jones (2020), 'Exploring the Impacts of COVID-19 on Rohingya Adolescents in Cox's Bazar: A Mixed-Methods Study', *Journal of Migration and Health*, 1–2: 100031.

Johnson, N. P. and J. Mueller (2002), 'Updating the Accounts: Global Mortality of the 1918–1920 "Spanish" Influenza Pandemic', *Bulletin of the History of Medicine*, 76(1): 105–15.

Kluge, H. H. P., Z. Jakab, J. Bartovic, V. D'Anna and S. Severoni (2020), 'Refugee and Migrant Health in the COVID-19 Response', *The Lancet*, 395(10232): 1237–9.

Kolstad, K. (2018), 'Cox's Bazar: The World's Largest Refugee Settlement', *NRC – Norwegian Refugee Council*, 24 August. https://www.nrc.no/news/2018/august/coxs-bazar-the-worlds-largest-refugee-settlement/

Kotowski, A. (2021), 'Four Things to Know about Covid in the World's Largest Refugee Camp', *Oxfam International*, 11 March. https://www.oxfam.org/en/blogs/four-things-know-about-covid-worlds-largest-refugee-camp

Kraut, A. M. (2010), 'Immigration, Ethnicity, and the Pandemic', *Public Health Reports (Washington, DC: 1974)*, 125(Suppl 3): 123–33.

MacGregor, M. (2021), 'More Than 30 COVID Cases in Lesbos Migrant Camp', *InfoMigrants*, 11 May. https://www.infomigrants.net/en/post/32137/more-than-30-covid-cases-in-lesbos-migrant-camp

Madden, D. and P. Marcuse (2016), *In Defence of Housing: The Politics of Crisis*, London and New York: Verso Books.

Murray-Atfield, Y. (2020), 'Melbourne Public Housing Tower Resident Says Community Is Being "Treated Like Criminals" amid Coronavirus Lockdown', *ABC News*, 5 July. https://www.abc.net.au/news/2020-07-05/coronavirus-lockdown-melbourne-public-housing-residents-speak/12423170

Oberti, C. (2021), '"It's Mental Torture": Daily Life in the Women's Section of the Kara Tepe Camp in Greece', *InfoMigrants*, 5 April. https://www.infomigrants.net/en/post/30983/its-mental-torture-daily-life-in-the-womens-section-of-the-kara-tepe-camp-in-greece

Om, J. (2020), 'Coronavirus Hard Lockdown of Melbourne Public Housing Towers Left Residents Feeling Like "Criminals", Inquiry Hears', *ABC News*, 25 August. https://www.abc.net.au/news/2020-08-25/coronavirus-melbourne-public-housing-tower-shutdown-inquiry/12589372

Rahman, F. (2019), '"I Find Comfort Here": Rohingya Women and *Taleems* in Bangladesh's Refugee Camps', *Journal of Refugee Studies*, 34(1): 874–89.

Raju, E. and S. Ayeb-Karlsson (2020), 'COVID-19: How Do You Self-Isolate in a Refugee Camp?' *International Journal of Public Health*, 65(5): 515–17.

Rielly, B. (2021), 'Living in This Constant Nightmare of Insecurity and Uncertainty', *The Civil Fleet*, 21 February. https://thecivilfleet.wordpress.com/2021/02/21/living-in-this-constant-nightmare-of-insecurity-and-uncertainty/

Refugee Council of Australia (2019), *Settling in Australia: The Challenges*, 26 December. https://www.refugeecouncil.org.au/settlement-challenges/2/

Simmons, M. (2021), '"We Thought we were Australian": Melbourne Tower Lockdown Lives on in Legacy of Trauma', *The Guardian*, 4 July. https://www.theguardian.com/australia-news/2021/jul/04/we-thought-we-were-australian-melbourne-tower-lockdown-lives-on-in-legacy-of-trauma

Victorian Ombudsman (2020), 'Investigation into the Detention and Treatment of Public Housing Residents Arising from a COVID-19 "Hard Lockdown" in July 2020', 7 December. https://www.ombudsman.vic.gov.au/our-impact/investigation-reports/investigation-into-the-detention-and-treatment-of-public-housing-residents-arising-from-a-covid-19-hard-lockdown-in-july-2020/

Weedon, A. (2020), 'Melbourne's Public Housing Coronavirus Lockdown Tells a Story of Two Cities', *ABC News*, 9 July. https://www.abc.net.au/news/2020-07-09/flemington-north-melbourne-public-housing-lockdown-two-cities/12431898

Ziersch, A., C. Due, M. Walsh and K. Arthurson (2017), *Belonging Begins at Home: Housing, Social Inclusion and Health and Wellbeing for People from Refugee and Asylum Seeking Backgrounds*, Flinders Press, Adelaide. https://anglicaresa.com.au/wp-content/uploads/1749_Belonging-begins-at-home-report_WEB-final.pdf

SECTION THREE

Representing the (in)visible

11

Tell don't show: The invisible plague in Dutch seventeenth-century paintings of the domestic interior

Irene Cieraad

Throughout most of the seventeenth century plague epidemics raged through Dutch cities and took their toll in an enormous loss of life. However, seventeenth-century paintings of domestic life do not show the sorrow or the death toll, but portray healthy, thriving mothers and children in sunlit interiors.[1] The sunny imagery of the seventeenth-century painting is so strong that it defies the historic reality of the countless plague victims. In a strange contradiction, up until today the Dutch language harbours numerous references to The Plague, or *pest* as it is called in Dutch. My perception of the glorious Dutch Golden Age, and the sunny imagery of seventeenth-century interior paintings in particular, changed after reading the published transcripts of seventeenth-century Dutch letters written by women to their husbands at sea (Van Gelder 2007).[2] What struck me most were the women's heart-breaking accounts of the loss of children due to The Plague. I have since tried to detect evidence of this daily reality in the paintings, given that art historians have warned against their deceptive realism (Cieraad 2016, 2019). According to Wayne Franits, it lures contemporary viewers into believing that the paintings represent slices of daily life in the seventeenth century (2004: 1–2).

In the future, art historians might face similar challenges relating the contrasting realities of the sunny interior photographs of family togetherness in lockdown with the distressing images of Covid patients in intensive care units (ICUs). Also, images of Covid patients isolating or recovering in their home environments might not be recognizable as such. Judging by their titles, no seventeenth-century Dutch painting is known to depict plague patients at home, but Covid-19 encourages a reflection on the representation of The Plague by Dutch painters at the time.[3] Gabriel Metsu's paintings *A Sick Woman and a Weeping Maidservant* (1657–59) and *The Sick Child* (1664–66) are now interpreted, considering their dating, as likely depictions of plague patients (Waiboer 2012: 69, 129).

The only known painting that explicitly illustrated the horrors of The Plague was commissioned by the governors of the Leiden plague hospice, a so-called pest house, to decorate their trustees' room (Figure 11.1). Pest houses were erected outside the city walls to isolate and contain plague patients who did not have any family members to take care of them. In showing the fatality of the disease, the painting is very instructive. Most prominent are the symptoms of bubonic plague, but invisible is the suffocation due to pneumonic plague. However, when the painting was ready in 1682 there seemed to be no need of a pest house anymore.

FIGURE 11.1 *Painting by Theodoor van der Schuer,* Pest Victims in a Pest House *1682. Museum De Lakenhal, Leiden.*

Also, Hendrick ten Oever's painting, dated 1670 and situated in Zwolle, a town in the east of the Netherlands, was most probably commissioned by the governors of an orphanage to decorate their trustees' room (Figure 11.2). It shows the exteriors of the private houses of plague patients, which were marked with a white cross painted on their façades. This so-called *pestkruis* had to warn potential visitors and passers-by to keep their distance in the same way as housemates of plague patients had to carry a white stick in public, not only as a warning to keep a safe distance, but also to be used as a pointer for the products they wanted to buy. Around 1650 it was common knowledge that The Plague was an infectious disease spreading not only

FIGURE 11.2 *Painting by Hendrick ten Oever,* The Slaughtered Pig *1670. Collectie Overijssel, Zwolle.*

through the air, but also through materials which had been in contact with an infected person (Noordegraaf and Valk 1996).

The disastrous consequences of the plague epidemics were more explicitly documented in drawings and etchings, which show corpses piling up in the streets and queues of funeral processions. However, in contrast to oil paintings, drawings and etchings were never used as wall decoration, but stored in albums. The watercolours made by Gesina ter Borch, the sister of the well-known painter Gerard ter Borch, which represented the death toll in her native town Zwolle, not only the deadly attack of a skeleton on a sweet little girl, dated 1656, but also the watercolour titled *Death at Ramshorst* (1660), are just one example (Figure 11.3). The affluent ter Borch family owned the Ramshorst mansion outside Zwolle, and like other families fortunate to own a countryseat, they fled the plague-invested city. But the watercolour shows that even the mansion was not a safe place. Death, in the guise of numerous skeletons, kidnaps dinner guests, who struggle to free themselves. Not only the view through the door, but also the drawing on the wall on the left of the picture, depict funeral processions. Skeletons are traditional symbols of death, while hourglasses, like the ones depicted on the floor, are so-called *vanitas* objects which carry the symbolic message 'remember (sooner or later) you will die' (Cheney 2018: 267).

FIGURE 11.3 *Watercolour by Gesina ter Borch*, Death at Ramshorst *1660. Rijksmuseum Amsterdam.*

Other references encoding the transience of life in seventeenth-century paintings are less known. For example, the children who inflate a pig's bladder in Hendrick ten Oever's painting symbolize the shortness of life as only a breath (Figure 11.2). Equally, the knitting of the adolescent girl that can be undone by simply pulling the thread represents the fragility of life. Knitting was at that time a craft mainly performed by orphaned girls. The slaughtered pig hanging on the ladder is a reference to death and dying. Slaughtered pigs or oxen were favourite subjects of painters during the plague epidemics, often in combination with children inflating a bladder. The presence of a broom in combination with the described objects, which either refer to death, The Plague,

FIGURE 11.4 *Painting by Samuel van Hoogstraten*, The Slippers *1658. Musée du Louvre, Paris.*

or life's fragility warrants, in my opinion, a related symbolic interpretation. In this interpretation the broom is key to the introduction of the concept of a liminal object as a boundary marker, in this case between life and death.

In my search more specifically for paintings of the interior which encode in the painted objects similar references to the transience of life I came across the intriguing painting by Samuel van Hoogstraten, titled *The Slippers* (1658), which creates the illusion of a view into an interior without anybody present (Figure 11.4). Not only does it prominently feature a broom leaning next to the doorpost, but also more liminal objects are visible, such as shoes, a door mat and a bunch of keys. In combination with the *vanitas* objects of an extinguished and leaning candle, a dark mirror and a closed book I want to make a case for a symbolic interpretation of the painting which points to the death of a housewife. The concept of the liminal object, however, is not restricted to the past but is also very useful in elucidating crucial objects in the current Covid-16 pandemic.

Telling letters, symbolic paintings

The letters from the women left behind to their men at sea shed light on the life histories of seamen's wives who had to cope financially and emotionally with the hardships of being lone mothers and wives in the rough times of plague epidemics. Most moving are the letters reporting the deaths of children due to The Plague. Such as a young mother describes her deepest sorrow on the death of her boy: 'My dearest and beloved husband I am so sad about our son's demise that I have been unable to write to you. When I think of him it is as if my heart bursts inside my body' (Braunius 1980: 19–20). In a letter dated 1664, a mother vividly describes the suffocation of her little girl due to pneumonic plague folded into a report of the general situation in Amsterdam: 'People are dying quick. One week alone between ten to eleven hundred people died, however with God's help it has been reduced to 445 this week. God our Lord has torched the fire of pestilence in our house and took our Anna within two days ... And only God knows if our suffering is enough for we are clearly punished for our sins' (Van Gelder 2008: 82–6). The end of the letter presents a common understanding that The Plague was a punishment of God.

Although the pestilences were seen as God's punishment they did not lead to biblical subjects of hell and damnation in the paintings (Loughman and Montias 2000: 54–5). On the contrary, the rise of genre paintings indicated a clear need for distraction, from naughty brothel scenes and jocular inn scenes to sunlit interiors of a mother nursing her child, a posh woman in the company of her maid, or simply a sweeping maid. The realism of seventeenth-century

Dutch paintings is a highly debated topic. Regarding the painters' omission of the sad reality of The Plague as described in the letters, this is certainly true. The numerous genre paintings which, according to the probate inventories and the accounts of foreign visitors decorated the interior spaces of Dutch houses in the seventeenth century, leave an impression of a nation desperately seeking distraction (Borzello 2006: 21).

For most art historians there is no reason to assume that Samuel van Hoogstraten's painting *The Slippers* (1658) would fall into another category than distraction (Figure 11.4). Van Hoogstraten, who at the end of his career wrote a book on the art of painting, stated that the work of a painter is to trick the viewer into believing an optical illusion (Van Hoogstraten in De Jongh 1976: 14–6). In the case of *The Slippers* he was creating the illusion of not only different materials, such as the leather upholstered chair, the satin tablecloth and the shiny tiles, but also of a view into several interior spaces. By the painter's artful brushstrokes and clever composition, the viewer believes that they are peeking through open doors into three interior spaces distinguished by different flooring. The beholder's view is directed to a partly visible painting on the wall of the interior which represents the painting *Woman Reading a Letter* created three years earlier by his contemporary Gerard ter Borch (Oczko 2021: 197–9). Copying a painting of a colleague into one's own work was not uncommon and is interpreted by art historians as a fraternal wink, but there is more in it than meets the eye.

Despite van Hoogstraten's realism in masterly representing different materials from the leather chair to the twig broom, the painting is misleading in its suggestion of the three linked spaces, which do not represent a common spatial arrangement in Dutch seventeenth-century houses.[4] As one of the very few paintings of interior spaces without human presence it has intrigued many viewers and led to different and often opposing interpretations, from a view into a brothel to a representation of a domestic interior of an absent but chaste housewife (Oczko 2021: 199–200; Kloek 2009: 75). In attempting to connect this painting to the historic reality of The Plague and the death toll it took, my interpretation will radically differ from previous ones.

In search for clues, I will start with the broom as the connecting object between Hendrick ten Oever's painting in which the broom is depicted next to the *pestkruis*, and Samuel van Hoogstraten's painting in which the broom is leaning next to the doorpost. A semiotic reading reveals that this interpretation connects with the iconographic tradition in explaining seventeenth-century Dutch genre painting, and in particular the work of the art historian Eddy de Jongh (1976). I will expand this interpretation by introducing the anthropological concept of the 'liminal object' (Thomassen 2015). By focusing on the depicted objects and their meaning I hope to move closer to the seventeenth-century layman's interpretation of this painting.

The broom and other liminal objects

The broom's omnipresence in Dutch seventeenth-century genre painting is the topic of a recent book by the Polish art historian Pjotr Oczko (2021), who understands the broom as an emblem of the Dutch culture representing domestic and moral cleanliness as performed in the ritual act of sweeping (2021: 407–11). Contrary to Oczko, I will stress the multifaceted meaning of the broom as a boundary marker which divides and unites opposites, not only inside and outside, but also clean and dirty, good and evil.[5] While sweeping away the dirt the broom as a cleaning instrument becomes at the same time dirty. Oczko stressed only the broom's positive metaphorical meaning of moral cleansing, while its opposite meaning of evil, in the sense of satanic defilement and as a vehicle of witches, was as much alive in the seventeenth century (Vervoort 2011).

Samuel van Hoogstraten painted in *The Slippers* the twig broom as a liminal object used to mark the boundary between two spaces with different degrees of interiority (Figure 11.4). The outer door (indicated by the handle on the right) opens to a space with a red and black tiled floor, which gives the impression of a scullery in the back of the house, separated by another door (indicated by a simple ring handle on the left) from a passageway laid with terracotta tiles. The concept of the liminal object is also helpful to describe other objects in the painting such as the doormat, the bunch of keys and the so-called slippers, which are in fact women's shoes only to be worn outside the house. The wooden soles of these shoes (*trippen*) would damage the fragile marble floor of the furnished room, like the coarse broom of twigs would never been used to sweep marble floors.

While the broom essentially marks the boundary between inside and outside, both the shoes and the doormat are indicative of a higher level of interiority.[6] Ever since the seventeenth century doormats have been used in front of entrance doors as interior markers of boundaries into representational spaces with more delicate flooring. As a liminal object the doormat serves to collect the dirt from shoes and keep the marble floor clean. Shoes are also liminal objects in keeping the feet clean and collecting dirt on their soles.

Samuel van Hoogstraten, the master of illusions, might suggest the following story: the woman of the house forgot something and hastily returned home leaving all the doors open. She kicked off her shoes, left her bunch of keys in the keyhole in order to relock the door within the minute after slipping into her shoes again and closed the doors behind her. In this narrative the beholder stands outside waiting for her return and is allowed to get a peek into the best room of the house. But on the symbolic level of the objects prominently displayed in *The Slippers* the painting tells another story.

The broom, in combination with the clean white cloth, reinforces the opposites of purity and dirt, of moral cleanliness and sinfulness. However, the depiction of a large white cloth on the foreground is very unusual. As Samuel van Hoogstraten was familiar with Catholic paraphernalia the white cloth and the keys will also be interpreted with Catholic iconography in mind.[7] In that vein the white cloth seems to be a reference to one of the medieval symbols of Mary's purity (Cieraad 1997: 14). The symbolism of the cloth, in combination with the broom seen as a primary boundary marker, not only between inside and outside, but also as inferred from Hendrick ten Oever's painting – also about life and death – leads to the Catholic interpretation of the deceased's passage to heaven (or hell) via the intermediate space of limbo. It explains the unusual arrangement of spaces characterized by different flooring. The intermediate space laid with terracotta tiles and marked with the liminal objects of the doormat and the shoes indicates a boundary with a space of higher interiority which needs to be opened by a key.

Not only is the dangling bunch of keys a symbolic reference to the woman of the house as the traditional key keeper, but a key is also a liminal object in its dual function of locking and unlocking, of closing and opening doors, and in allowing or inhibiting access. Within Catholic iconography, however, the key is the symbol of Saint Peter who opens the heavenly gate only to the morally just. Adding to my symbolic interpretation of the painting are the *vanitas* symbols of an extinguished and leaning candle and a closed book which occupy the centre of the image (De Jongh 1967: 20). Van Hoogstraten played with Gerard ter Borch's painting *Woman Reading a Letter* which he only partly depicted. The invisible part of ter Borch's painting includes the same silver candlestick with a leaning candle that is depicted next to a small dark mirror.[8] By adding the enlarged part of the dark mirror above the two *vanitas* symbols van Hoogstraten conveys, in my opinion, the passing of the woman of the house. The view through the open 'gate of Heaven' into a sunlit interior expresses the hope for the woman's peaceful rest. As such this painting would have presented a soothing image in times of The Plague.

Conclusion

The letters emphasize the grim daily reality in the seventeenth century when many plague epidemics struck the country. Holland was at that time the most urbanized part of the world, and like any infectious disease, The Plague spread easily in densely populated areas. The rich tried to escape the plague-infected cities, but as Gesina ter Borch showed in her watercolours, nobody was safe. Drawings, etches and watercolours documented the horrors, but were put away in albums, while canvases of different sizes and subjects were common wall decorations in all main rooms of the house. Especially the popularity of paintings of healthy women and children in a peaceful domestic setting seem to emphasize a need for distraction. Their compensatory relation to the historic reality of epidemics and wars in the seventeenth century may explain why these subjects no longer featured in eighteenth-century painting.

Not only a similar need for distraction in the present Covid-19 pandemic, but also more similarities with The Plague epidemics has engendered a curiosity about the impact of the pestilences on seventeenth-century society. My knowledge of the letters made me search for more hidden references to death and bereavement in paintings of domestic scenes. In that search Samuel van Hoogstraten's intriguing painting *The Slippers* came to the fore. Not only did he depict a domestic interior without human presence, but also his foregrounding of the broom directed me to make a link between the broom depicted next to the pest cross in ten Oever's painting.

The broom, in combination with several *vanitas* objects in the centre of the painting, convinced me of a symbolic interpretation of the painting which concerns the passing of a housewife. It is uncertain if she died from The Plague, but the dating of the painting makes it plausible. Like all symbolic interpretations my interpretation is speculative, but with solid foundations in anthropological literature on liminality. With the broom as key in my definition of the liminal object, which is not only a boundary marker but also a union of opposites, three more objects in the painting have been identified as liminal: the shoes, the doormat and the bunch of keys.

My symbolic interpretation of *The Slippers* may seem farfetched, but we must realize that religion, whether the Catholic or the Protestant faith, was the dominant ideology and concerns about the afterlife were often more compelling than those about daily existence. According to the iconographic tradition in art history, seventeenth-century beholders were able readers of the symbolism of not only daily objects, but also *vanitas* objects, as well as religious iconography. The relevance of the symbolism in seventeenth-century paintings for today's beholders may be minimal, but the concept of the liminal object has as much relevance now as it had then in pointing to critical boundaries.

In these pandemic times there are liminal objects which point to the critical boundary of a Covid-19 infection. A perfect example is the face mask which protects people against an airborne Covid-19 infection and marks the critical physical boundary of nose and mouth. When in use the mask is clean on the inside but potentially dirty on the outside by the blocked virus particles. Also, the disposable gloves and aprons worn by medical staff when treating Covid-19 patients point at the critical boundary between health and a potentially deadly disease. In uniting the opposites of clean and dirty, present-day liminal objects such as face masks, gloves and aprons are disposable, which mark a fast transgression of the critical societal boundary between new products and waste.

Notes

1. In their assumed depiction of reality these Dutch paintings have played a crucial role in the modern historiography of home and domesticity (Flanders 2015).
2. These letters, locked away for centuries in the British National Archives, were once found on Dutch ships captured by the English in sea battles (1652–74) between the two nations, which were simultaneous with the last three epidemics of the century (Van Gelder 2008). References to all publications on the transcribed letters are in Cieraad 2019.
3. In origin seventeenth-century paintings did not have titles but were endowed with descriptive titles in the nineteenth century.
4. Another painting, titled *View into a Hallway* (*ca.* 1662), also presents an uncommon arrangement of interior spaces, but in this case we know that it was used to surprise the guests of his London client Thomas Povey who had put the painting behind a closet door (Oczko 2021: 196).
5. Oczko does not discuss Hendrick ten Oever's painting.
6. The broom seems a common painterly object to alert seventeenth-century beholders of a view into the interior.
7. Although registered as Protestant (Dutch state religion), he depicted the Catholic rosary as celebration of the Blessed Virgin Mary twice during his stay in Vienna, most prominently in Feigned letter rack (*ca.* 1655) in possession of Prague Castle Picture Gallery, which gives the impression that he secretly converted to Catholicism.
8. Research indicated that van Hoogstraten copied the original, gloomier version of Gerard ter Borch's painting, which was later on brightened up by changing amongst others the red tablecloth into a colourful Persian tapestry (Oczko 2021: 198–9).

References

Borzello, F. (2006), *At Home: The Domestic Interior in Art*, New York: Thames & Hudson.

Braunius, S. W. P. C. (1980), 'Het leven van de zeventiende-eeuwse zeeman: valse romantiek of werkelijkheid?' (Life of a 17th century sailor: false romanticism or reality?), *Mededelingen van de Nederlandse Vereniging voor Zeegeschiedenis*, 40/41: 11–22.

Brusati, C. (2013), 'Paradoxical Passages: The Work of Framing in the Art of Samuel van Hoogstraten', in Th. Weststeijn (ed.), *The Universal Art of Samuel van Hoogstraten (1627–1678): Painter, Writer, and Courtier*, 53–75, Amsterdam: Amsterdam University Press.

Cheney, L. D. (2018), 'The Symbolism of the Skull in Vanitas: Homo Bulla Est', *Cultural and Religious Studies*, 6(5): 267–84.

Cieraad, I. (1997), 'Nederland: een bewoond gordijn. Een symbolische analyse van de rol van het gordijn in het Nederlandse interieur' (a symbolic analysis of the curtain in the Dutch interior), *Textielhistorische Bijdragen*, 37: 12–40.

Cieraad, I. (2016), 'Writing Home, Painting Home: Seventeenth-Century Dutch Genre Painting and "The Sailing Letters"', in C. Sandten and K. A. Tan (eds), *Home: Concepts, Constructions, Contexts*, 45–62, Trier: Wissenschaftlicher Verlag Trier.

Cieraad, I. (2019), 'Rocking the Cradle of Dutch Domesticity: A Radical Reinterpretation of Seventeenth-Century "Homescape"', *Home Cultures*, 15(1): 73–102.

De Jongh, E. (1967), *Zinne- en minnebeelden in de schilderkunst van de zeventiende eeuw* (on iconography in 17th century painting), Amsterdam: Nederlandse Stichting Openbaar Kunstbezit.

De Jongh, E. (1976), *Tot lering en vermaak. Betekenissen van Hollandse genrevoorstellingen uit de zeventiende eeuw* (on the meaning of 17th-century Dutch genre painting), Amsterdam: Rijksmuseum.

Flanders, J. (2015), *The Making of Home: The 500-Year Story of How Our Houses Became Homes*, London: Atlantic Books.

Franits, W. (2004), *Dutch Seventeenth-Century Genre Painting: Its Stylistic and Thematic Evolution*, New Haven: Yale University Press.

Kloek, E. (2009), *Vrouw des huizes. Een cultuurgeschiedenis van de Hollandse huisvrouw* (woman of the house: a cultural history of the Dutch housewife), Amsterdam: Uitgeverij Balans.

Loughman, J. and J. M. Montias (2000), *Public and Private Space: Works of Art in Seventeenth-Century Dutch House*, Zwolle: Waanders.

Noordegraaf, L. and G. Valk (1996), *De gave Gods. De pest in Holland vanaf de late middeleeuwen* (on The Plague in Holland since the Middle Ages), Amsterdam: Bert Bakker.

Oczko, P. (2021), *Bezem & Kruis. De Hollandse schoonmaakcultuur of de geschiedenis van een obsessie* (English summary Broom & Cross. The Culture of Cleanliness in Holland, or The History of an Obsession, 405–11), Leiden: Primavera Pers.

Thomassen, B. (2015), 'Thinking with Liminality. To the Boundaries of an Anthropological Concept', in A. Horvath, B. Thomassen and H. Wydra (eds), *Breaking Boundaries: Varieties of Liminality*, 39–58, New York: Berghahn Books.

Van Gelder, R. (2007), 'Letters, Journals and Seeds: Forgotten Dutch Mail in the National Archives in London', in N. Worden (ed.), *Contingent Lives: Social Identity and Material Culture in the VOC World*, 538–45, Cape Town: ABC Press.

Van Gelder, R. (2008), *Zeepost: nooit bezorgde brieven uit de 17de en 18de eeuw* (Oversea mail: never delivered letters from the 17th and 18th centuries), Amsterdam: Uitgeverij Atlas.

Vervoort, R. (2011), *'Vrouwen op den besem en derghelijck ghespoock' over Pieter Brueghel en de traditie van heksenvoorstellingen in de Nederlanden tussen 1450 en 1700* (on representations of witches in Dutch paintings from the 15th till the 17th century), PhD-thesis Radboud University Nijmegen.

Waiboer, A. E. (2012), *Gabriel Metsu Life and Work: A Catalogue Raisonné*, New Haven: Yale University Press.

12

Lockdown portraits: Resituating the self

Inga Bryden

During lockdowns – a response to the Covid-19 pandemic – people spent longer periods of time at home, confined to the space of the domestic interior. By contrast, public urban spaces were de-peopled. A fascination with the absence of the human at a time of crisis was evident in increased popular cultural interest in photographs of empty urban spaces. Such representations of deserted spaces highlight impermanence and evoke feelings of the uncanny. As Anthony Vidler (1992) has suggested, abandoned, empty spaces render the familiar, unfamiliar.

This chapter explores in more detail the notions of familiarity and unfamiliarity in relation to the domestic interior during a period of crisis; what might be termed a flight from the exterior to the interior. In particular, it discusses whether the familiar spaces of the home have been made more familiar through portraiture, as a means of reinstating the human subject in a known, arguably more controllable, space, connecting with others and examining the self. In this sense creating a portrait is a response to a perceived external threat of instability, social distancing and a lack of human, intimate presence.

During lockdown in the UK there was a heightened interest in portrait painting over the internet, in the context of a renewed popularity in undertaking arts and crafts activities at home. The chapter considers examples of how depicting the human subject in the interior space – or on the threshold of it – has been approached using portraiture: portrait photographs created over the internet (or in the home) by professional artists; painted and photographic self-portraits exploring the daily effects of lockdown, and creative initiatives engaging the public or a community, exhibited online or in spaces external to the home. The lockdown portraits discussed refer, then, to individual representations and, collectively, to a portrait of a nation 'at home'.

In their essay published in *The Conversation* on 19 March 2020, Cherine Fahd and Sara Oscar discuss the ubiquity of photographs of empty public spaces as a means of documenting and responding to the first national lockdown (Fahd and Oscar 2020). Such images can be set in a tradition of depicting the built environment devoid of human presence, from Giorgio de Chirico's early cityscape paintings to Christian Richter's *Abandoned* series of photographs of vacant, decaying, unstable buildings. This notion of the 'architectural uncanny' as explored by Vidler is useful to consider in relation to the dynamic between the self and interior space. Of particular relevance here is Vidler's extension of the association of the uncanny with the unstable nature of the house and home as articulated by Ernst Jentsch and then Sigmund Freud (Vidler 1992: 23) to spatial conditions – environment – more generally. The uncanny also arose from urban space and was linked to both feelings of insecurity due to a lack of orientation in one's environment and a sense of something familiar appearing in 'new' ways. In other words, a key aspect of the uncanny is that it leads to reflection on individual and social estrangement and on the relationship between self, home and community. As a metaphor for the unease of the modern condition, the uncanny seems apt for Covid-19 times.

The mechanical eye of photography is integral to visualizing this sense of disorientation and unease, particularly when photographs of empty public spaces capture a departure from or absence of the everyday. During lockdown the images produced by news photographers exposed 'how our surroundings can suddenly become something other – something fragile and tenuous' (Fahd and Oscar 2020: 1). As a counterpoint to such images and the pandemic practice of social distancing, it can be suggested that the home became a focus for reorientating and resituating oneself, signifying retreat and slowing down. The home has, since the nineteenth-century construction of it as a refuge – 'a place that separates the safe from the unsafe' (Taylor 2013: 157) – been associated with concepts of ease, intimacy, security and familiarity. The representations of how individuals try to make themselves 'at home' discussed here illustrate the changing spatial and social configurations brought about by the impact of the Covid-19 pandemic.

The deep-seated connection of the home or house with an inhabitant's identity and especially with a sense of stability is evident in the phenomenological line of enquiry within cultural geography, itself concerned with examining cultural practices relating to how people make sense of place. The philosopher Gaston Bachelard ([1958] 1994: 3) acknowledges that the house 'is a privileged entity for a phenomenological study of the intimate values of inside space'. He sees the house itself as a 'psychic state' (72) which evokes deep feelings of value and caring. Such sentiments gained cultural currency during the first UK lockdown, for example, with the Clap for Our Carers campaign in support of the National Health Service (NHS) when people connected with neighbours through windows and by coming out onto their doorsteps. Yet just as a house embodies intimacy and encloses memories, it is, Bachelard notes, being constantly reimagined and thus gives 'proofs or illusions of stability' (16).

Memory, familiarity with the interior space of a home and the dynamic between people and things are further complicated with the ubiquity of screens in the home and our interaction with them. As Edward Hollis ([2013] 2014: 259) observes, 'screens are everywhere now, and nowhere'. The screen 'elides fact and fantasy' (260) and yet the human reliance on it intensified during periods of being quarantined at home and with the impacts of the pandemic. Connecting with others through the digital space of a laptop, tablet or iPhone provided a means of reinstating the presence of the human subject and of reflecting on the self and its surroundings. Notably, portrait painting over the internet increased during lockdown in the UK; part of a renewed cultural focus on making things in the home and on creativity itself as a means of re-establishing community. The popular television programme, *Grayson's Art Club*, shown on Channel 4 in 2020 and 2021, had portraits as the theme of its first episode.

From March 2020 the shift to working from home online using a webcam brought a preoccupation with self-presentation and the appearance of one's backdrop, the objects and spaces of the home interior. Essays and commentaries considered how to simultaneously project professionalism and domestic ease, providing in effect a guide to Zoom self-portraiture. Commentators acknowledge that setting up the composition of a live self-portrait in preparation for an encounter has become routine, whilst also noting the unease about confronting one's own image on screen. The online face in motion, suggests Eva Wiseman (2021: 5), exposes the 'fragility of our unfinished selves' and the limits to how identity can be manipulated, even as technology allows portraits of the self to be edited.

Unease, then, can be generated by something – our own face – which should be familiar. Or rather, the disorientation stems from the unfamiliar experience of extending self-consciousness beyond the body and into the space framed by a laptop and digitally mediated. This altered relation to space, brought about by social distancing and lockdown, has led to a blurring of virtual space and actual domestic setting, of self-representation and daily living. Richard Mapes (2020: 1) sees this as 'uncanny … destabilizing attempts to produce controlled readings of one's self'.

At the same time, situating the self in digital and actual domestic space brings creative possibilities. As the symbolism in Renaissance portraits might be analysed, so the interiors and bookshelves behind the Zoom sitter can be curated – or downloaded – and read. For the purposes of this chapter, the interaction between background and figure should be emphasized: both place (environment or surroundings) and the placing of the subject have an important role to play. This dynamism can be noted in Italian Renaissance portraiture with the incorporation of glimpses of domestic interiors which interacted with the subject, in contrast to the more passive, flat, dark backgrounds which threw the subject's profile into relief (Pelletier 2021).

The genre of portraiture is historically bound with the notion of likeness; of attempting to capture or represent a person from life; to render them recognizable and familiar. Yet, as Shearer West (2004: 12) points out, all portraits show a 'distorted, ideal, or partial view of the sitter'. Likeness is 'not a stable concept' (22). It can be suggested that one means of 'stabilizing' the self or human subject is to surround it with meaningful objects or to place it in a detailed, framed setting. In a time of enforced residence at home, engaging with portraits and portraiture allows investigation of both internal and external aspects of identity. West asserts that a portrait can 'probe the uniqueness of an individual in a way that sets the sitter apart from his or her context' (21). Yet equally the subject can be resituated and interpreted within that context; the objects and props being integral to the reading.

Portraiture predominantly represents a particular moment or occasion and is often associated with the past, a memorial to a particular time or person. In this it articulates a tension between absence and presence, the temporal and the permanent. In the context of Covid-19, photographic portraiture was particularly in evidence as a means of documenting a period of crisis. Drawing on theories of photography is useful in highlighting the resonances between this medium of portraiture and cultural responses to the conditions of lockdown. It can be argued that photographs and photography help to situate people and have a stabilizing effect where, in effect, space is owned and controlled. As Susan Sontag ([1977] 1979: 9) comments, 'As photographs give people an imaginary possession of a past that is unreal, they also help people to take possession of space in which they are insecure'. The image also offers certainty and fixity in contrast to the uncertainty of real-world events – heightened in times of crisis – and spatial disorientation. Moreover, the activity of taking photographs of oneself or others can be 'soothing, and assuages general feelings of disorientation' (9–10). Taken as a group situated across time, photographs form a kind of 'portrait-chronicle' (8), evidence of connection between individuals and of connectedness.

Viewed as a response to the absence of citizens in public spaces during the pandemic, photography '*authenticates* the existence of a certain being' (Barthes [1980] 1984: 107) inhabiting an interior space. However, there are limitations to establishing a stable individual identity. Whilst a photographic portrait appears 'to provide a foolproof means of conveying likeness' (West: 189), the viewer 'can only sweep it with [a] glance, like a smooth surface' (Barthes: 106). In other words, the viewer is unable to access the interior space or innermost being, a distancing enhanced by the laptop screen. At the same time photographic portraits created over the internet during lockdowns offered new creative possibilities, particularly for adapting the conventional props of portraiture whereby sitters would occupy 'anonymous spaces' with 'artificial elements' (West: 190).

Freelance portrait photographer Fran Monks began photographing her subjects over the internet during the first UK lockdown for financial reasons, but also because she wanted to document the experience of being isolated at home and socially distanced. It is clear from Monks's website, blog and media articles that, for her, confinement to the interior and use of technology facilitated expansion and connection. Emphasizing the collaborative and improvised nature of the relationship between the photographer and subject (in their respective homes), Monks increasingly realized the significance of including more of the environment or domestic surroundings in the portrait. Environment also refers to the laptop screen itself, incorporated in the final image. Monks ('Coronavirus: Isolation Portraits' 2020) refers to the 'black border of the computer screen [being] somewhat reminiscent of a darkroom print from a negative' and to the 'strange artefacts which appear'. The latter includes a small-screen image of the photographer holding up her camera, in the top right-hand corner of the photograph (Figure 12.1). Although the intrusion of an artefact such as a 'selfie-signature' (Monks 2021) made

FIGURE 12.1 *'Sally' by Fran Monks*, Social Distance – Lockdown Mark I, *2020.* © *Fran Monks.*

'strange' suggests the uncanny, Monks argues that Zoom enhances the effect of a relaxed, familiar home environment which, in turn, produces a more unique portrait. Moreover, the sitter is more in control of the domestic space, positioning the camera and selecting what is seen in the frame.

Other photographic lockdown portraits focused on the doorstep, rather than being set in the home. During the first UK lockdown, photographer Birgitta Zoutman documented her local community in a series of portraits taken within a twenty-minute cycle ride from her home, using a zoom camera lens to ensure social distancing (allowing reframing of a scene whilst remaining in the same physical position). Shared on her Facebook page, the informal portraits of neighbours and families evoke connectedness and contributed to the community in material ways (with donations going to a local food bank). The intimate family groupings on the threshold of their homes, surrounded by ordinary, familiar things, recall eighteenth-century British informal group portraiture, or middle-class family portraits which emphasized the seemingly trivial and familiar qualities of the scene (West: 83). The pets (dogs) in Zoutman's portraits represent qualities such as loyalty and protection, taking on a particular significance in the context of Covid-19. Similarly, the rainbow, seen in windows or by doors, came to symbolize support for NHS workers and a way of communicating solidarity with people from a distance.

Creating self-portraits in the home (or studio) over a period of sudden change and instability is a particularly effective means of documenting the daily effects of lockdown and exploring self-identity. As a genre, self-portraiture has a 'chameleonic potential' and can accommodate 'expanding definitions of identity and shifting notions of selfhood' (Rudd 2021: 7). Its purposes are multifarious: to capture a likeness; convey an inner state; play; hide; or transform. Self-portraiture using flat mirrors (objects widely referenced in painted self-portraits) and requiring long sittings changed with photography and the ubiquitous selfie has in a sense democratized it. The notion of the uncanny is relevant here, since a self-portrait involves the artist creating a 'double' of themselves. The photographer Martin Parr has highlighted the strange or disorientating aspects of the process through an ironic focus on background and the construction of interiors. The self in *Autoportrait* ([2000] 2016) is situated in elaborate studio sets (evoking the gimmicks and props used by early studio photographers) or in digitally manipulated fantastical situations.

During the third UK lockdown commercial photographer Mike Sewell produced a daily self-portrait as a creative challenge, posting it on social media. In *Egg Head* (2020), set in the space of the kitchen, perspective and scale are played with: a close-up of the photographer's bald, bespectacled head appears flanked by two eggs in a ceramic holder, the three 'eggs' dominating the scene. In these portraits interesting angles are created using an iPhone (with a remote control) or Nikon (with self-timer) cameras. Everyday objects in a familiar domestic interior thus appear unfamiliar, as if taking on a new agency (albeit with a touch of humour). Yet, at the same time, the creative process itself provides reassurance and routine amidst the 'chaos' of the pandemic.

The notion of not being entirely at home 'at home' can also be extended to a sense of not being at ease within the self. Artist Gillian Wearing was motivated by the isolation of lockdown to embark on an exploration of her image and to focus on how the medium of paint (which she hadn't used for thirty-three years) could affect the representation of self. The resulting series of self-portraits in watercolour and oils, plus other works, formed the *Lockdown* exhibition at the Maureen Paley gallery, London (16 September to 1 December 2020). If the motif of doubling sees the 'other' as a replica of the self, Wearing extends this to investigate the notion of masking. The sculpture *Mask Masked* comprises a wax mask of the face, with nose and mouth covered by a cloth mask (referencing face masks worn as protection against the virus), held aloft on a steel rod. Collectively, the painted self-portraits reveal an inward journey, documenting what Martin Herbert (2021: 1) describes as 'a spectrum of moods'. Wearing is 'thrown back on herself in a way that feels painfully familiar' to the viewer. The different poses and inward or off-centre gaze (countering a more traditional portrait pose) delineate layers of self-alienation. However, it can also be suggested that the neutral backgrounds and interiors devoid of objects resonate with the particular circumstances of physical disconnection experienced during periods of lockdown. Paradoxically, the exhibition in a public gallery allows the (re)adoption of social personas. Herbert (2021: 1) argues that Wearing sees the performance of socialized roles as a form of freedom, which allows, 'if you change the mask, for escaping the prison of selfhood, of fixed identity'.

The role of portraiture in affirming social connection or group identity during lockdowns was especially notable in the range of public initiatives, community projects and creative challenges launched by individuals and museums. British portrait artist Thomas Croft posted a video on Instagram offering a free portrait to the first NHS Key Worker to contact him. The portrait of Harriet Durkin, a nurse at Manchester Royal Infirmary, wearing PPE (personal protective equipment) was the first in what became a virtual exhibition and global art project. 'Portraits for NHS Heroes' can be placed in the tradition of 'occupational portraits'; a Covid-19-specific situating of the individual and, collectively, an institution to represent the 'tropes of solidarity, equality, and individuality' (West: 121).

With the similar aim of creating a collective portrait of the UK during lockdown, the 'Hold Still' community project led by the Duchess of Cambridge, Patron of the National Portrait Gallery, involved members of the public submitting a photographic portrait of their experience of lockdown during May and June 2020. It is striking how many of the hundred portraits, selected from over 31,000 submissions, feature windows; the glass pane both framing and separating the individual from others (as in 'Behind the Glass' by Lyndsey Adams). Furthermore, the window symbolizes the act of looking from the outside in, and vice versa, reflected in the title of Sara Lincoln's photograph: *Justin, from the Outside In* (Figure 12.2).

The 'Hold Still' lockdown portraits depict ordinary domestic activities – familiar, yet unfamiliar due to the extraordinary circumstances. With art galleries closed, artists could perhaps retreat to their studios; in a wider sense the home became a site for creativity. The domestic space was the focus of a creative challenge tweeted by the Getty Museum on 25 March 2020: for inhabitants to recreate a work of art using three items from their home. Inspired by Dutch Instagram user @tussenkunstenquarantaine (which translates as 'between art and quarantine') the initiative is an example of creative (self)-fashioning and adaptation of the interior as both a refuge from uncertainty and a means of sharing and enjoying art beyond the confines of the home.

The domestic interior as a space ripe for creative reinvention is evident in street photographer Enda Burke's lockdown portraits of his parents in their home (where he stayed during lockdown). Since the streets were emptied of the usual photographic subjects, Burke focused on family and the familiar.

FIGURE 12.2 Hold Still: A Portrait of Our Nation in 2020 – *'Justin, from the outside in' by Sara Lincoln. National Portrait Gallery, London. © Sara Lincoln.*

LOCKDOWN PORTRAITS: RESITUATING THE SELF

Rather than recreating a work of art, the award-winning series *Homebound with My Parents* arguably turns the home and its inhabitants *into* art. More specifically, the photographs depict lockdown existence as theatrical and seemingly ordinary activities (watching television; drinking a milkshake; ironing) as faintly ludicrous (Figure 12.3).

A key aspect of the project, it can be suggested, was to juxtapose the ordinary and familiar with the exotic and marvellous. Burke (2021: 1) comments: 'I am drawn to the monotony associated with family life during the pandemic, exploring how small details of color and play can become marvels in monotonous settings.' Using nostalgia as a form of escapism from the pandemic (a widely reported lockdown phenomenon), Burke constructed sets out of retro objects, vibrantly coloured furnishings and Catholic religious iconography, at the same time 'constructing narratives' with his parents as the protagonists. This element of role playing resonates with Wearing's investigation of adopting personas. It can be suggested, though, that the paraphernalia of place (Monks's 'environment') and the placing of – and interaction with – the subjects is equally important.

FIGURE 12.3 *'Tesco Value Dad' by Enda Burke*, Homebound with My Parents, *2020*. © *Enda Burke.*

This chapter has explored the complexities of resituating the self in the interior at a time of crisis, focusing on portraiture as an assertion of identity and a reaching for human connection, albeit mediated by the lens and framed by the screen. Whereas lockdown photographs of empty urban public spaces capture a sense of estrangement from space, portraits of the subject in their home or domestic space reconnect the self with the materiality and familiarity of the interior. In this sense the interior space is culturally repositioned as a site of both self-making and place-making. In the era of Covid-19 this reveals new perspectives on the interrelation of identity and space, and absence and presence. However, the familiar spaces of the home have not necessarily been rendered more familiar through this process. Whilst technology has facilitated collaboration, connection with a wider community, or control of the home environment, it has also produced unfamiliar perspectives: 'the camera makes exotic things near, intimate; and familiar things small, abstract, strange, much farther away. It offers … both participation and alienation in our own lives and those of others.' (Sontag 1977 [1979]: 167). Moreover, the restrictions of being quarantined at home during lockdown and the limitations of the laptop screen or camera frame have been shown to inspire and facilitate creativity. This has involved, for example, greater interaction or collaboration between the room (and objects therein), the subject and the portrait photographer. Resituating the self in lockdown has revealed new ways of working for artists and has enhanced public understanding of pictorial composition and self-presentation.

References

Bachelard, G. ([1958] 1994), *The Poetics of Space*, trans. M. Jolas, Boston: Beacon Press.

Barthes, R. ([1980] 1984), *Camera Lucida: Reflections on Photography*, trans. R. Howard, London: Fontana.

Burke, E. (2021), 'Homebound with My Parents', *LensCulture*. https://www.lensculture.com/articles/enda-burke-homebound-with-my-parents

'Coronavirus: Isolation Portraits over the Internet' (2020), *BBC News In Pictures*, 15 April. https://www.bbc.co.uk/news/in-pictures-52284371

'Coronavirus: Photographer Captures Lockdown Life in Doorstep Portraits' (2020), *BBC News*, 14 April. https://www.bbc.co.uk/news/uk-england-shropshire-52270585

Croft, T. (2020), *Portraits for NHS Heroes*, London: Bloomsbury Caravel.

Fahd, C. and S. Oscar (2020), 'The Uncanny Melancholy of Empty Photographs in the Time of Coronavirus', *The Conversation*, 19 March.

Herbert, M. (2021), 'Behind the Mask? An Interview with Gillian Wearing', *Apollo Magazine*, 6 March.

Hold Still: A Portrait of Our Nation in 2020 (2021), intro. The Duchess of Cambridge, London: National Portrait Gallery.

Hollis, E. ([2013] 2014), *The Memory Palace: A Book of Lost Interiors*, London: Portobello.
Mapes, R. (2020), 'A Guide to Zoom Self-Portraiture', *Places*, August.
Monks, F. (2021), 'What Might Be Worth Keeping from This Lockdown Experience?', *Fran's Blog*, 12 February. https://www.franmonks.com/blog/whats-worth-keeping-from-this-lockdown-experience
Parr, M. ([2000] 2016), *Autoportrait*, Stockport: Dewi Lewis.
Pelletier, C. M. (2021), 'On Background: From the Renaissance to Zoom', *Genealogies of Modernity*, 5 March. https://genealogiesofmodernity.org/journal/2021/3/3/on-background-zoom-and-the-italian-renaissance-portrait
Rudd, N. (2021), *The Self-Portrait*, London: Thames and Hudson.
Sontag, S. ([1977] 1979), *On Photography*, London: Penguin.
Taylor, M. (2013), 'Hidden Spaces: Cavities, Attics and Cellars – Morbid Secrets and Threatening Discoveries', in G. Downey (ed.), *Domestic Interiors: Representing Homes from the Victorians to the Moderns*, 147–58, London: Bloomsbury.
Vidler, A. (1992), *The Architectural Uncanny: Essays in the Modern Unhomely*, Cambridge, MA: MIT Press.
West, S. (2004), *Portraiture*, Oxford: Oxford University Press.
Wiseman, E. (2021), 'Zoom Meetings Mean You Have to Face Your Own Face', *The Observer Magazine*, 5 September: 5.

13

Fiction: IKEA's saleable living for pandemic life

Rebecca Carrai

In 2020, returning from a fieldtrip to the IKEA museum and hotel in Älmhult, Sweden, and reading the furnishing company's recent publication, *Democratic Design* (2020), it struck me that I felt as if there was no ongoing pandemic. Did we dream it? Was the virus a reality or imagined? This chapter is driven by the exploration of the role of fiction within IKEA's history, culminating in a theorization of the furniture retailer's impact on the home interior during Covid-19. Through a historical exploration, the chapter illustrates IKEA's increased jeopardization of reality by means of technologies. Intended broadly as *logos*, an utterance of *techne*, techniques, arts, skills and crafts, technologies have been adopted by the company to distort corporeality from the mid-1950s and exacerbated during Covid-19.

Fiction is embedded in IKEA's history. As former IKEA designer Lotta Hahn posits, 'IKEA homerooms were never realistic but aspirational' (Hahn, 4 October 2021). They represented life-like situations, but their content was futuristic compared with people's living standards. The continuous construction of desirable images has historically aided IKEA in disseminating notions of domesticity, suggesting lifestyles, trends and influencing consumer behaviour. Initially, this mediation occurred by publishing photographs of home interiors in their printed catalogues. Those pages were populated with colourful, attractive media spaces communicating their own architectural realities. Later, mediation was applied to the three-dimensional spaces within the stores and with the launch of the company's website domestic space was disseminated online.

Through the examination of documents held in the company archive and oral information from interviews with IKEA staff, this chapter problematizes IKEA's ongoing project to dematerialize and craftily reconstruct the real, tangible interior into a mediated saleable product.[1] The chapter specifically illustrates its peak during Covid-19 through the case study of Italy. It unpacks how the Swedish company responded to Italian society by implementing site-specific commercial strategies, embracing the health, financial and social crisis as an opportunity to profit from being the first European country experiencing the spread of the virus.

The Instagrammable home

Arguably, the Instagrammable home existed before the arrival of social media. In 1953, two years after the launch of the initially mail-order catalogue, IKEA's founder, Ingvar Kamprad, director of a still small-scale, local business, made Gillis Lundgren responsible for merchandising design, setting shots and, above all, catalogue production. While the previous brochure, *ikéa-nytt*, and early 1950s catalogues featured basic, sales-oriented graphics, the 1955 edition presented an illustration of a house plan and a rendering of a living room (Bjarnestam 2013; Torekull and Kamprad 1998). Lundgren's contribution consisted of perceiving the image as an object of mediation of a recognizable, domestic environment and the company not as a mere furniture retailer but as an adviser on home life. Since then, representations of living spaces were to dominate the catalogue and life-like situations were widely depicted (Seits 2018). Intelligently juxtaposed with logo and textual information, they communicated the home in dreamy domestic displays as affordable and desirable to all customers. Images started to exercise soft powers in appealing to and shaping the preferences of the viewer while simultaneously promoting the merchandise on sale.

This is the initiation of IKEA's ongoing 'home communication project', in which a clever combination of texts and visual associations takes over the meaning of physical space with model rooms – three-dimensional, almost-real spaces – hosting a fictional reality. IKEA's catalogue images reflected a complex network of 'mentalities' (Frichot 2018). A set of different relations between human and non-humans' subjectivities took place even behind the scenes. Starting with the design and construction of a home room, the scene was then inhabited by domestic performances – usually by IKEA staff – who were to be photographed and displayed in the catalogue. These images often depicted happy family 'melodramas' but simultaneously, mixed scenography with instructions on how to furnish one's rooms (Seits 2018: 417–9). To picture the IKEA home required no shift from image to reality, but the images intended to hide a set of different translations, from the company's configuration of a carefully designed, three-dimensional space, with furniture suggesting a variety of uses with the aim of engaging the consumers' desires and belief that they could 'do-it-themselves' (Figure 13.1). As this persuasion took place across the catalogue pages, a similar phenomenon could be observed in the shopping experience since the first showroom-store in 1958, where the fiction was translated with the added allure of sensual experience.

From the mid-1970s, with the expansion of the business and the 'transition from the industrial, product-driven economy of modernity to a new political economy structured by the primacy of sign' (Holt 2016: 56), IKEA increasingly nurtured its visual marketing strategy. Traces of human life – a set table, unfinished meals, crumpled blankets, etc. – were staged to recall home rituals. Abstract close-ups were juxtaposed with domestic scenarios, family life embodied by and staged in various household types and rooms, which, given their diversity and generality, could appeal to a wide audience IKEA's images encouraged a form of domestic neoliberalism (Ledin and Machin 2019) by placing viewers at the centre of their narrative and enabling them to relate to increasingly diverse realistic situations. The mediated interior became, both in the catalogue and the store, a platform extending beyond the mere publicizing of products but tickling the viewer's imagination and triggering consumption desires. It led the reader of this theatrical space to 'experience' and want the seemingly real content that it could see.

FIGURE 13.1 *Backstage for 1974/75 catalogue. © Inter IKEA Systems B.V.*

IKEA's digital turn

With the launch of the company's website in 1997, and the introduction of social media in 2007, IKEA engaged with digitalization, including the collection, processing and analysis of data, such as in the Life at Home reports. IKEA's rooms started to appear on the web and colonize immaterial places. Especially in the social media, they became pocketable, multiformat and proliferated even on to digital platforms that were not directly tied to the company, from unofficial to others run by users or less explicitly sponsored by firms like IKANO Bostad. Technology affected not only the dissemination of IKEA's saleable interiors, but also the mediation, the modification of their design and construction methods as well as architectural changes to the company's work environments, including the several relocations of their photo studio and the continuous expansion of their headquarters (Tony Nilsson, 26 January 2022).

Whereas furniture production increasingly occurred outside the Swedish headquarters, these, in turn, required larger spaces for administration, IT departments, import/export and, mostly, image production. Later, in the mid-1980s, IKEA installed a new global network called Dec-net IKEA. This enabled direct computer connection for Macintosh and IBM PC and server to server transmissions of files, greatly speeding up the catalogue production (Björn Zitting, 2 October 2021). Since 2000, IKEA's photos have been gradually replaced by computer-generated images. IKEA's Marketing & Communication department (IMC) is now in charge of building both physical and digital models to produce influential media architectures which decreasingly requires setting up a physical prototype. A library of several hundred virtual architectural elements is available to construct possible scenarios. This digital library, IKEA Media Content Center (IMCC), provides IKEA worldwide access to domestic images for publication first on catalogues, later social media platforms – representations adapted from country to country to respond to geo-specific home micropolitics as showcased during Covid-19.

In 2010, IKEA started experimenting with Virtual Reality, especially Real Time, operations simultaneous with users' responsiveness. According to IKEA's Innovation Manager, Enthed Martin, the aim of using such advanced technology was to keep people in front of their screens for hours and engage with IKEA's imagery, regardless of their interest in shopping. In 2017, IKEA's Place app was released in collaboration with Apple (*IKEA VR, AR, MR and Meatballs* 2017) (Figure 13.2). This software enables users to photograph an interior, place IKEA furniture to scale in the framed digital reality and receive furnishing advice from an algorithm. The app aims to bridge the so-called 'imagination gap' by 'delegating' decisions from the prospective user to the algorithm ('IKEA Place: Bridging the Imagination Gap With AR' 2017). In

FIGURE 13.2 *IKEA Place App commercial from 2017.* © *Inter IKEA Systems B.V.*

addition, the app enhanced the normalization of increasingly fast, neoliberal and consumerist lifestyles. Amassing more stuff despite living in smaller spaces became a focus for IKEA suggesting how to continue shopping while filling unused space. Accordingly, the former representation of model interiors became an unfolded view of multiple planes as potential spaces for furniture.

While IKEA's representations of domestic spaces were previously created in the studio as well as in the stores with model rooms as props, recent decades have increasingly focused on the augmentation of the virtual. PR and marketing leader, Raphael Bartke, describes: 'attention spans have decreased significantly, and customers' behaviour has changed: digital images are more attractive than photographic ones, luring the viewer into an addictive flow of home inspiration and engagement with the displayed object' (Bartke, 14 September 2021). The pinnacle of IKEA's adaptation to these changes in society could be seen in the recent decision to cease printing the iconic catalogue following a gradual decline in readership. The last edition in 2020, produced as usual one year earlier, avoided the upheavals hitting humanity in mid-pandemic, and obscured the transformative societal changes that were happening by keeping the focus on the home environment as a safe and happy place. When most of the world's population was in a state of complete lockdown, and social distancing was the norm, the company successfully reinforced its fiction. Despite the closure of 10 per cent of its stores in various lockdowns the firm increased its income by 13 per cent (*Retail Detail*, 4 November 2020) through implementing its 'click & collect' service. IKEA's website has been recognized as one of the top-performing e-commerce sites during the pandemic (Berthiaume 2020). While physical interaction seemed to stop, shopping did not – it evolved. IKEA continuously engaged its clients with digital activities, from workshops to live streaming on social media, from e-commerce sites to video-counselling services. 'Connect and buy' became a new paradigm.

Social distancing

Whereas Italian customers, in particular, had previously preferred the heady sensorial experience of in-store homerooms, they learned during the pandemic to equally appreciate and trust online shopping at home, investing ever higher amounts of money with a few clicks. While the IKEA shopping ritual was previously seen as an act of socialization and involved the experience of scenographies, food areas and even a motel in Älmhult, digitalization turned shopping into a more frequent and individualistic experience. If reconsidering the store concept might have already been on the company's agenda, the pandemic prompted IKEA to look for new shopping formats, including forms of entertainment other than the traditional 'maze of aisles' (Deighton 2021). A peculiar phenomenon impacted specifically the Italian franchise: the harder the pandemic hit the population, the greater became the influence of the furniture retailer's sales strategies. One of them was a video-call helpline, which had been introduced to assist customers with rearranging and decorating their interiors while in-store shopping was forbidden. It was enthusiastically received as confirmed by IKEA Italia's remote sales leader (Arianna Diegoli, 21 May 2021). Since the first lockdown, IKEA counselling services have been growing in number, places of dissemination and functions, from video calls, YouTube clips to visual contents extending beyond bedroom, living room and kitchen designs. If the helpline service had been offered cost-free to the prospective customer earlier, the pandemic turned it into a novel income source and a quick fix for home design. For a charge of a minimum of nine euros per call and extending consultancy to bathroom design and décor tips for the whole interior, the video call service guides customers through the homemaking via the screen, a service that can be reimbursed after the purchase. Moreover, an incentive to call IKEA and shop online was a new law, Legge di Bilancio 2021 (art 1, comma 58, b.2), which allows residents to use a bonus of 50 per cent for the purchase of furniture and electronic components and relates to the 'bonus casa' decreed by the Italian Government encouraging sustainable properties renovation ('Bonus Mobili 2021' 2020).

If digitalization resulted in IKEA witnessing an average increase in income during lockdown – with a share of 39 per cent for kitchen purchases, 16 per cent for bedrooms, 8 per cent for home workspace items and 45 per cent of total remote sales – it is important to note that the increased numbers necessitated new labour and consumption practices with impact on social behaviours and public functions of a city. Confirming that shopping didn't require a visit to the store but could be performed anywhere virtually, during the pandemic many Italians abandoned the metropolis – emptied of social and leisure activities – to follow the city-quitters trend affecting the deurbanization of the major urban centres and causing overpopulation in less dense, greener, peripherical areas. Digitalization stimulated by the pandemic accelerated the existing transition from the 'physical to digital' which also called for a rethinking within IKEA's former activities, from in-store shopping to the organization of work-spaces. Previously behind a desk, and ready to help the prospective buyer, staff have been increasingly distanced from the consumer and the latter from the desired object. As IKEA Italia's staff reported, video calls and live streaming on Instagram and social media posts compensated for the lack of physical proximity and strengthened the closeness between the company and customers by enabling timesaving, more informal, instant communication. However, correspondences between IKEA and its customers can be traced back to the 1955 IKEA questionnaire, a tool granting users a voice with which to express their domestic preferences and mail the company about them (IKEA catalogue 1955). Throughout the pandemic, and as a result of the dynamic digital content, exchanges occurred so frequently that an average of sixteen customers contacted IKEA after an Instagram live streaming, asking for the specifics of a product on display or details on a potential purchase.

Sanitizing the interior

When, on 12 March 2020, IKEA Italia followed governmental regulations and closed its (store) doors, but kept the digital gates open, the hashtag #RipartiamoDaCasa (Let's re-start from home) began to circulate online with posts and live streaming on Instagram together with a homonym YouTube playlist (*IKEA – #Ripartiamo da casa* 2020). 'In this period, home is the best place to stay', claimed the Italian franchise in the heyday of the pandemic when the flood of online recordings and images engulfed the web (IKEA Italia (2020) [Instagram] 12 March).[2] Tracking the IKEA Italia pandemic motto on the web led to videoclips on how to 'Fight chaos in your home', 'Work in pyjamas from home', 'Customise the house according to your taste' and others. What features in the pandemic saga is a clear, widespread optimistic tone combined with instructive, pedagogical content, yet always also based on commercial goals. Despite the company's intention to render the home a 'better place for many people', and help the population to stay positive, one cannot overlook their opportunism in increasingly indoctrinating customers and marketing the image of the domestic interior as the place where people were confined. This was particularly the case in Italy due to severe mobility restrictions, and which, indisputably, caused significant functional, structural and aesthetic transformation. Coincidentally, IKEA's clips and posts were not limited to showing users how to optimize home spaces or suggesting furniture, but 'convert(ed) more and more areas of the economy into these new digital realms' (Robinson 2020: 5). They gave convincing advice on parenting, cooking, family relationships – arguably not the competence of a furnishing company – such as in a YouTube film offering suggestions on how to organize kids' remote education desks or encourage the correct sitting position.

On top of this, IKEA Italia's Instagram posts started to sanitize the chaotic, messy reality of the home, turning it into sleek, digitally crafted pictures. A post from 13 March features a computer-generated image portraying a tidy, light, peaceful room. Here, the mediated interior is inhabited by children – perhaps real actors, perhaps virtual profiles – who are unsupervised and seem to help each other with remote school lessons. This framing of domestic life suggests both visually and verbally that through IKEA's products and decluttering solutions harmony can be achieved at home. It claims that '(w)ith an organized space for playing, drawing, and studying, you can find the ideal balance for your children' (IKEA Italia (2020) [Instagram], 13 March). The image subtly endows IKEA with superpowers concerning domestic life and management while convincing the audience that it can live in such unrealistic reality

FIGURE 13.3 *IKEA Italia, (2020) [Instagram] 15 March.*

through the mere purchase of a product. Instagram clips published during the lockdown portray idyllic family life while omitting tensions, overlooking the lack of space, depression, gender disparities, social inequality and other kinds of domestic and emotional problems people experienced, and which were exacerbated during the pandemic (Figure 13.3). In favouring the fiction of a picture-perfect society, where positivity is boosted and problems avoided, the company spared no effort to keep the dreamt normality alive. Adopting visuals cleverly mixed with perspicacious captions, IKEA's online campaigns utterly neglected the thunderstorm hitting the real domestic interior where people found themselves co-existing in a limited space, or parents juggled work, childcare and remote education responsibilities.

IKEA was aware of people's feelings of anxiety, search for comfort, fluid spaces at home and more virtual connections which increased by 35 per cent (Figure 13.4). Through the three Life at Home Reports conducted to study closely pandemic life, the company managed to tap into the everyday existence of several households from different countries ('Life at Home Report 2020' 2021).[3] IKEA's remote sales leader confirms that people were longing for an adjustment from the interior to the office, shifting to this unprecedented co-mingling of living and working, and desperately looking for extra space in which

FIGURE 13.4 *Third 2020 Life at Home Report*, The Big Home Reboot.

to place equipment that was usually absent from the home. Consequently, people's challenged lives were countered by IKEA with recordings, videocall services calming the urgent requests and floods of digital pictures 'purifying' the home from all its imperfections and everyday life problematics.

During the first pandemic wave when Italians were confined to their homes, with ambulance sirens outside, and no social gatherings, including funeral ceremonies, IKEA engineered another form of estrangement from the mediated object (home) through a fairy-tale, utopian and largely falsified picture of reality. They boosted their 'happy ending narrative'. Drawn from a Manichaeistic, good and bad scenario, this narration contributes to portraying IKEA as the hero while infantilizing the audience, trivializing the complexity of reality and distracting the spectator from the actual, physical space. This fiction, observable at IKEA from the frictionless domestic imagery to the seemingly Covid-free headquarters atmosphere, enables a temporary suspension of critical thinking. It supports a state of inebriation and avoidance of reality that allows people to seek distraction in consumption.

Design by *fiction*

Virtual domestic constructions can prompt their encoded messages with no limits of target or geography for interpretation by gigantic, global communities. Before Covid-19, online sites were increasingly becoming a reality, the virtual was gradually replacing the physical and the smartphone allowed escape into digital worlds at the expense of tangible, corporeal life. With the advent of the pandemic, humanity faced an amplified 'cyber metamorphosis' (Andreoli 2021).

Although an element of fiction can be retraced throughout the entire history of IKEA, a departure from and manipulation of reality, through the increased technologization that occurred during the pandemic, IKEA played a major role in triggering a radical shift to a semiotic commodification. Digitization allowed the company to break all boundaries between things, commodity forms and exchange values. The pandemic exposed and exacerbated that process, when ever-greater power was achieved by coordinating immaterial production and consumption globally. IKEA's continuous feeding of the domestic interior with additional symbols and associations allowed a re-interpretation of the interior and all its elements into a 'total signification' (Holt 2016). Since March 2020, the multinational has tapped into additional fields of political economy by centralizing more functions and using new technologies. An assemblage of palliative and unrealistic images contributes to submerging the viewer into a novel hyperreality; helplines and YouTube videos support the vision of the furniture retailer as the holy grail of home design and 24/7 saviour, the 'one' capable of responding to users' rapidly changing needs. An exemplary representative of twenty-first-century neoliberal structures, IKEA has taken full advantage of the ongoing health, financial and social crisis.

Besides the objective success of IKEA's pandemic digitalization, noticeably the boost of online sales and changes in consumer's behaviour, the amplification of fiction allowed the persuasion of costumers in a way that brought them closer to the company. Despite the difficulty in predicting the long-term consequences of the pandemic on our lives, this chapter foregrounded IKEA's use of fiction to bring an awareness of its savvy transmission of domestic design. During the pandemic, IKEA demonstrates a remarkable capacity to understand and benefit from radical social transformations. This success goes back to strategies the company had been implementing at the core of its philosophy since the mid-1950s. Sara Kristofferson argues that the multinational's geniality doesn't lie in the morphology or features of a specific furnishing set but in its conception of design (2014). This concept embraces all areas of practice from IKEA's appropriation of Swedishness to create self-images to its use of humour in advertising campaigns addressing contemporary discourses (Kristofferson 2014). Design – not in its product state – is fiction at IKEA as it demonstrates the ability to morph and mediate an image of interior architecture, to embody ethos, age or ideology – increasingly so through technological tweaks and imagination. As Irina Seits posits, at IKEA, '(t)he main object on display is not material – it is an idea' (2016: 123). In its dissemination of futuristic images, from catalogue photos to Instagram's posts, IKEA has affected the way domestic space is perceived, experienced and imagined.

Yet the IKEA home is not concrete, nor is it a specific object or style. Rather, design stands for the spirit of being ready for change and the ability to adapt to different domestic functions. Neither rigid nor monolithic, implying long construction processes, IKEA's design mutates quickly and exploits fiction at maximum capacity to codify, project and transmit domestic ideas.

Notes

1. This chapter analysis draws from the author's doctoral research project, *The IKEA Home*, she has been carrying out at KU Leuven, Belgium. The archival sources relative to the IKEA company are held by (IHA) IKEA Historical Archives and were accessed with the permission of Inter IKEA Systems B.V. Most of the analysis is based on the study of the IKEA catalogues, Swedish edition, from 1951 to 2015 and Italian editions from 1989 to 2020.
2. Besides the YouTube playlist, this analysis is based on all the IKEA Italia Instagram posts published during the first Italian lockdown, from 12 March, as the date the company starts addressing the pandemic in its social media, to 18 May 2020 when the Covid restrictions were revised by the Government. All translations from Italian to English are by the author.
3. It is important to stress that the three reports conducted by IKEA in 2020 entitled *Life at Home 2020: Pulse Report #1*, *Life at Home 2020: Pulse Report #2* and *The Big Home Reboot* constitute the company's most extensive market research regarding domestic life. They looked closely at the health crisis effect on domestic space by analysing the phenomenon at the beginning, throughout its course and in its latest stage. The survey included 37 different countries and over 38,000 people. Italy was one of the countries considered. 83 per cent of Italians reported that the home had represented a 'sanctuary' during pandemic life.

References

Andreoli, V. (2021), *La famiglia digitale. Come la tecnologia ci sta cambiando*, Milan: Solferino.

Berthiaume, D. (2020), 'The Top-Performing e-commerce Site during COVID-19 Is…', *Chain Store Age. The Business of Retail*, 6 April. https://chainstoreage.com/top-performing-e-commerce-site-during-covid-19 (accessed 11 January 2022).

Bjarnestam, E. A. (2013), *IKEA. Design & Identity*, Italy: TITEL Books AB for IKEA of Sweden.

'Bonus Mobili 2021: limite di spesa innalzato a 16.000 euro' (2020), *Lavori pubblici*, 31 December. https://www.lavoripubblici.it/news/Bonus-Mobili-2021-limite-di-spesa-innalzato-a-16-000-euro-24950 (accessed 11 January 2022).

Deighton, K. (2021), 'IKEA Tests New Store Formats That Free Shoppers from the Maze of Aisles', *Experience Report*, 24 August. https://www.wsj.com/articles/ikea-tests-new-store-formats-that-free-shoppers-from-the-maze-of-aisles-11629843814 (accessed 11 January 2022).

Frichot, H. (2018), *Creative Ecologies: Theorizing the Practice of Architecture*, London and New York: Bloomsbury. Ebook.

Holt, M. (2016), 'Baudrillard and the Bauhaus: The Political Economy of Design', *Design Issues*, 32(3): 55–66.

IKEA – #Ripartiamo da casa (2020), '[Playlist] YouTube, 4 May. Available online: https://www.youtube.com/playlist?list=PLA_B__IczTYDGP9VAGq6i-6VvHw18SHHZ (accessed 11 January 2022).

IKEA Democratic Design (2020), Älmhult, Sweden: IKEA Museum. IKEA of Sweden Älmhult.

IKEA Italia (2020), '#RipartiamoDaCasa', [Instagram] 12 March. https://www.instagram.com/p/B9oJnOJIyrz/ (accessed 11 January 2022).

IKEA Italia (2020), 'Con uno spazio organizzato dove giocare, disegnare e studiare, si può trovare l'equilibrio ideale per i vostri bambini', [Instagram] 13 March. https://www.instagram.com/p/B9rt7OJIWic/ (accessed 11 January 2022).

'IKEA Life at Home Report 2020' (2021), *IKEA.com*, 15 June. https://www.ikea.com/it/it/newsroom/corporate-news/ikea-life-at-home-report-2020-pub3910e757 (accessed 11 January 2022).

'IKEA Place: Bridging the Imagination Gap with AR' (2017), *SPACE10*, 21 December. Available online: https://space10.com/project/ikea-place/ (accessed 11 January 2022).

'Ikea Sees Profit Rise, Helped by Corona Pandemic' (2020), *Retail Detail*, 4 November. https://www.retaildetail.eu/en/news/furniture/ikea-sees-profit-rise-helped-corona-pandemic (accessed 11 January 2022).

IKEA VR, AR, MR and Meatballs (2017), [Video] Vimeo, 21 November. https://vimeo.com/243860738 (accessed 11 January 2022).

Kristoffersson, S. (2014), *Design by IKEA. A Cultural History*, London and New York: Bloomsbury.

Ledin, P. and D. Machin (2019), 'Forty Years of IKEA Kitchens and the Rise of a Neoliberal Control of Domestic Space', *Visual communication (London, England)*, 18(2): 165–87.

Robinson, W. I. (2020), 'Global Capitalism Post-pandemic', *Race & Class*, 62(2): 3–13.

Seits, I. (2016), 'What Is the Aesthetics of the Everyday?', *Södertörn Philosophical Studies* (24, Matrial: Filosofi, Estetik, Arkitektur): 111–24.

Seits, I. (2018), 'Architectures of Life-Building in the Twentieth Century Russia, Germany, Sweden', Doctoral Dissertation, Södertörn University, Stockholm.

Torekull, B. and I. Kamprad (1998), *Leading by Design. The IKEA Story*, New York: Harper Business.

Oral information and interviews

Arianna Diegoli, Spring–Autumn 2021.
Björn Zitting, September–October 2021.
Lotta Hahn, September–October 2021.
Raphael Bartke, September–October 2021.
Tony Nilsson, September 2021–January 2022.

14

Nice white spaces: Race and class in domestic cleaning ads during Covid-19

Rachele Dini

In the twenty months since the first national lockdowns of March 2020, the British and US media have woven a narrative about Covid-19 that draws on all-too-familiar tropes. It is a story about the home's transformation into a school-qua-office-qua-gym, and about harried professionals balancing the conflicting duties of parenting, paid work and housework. And it is a story that skews white, middle class and hetero – while perniciously reinforcing conservative notions of domesticity. The controversy that became known as #cleanergate, when in June 2020 certain white middle-class feminist columnists criticized pleas for households to pay their cleaners to stay home, is an apt example (Cox 2020). These feminists reinforced the assumption that men and children were incapable of housework, while implying that the safety of some women (the working-class, immigrant, and women of colour who comprise the majority of professional cleaners) was worth sacrificing for the sake of others (wealthy white ones). This tendency has been common across popular media, and nowhere more so than in ads for cleaning products, where in time-honoured fashion, messages have centred on the safety and hygiene of white middle-class bodies and bodies coded as white. Where domestic and personal hygiene industries in the nineteenth century directly contributed to the framing of white bodies as 'paragons of purity' and the bodies of minorities, immigrants and the working class as unclean, ads in 2020–2021 have reinforced the message that the homes in need of most protecting are white middle-class ones (Shove 2003).[1]

This chapter examines a selection of online and television advertising campaigns for cleaning products released to the UK and US audiences between April 2020, when the UK was in its first lockdown and a rise in anti-Asian racism was recorded in both countries, and August 2021, a year after the height of the #BlackLivesMatter protests that took place in response to George Floyd's murder. The ads I examine are representative of a wider pattern I have identified from surveying the campaigns of twenty-five brands across the US and UK markets.

Analysing the Covid-19 advertising landscape for cleaning products offers the opportunity to discern how major corporations have capitalized on a pandemic that forced millions of people to spend more time at home and resulted in increased time watching television and browsing online (thereby rendering them captive audiences for commercial messages). Consider, for example, that British and US cleaning product brands accounted for some of the biggest adspend in the first year of the pandemic. Consider too that Proctor & Gamble (parent company of Fairy, Ariel, Bold, Daz and Flash) alone increased its adspend from $900m to $8.2bn between June 2020 and June 2021 (Gray 2021).

Analysing these ads also enables us to consider the cleaning product industry's ongoing reliance on aspirational imagery premised on racial and classist othering, even (and arguably, especially) in messaging that ostensibly attempts to be inclusive. The greater frequency of men in cleaning product ads than even a decade ago indicates ad agencies' awareness of the profitability of responding to media headlines about women's disproportionate shouldering of cleaning and childcare duties during lockdown (Lungumbu and Butterly 2020) with depictions of men doing housework. Similarly, the heightened environmentalist emphasis apparent across the sector indicates an (albeit tokenistic) effort to extend the concept of 'home' to the planet as a whole. However, the two industries' long-standing reliance on more or less racist and classist tropes remains unchanged.

In making these claims, I rely on Delgado and Stefancic's articulation of white supremacy as a hegemonic discourse that normalizes white wealth, power, cultural norms and social standing (2017), and Shankar's definition of 'diversity' as 'index[ing] difference in unspecific and nonthreatening ways' that ultimately 'pul[l] focus back to a white mainstream,' and of 'diversity work' in advertising as work that 'champions difference as a strength in capitalist and institutional logics' (2019: 113–4).

What kind of home? Persil (Unilever) and Dettol (Reckitt Benckiser)

British laundry detergent manufacturer Persil was among the first brands to launch a Covid-themed campaign. In April 2020, ten days after the British government's announcement of a national lockdown, the brand launched 'Home Is Good' to international markets, pivoting away from its long-standing emphasis on the benefits of outdoor play ('Dirt Is Good') to encourage families to respect the lockdown rules. A twenty-second online and television ad spot invited children to visit a Persil-sponsored hub on the National Geographic Kids website for ideas of activities to do at home. Notably, however, the ad itself portrayed an empty play park in Toronto surrounded by mid-market apartment buildings and skyscrapers, and two white children painting rainbows in an upmarket interior. A second ad released the following month included two children of East Asian descent, but again in homes spacious enough for raucous play. It closed on two white children drawing a rainbow on a large outdoor deck. In just twenty seconds, each of these ads established 'home' as a white middle-class space and conjured an image of lockdown premised on the experiences of white middle-class professionals with access to a private garden. The offer of advice for stay-at-home games was likewise paradoxical: middle-class parents would likely have the resources to entertain their children without Persil's help, while low-income parents, whom studies show have the least time and resources to play with their children let alone home-school them (and therefore might ostensibly benefit from assistance), were also the most likely to be key workers (Parker et al. 2020; Warren et al. 2020). The challenge for these households would not have been keeping children busy so much as arranging childcare and affording an internet connection powerful enough to access online learning resources (Human Rights Watch 2021; Vogels 2020).

A similar white middle-class-centricity is apparent in Dettol UK's campaigns, 'Keep Protecting', 'Tru Clean' and 'Helping Protect What We Love Since 1933', which were launched, respectively, in July 2020 to coincide with the end of the first UK lockdown, in May 2021 for its first plant-based antibacterial range, and in June 2021 in anticipation of the end of the third UK lockdown. In the first campaign, spots such as 'For the Deliveries' (showing a disembodied white female hand spraying a package) and 'For Your Electronics' (the same hand spraying a laptop and smartphone) showcase a series of upmarket open-plan interiors being kept safe by a product that promises to 'kill the flu-causing virus in seconds' (Dettol 2021). The visual imagery frames the pandemic as a mild inconvenience whose only material effect has been to move shopping online and paid work to the living room.

Meanwhile the disembodied white hand – a long-standing trope in food and domestic hygiene ads since the Second World War – communicates, even in the absence of actual people, that this is a white space. As I have written elsewhere, the white female hand ubiquitous to ads centred on the home promotes white femininity as aspirational, while inadvertently allegorizing capitalism's reduction of human subjects to interchangeable appendages of one-of-a-kind consumer goods (Dini 2021b). As we shall see that hand surfaces in several other ads from this period.

Dettol's second campaign, 'Tru Clean' (2021), positions the power of nature being harnessed for the benefit of a wealthy home that while ostensibly peopled by minorities nevertheless codes white. The longest of these ads (thirty-five seconds) shows the transformation of a seedling into an antibacterial spray gracing the countertop of a sunlit kitchen-living space replete with green plants. Here it is picked up by a man of East Asian descent to wipe the surface where he has just fixed his daughter's breakfast. The placement of the child's mother, who is white, in the background overtly frames housework and parenting as tasks to be shared equally, while the portrayal of the East Asian father and daughter recalls what Shankar describes as the 'racial naturalisation' of Asian Americans in contemporary US advertising (Shankar 2012). Their transformation, that is, from 'model minority' workers to 'sophisticated, upwardly mobile model minority consumers' within a neoliberal framework where 'meanings of race and ethnicity that are rooted in political economy are recoded simply as "differences" that can be considered equal' (Shankar 2012). While Shankar's research focuses on the US market, these ideas are readily applicable to contemporary UK advertising, which frequently draws on narrative formulae, stereotypes, tropes and memes whose origins can be traced to US popular culture. I would add that in the context of Covid and rising anti-East Asian racism (Gao 2021; Hahm et al. 2021), the use of this minority group in cleaning product ads also serves a placating function, reassuring East Asian audiences that the brand is 'on their side' and white audiences that they are not harbingers of disease. In this case, the latter is partly achieved via a visual vocabulary that plays on white Western stereotypes about Asians' greater affinity to nature – a form of fetishization that Larry Lohmann calls 'Green Orientalism' (1993).

The most interesting of Dettol's ads however is 'House Proud', from the campaign 'Helping Protect What We Love Since 1933' (2021), launched just under a year after the #BlackLivesMatter protests. The visual vocabulary of this ad conflates race, taste and what I'll refer to here as 'quirkiness'. By this I mean a form of femininity that has gained prominence in popular media portrayals of young women since the early 2000s. As exemplified by white celebrities such as Zoe Deschanel, Alexa Chung and Aisling Bea, the 'quirky girl' is defined by an aesthetic appearance and self-presentation that, while pitched as unconventional, is in fact characterized by its legibility, non-threatening qualities and assimilability into normative narratives – while her personality is reflected in aspirational lifestyle brands such as Anthropologie, Oliver Bonas and Maisons du Monde, which allow her to express her 'quirkiness' in her home.

In this ad, we see a young Black woman disinfecting her home in advance of a visit from two close female friends, one white, one of East Asian descent, who are shown together with her in two framed photographs on the mantelpiece at the ad's outset. The closing sequence shows the three squealing in delight as she opens the door, followed by a shot of three cans of Dettol spray – yellow, blue and pink – standing on a coffee table in front of her brown leather sofa. Like the campaign's other spots, which included stories about people in care homes, shop owners and teenagers playing contact sports, the ad speaks to the longing felt by those separated from loved ones during the various lockdowns. But it does so via a series of images that enlist the concept of home to reinforce the conflation of personal identity, racial identity and feminine independence with consumer preferences, and that portray racial difference itself as a 'quirk'. More specifically, the interior furnished with a rattan chair, zebra-patterned cushions and 'ethnic' rug simultaneously mirrors the aesthetics of mainstream interior design of the late 2010s/early 2020s and, paradoxically, communicates the woman's subtly racialized tastes. She is at once exotic and legible to a majority-white audience (Figure 14.1). Indeed, the closing shot of the diverse Dettol range overtly references the diversity of the friendship group. The image literalizes the idea

FIGURE 14.1 *In 'House Proud' Dettol turns so-called diversity into a quirk. Author's own.*

FIGURE 14.2 *The closing shot of Dettol 'House Proud' (2021) inadvertently allegorizes the dehumanizing effects of reducing people to their consumer preferences. Author's own.*

that you are what you buy – and that consumer goods are the best expression of both one's personality and one's affection for others – while inadvertently allegorizing the dehumanizing effects of such reductive thinking. The yellow, blue and pink cans standing proudly in this interior, like the opening shot of the three women in the framed photographs, aptly express the logical endpoint of treating people as consumer segments (Figure 14.2).

Allegories of white supremacy: Fairy (Proctor and Gamble) and Finish (Reckitt Benckiser)

In what remains of this chapter, I examine two campaigns in which racialized themes appear calibrated to distract from the pandemic, which is glaringly absent. Released in November 2020, Fairy's TV spot, 'For an Effortless Clean', was clearly designed to appeal to a British public beset by lockdown fatigue. The ad opens onto a disembodied white woman's hand placing a bottle of Fairy Liquid soap onto a countertop to the tune of Bob Marley's 'Three Little Birds'. As Marley sings, 'Don't worry, about a thing/ 'Cause every little thing, gonna be all right', an animated version of Bizzie, Fairy's iconic white baby mascot, jumps out from the bottle's label and onto a soapy sponge, which he rides down a heap of dirty dishes before swinging from a sink plug chain onto a stack of clean white plates. It is the pandemic home worker and home-schooling parent's dream come true – wherein both housework and Covid have disappeared – but it is also a racialized one.

As attested by Fairy's very name, cleaning product manufacturers have long relied on animism to inject excitement into household drudgery, while deflecting from the question of who should be doing this labour (Dini 2021a; Neuhaus 2011). It is in fact noteworthy that the rise in the 1930s of animism in British and US cleaning product ads coincided with a shortage in domestic workers and a period of heightened racial and class anxieties (Dunlap 2011; Strasser 1982). Likewise, the tenor of such mystification reads differently when one examines the preponderance of portrayals of appliances and cleaning products as either magical or bestowed upon white housewives by magical beings alongside the myriad ads in the same period that portrayed these items as servants or slaves (Dini 2021a). Analysing these two genres of ads alongside each other reveals the extent to which the fantasy of the magical cleaning product or imaginary friend that renders cleaning effortless is modelled on the master/slave relationship.

That fantasy is embedded in the visual and aural vocabulary of Fairy's ad. Indeed, the appropriation of reggae (a genre that emerged in response to Jamaica's emancipation from British rule), and of a song from Bob Marley's most explicitly political album, is especially startling in light of the timing of the ad's release, mere months after a summer of international public protests against institutional racism and police brutality, and at a time of heightened awareness of the threat of white supremacist violence – not to mention the #tradwife movement's ongoing calls to 'make white babies'(Kelly 2018). While the use of Marley was perhaps conceived, in response to the protests, as an homage to Black culture, it's difficult to see the execution as communicating anything but a fantasy of white fortitude surviving both the pandemic and dishwashing drudgery thanks to the magic of Fairy Liquid and an encouraging but invisible Black 'other'. The final image of Brizzie standing triumphantly atop a mountain of white plates, surrounded by white dishes freed from the brown stains that beset them at the ad's start, is ultimately a white supremacist vision (Figure 14.3).

Dishwashing detergent brand Finish's US-based campaign, #SkipTheRinse, launched in late July 2020, also deflected attention from the pandemic via a series of three-minute 'digital short stories' produced in partnership with National Geographic. These enlist people of colour, issues of social justice and identity politics, and the concept of home in ways that while purportedly aimed at raising awareness of environmental issues ultimately obscure broader forms of inequality.

The first, 'Triarchy', features Adam Taubenfligel, the white male founder of a sustainable denim company. The second, 'Matika Wilbur', focuses on a

FIGURE 14.3 *Fairy's white baby mascot surrounded by white plates plays on longstanding racist tropes. Author's own.*

female Native American photographer for National Geographic whose work documents the effects of environmental degradation on her people. The third, 'Emily Tianshi', showcases a young Asian-American woman who at the age of thirteen developed a prototype to enable households to produce water during droughts. In each, visually arresting images of the individual at work are juxtaposed with scenes of them at home, loading the dishwasher without pre-rinsing the dishes. Each story ends with the statement, 'You can play your part at home. Join the Millions and #SkipTheRinse', overlaid on a tessellation of images of individual water taps being closed by white hands – effectively reducing the environmental crisis to a problem for the individual rather than the corporation or state to solve, and from the comfort of their own homes no less (Figure 14.4).

Each short in turn portrays home, work and self as seamlessly integrated – wherein skipping the rinse is less a good deed than an act coherent with the optimized neoliberal self. Thus, in 'Triarchy', Adam's assertion, 'It's impossible for what I do at work to not follow me home; when I run the dishwasher, I don't rinse dishes in the sink', reframes the eroded distinction between work and home experienced by many during the various lockdowns as claustrophobic (or conducive to longer working hours) as a personal choice reflecting coherent morals. The closing sequence, which shows him photographing a Black female model against a graffiti-covered wall to demonstrate his alertness to what's cool, inadvertently illustrates what Naomi Klein famously described, in No Logo (1999), as fashion brands' 'aggressive[e] min[ing]' of street art and Black

FIGURE 14.4 *Finish '#SkipTheRinse' frames the environmental crisis as a problem for reified, atomized individuals to solve from home. Author's own.*

youth culture'. 'Emily Tianshi' likewise relies on the 'model minority/model consumer' trope discussed earlier.

But it is on 'Matika Wilbu' that I want to linger. Here, the photographer's moving portrayal of the threat that climate change poses to her community, and her articulation of home as a state of equilibrium between human beings and the wider ecosystem, is undermined by the short's visual vocabulary. Where early issues of National Geographic entertained white readers with images of exotic 'others' in far-flung lands to affirm the superiority of nation state and empire, this film subsumes indigenous identities, indigenous conceptions of home, and the environmental devastation threatening both, into a message that appeals to a white saviour instinct.

This impression is amplified by the scenes of Matika in the interview, which take place in a home office decorated in a mid-century modern style, and the scenes of her in her kitchen, where the camera hovers over the KitchenAid and LeCreuset pots on her countertop. These objects establish for white viewers that Matika is the 'good' kind of person of colour – educated, moneyed, fluent enough in the language of middle-class consumer culture to demonstrate she is not a radical – while providing a different kind of evidence of what she calls the 'modern infrastructure [that] has impacted [her people's] identities'. Like the corporations with dubious histories (Rothenberg 2007) that pay her, these domestic objects reveal the web of life to be entangled with the web of global corporatism. The home that is her people's land has been colonized not only by white settlers, but by their idea of domesticity. The iconography of racial capitalism is everywhere in this short.

This is not to criticize Matika for seizing the opportunities offered by Finish and National Geographic – or, indeed, for not renouncing industrial modernity. After all, judging Indigenous people negatively for using modern technology, and expecting them to be 'what the West is not' is, itself, a form of Green Orientalism (Lohmann 1993; Ray 2013; Zehle 2002). Nor am I suggesting that Matika believes 'skipping the rinse' is the way to solve the water shortage crisis. My point, rather, is that this film short is at once a case study in Green Orientalism and corporate greenwashing, and an inadvertent record of the ubiquity of a capitalist consumerist understanding of domesticity, and the inescapability of the very networks of labour and consumption that are responsible for the climate crisis.

In each of Finish's 'digital short stories', the communication of the importance of conserving water at home at once capitalizes on the powerlessness felt by many in the face of both the climate crisis and the ongoing pandemic, while replicating the rhetoric long used by National Geographic to domesticate the world for Americans' consumption. Finish draws on a series of tropes calibrated to evince an empathy for the wildlife and communities whose homes are under threat that does not, however, extend to questioning the underlying causes of the threat, or to provoking other forms of social organization. Home remains at once abstracted – something that all living beings need – and specific in such a way as to resist reimagining.

Conclusion

The ads examined here comprise a miniscule sample of the commercial messages with which cleaning product companies – and their agencies – have bombarded the British and US public in 2020 and 2021 to capitalize on the heightened fear of germs and increased time spent in the home. One of the interesting aspects of our current moment is the tension between advertising's historical effort to speak to, and shape, consumers' fantasies, and the increased demand, at least among some (usually younger and left leaning) demographics, for advertising that responds to their values and reflects their experience, even when it is not idyllic. That demand is arguably more difficult to reconcile when it comes to selling products for a pursuit that for all the efforts of #cleaninfluencers and #tradwives remains associated with drudgery, menial labour and lower status. Put differently, the endurance of racist and classist tropes in cleaning ads is not only due to the demographic makeup of agencies, which remain overwhelmingly white. Nor is it solely attributable to the fact ad agencies' largest accounts are with companies that target a white majority audience. Rather, it is attributable to Britain and the US' enduring investment in the association of cleanliness and taste with wealth, status and whiteness. For it is an association that appeals to large swathes of both nation's populations, that pays dividends, and that, as the rise of far-right movements around the world attest, grows stronger during times of crisis. Nice white spaces continue to serve as powerful function as vessels of desire and oppression.

Note

1 The assimilation of immigrants to the United States in the nineteenth century was linked to learning American modes of hygiene (Hoy 1995). Shankar notes that 'soap and hygiene products [...] routinely featured white bodies as paragons of purity' (2019). Mclintock notes that hygiene was framed in nineteenth-century British advertising as 'restor[ing] the threatened potency of the imperial body politic and the race' (1994: 509–10). Cox argues that 'the perceived dirtiness of others, whether they be "the great unwashed" [...] or "smelly foreigners," reinforces dominant value systems and social boundaries' (2016: 97–116).

References

Bedford, E. (2021a), 'Cleaning Product Sales Growth from the Coronavirus in the US in March 2020', *Statista*, 6 January.
Bedford, E. (2021b), 'Consumers Buy More Cleaning Products Due to Covid-19 in the United Kingdom from March 2020 to February 2021', *Statista*, 24 November.
Robinson, C. J. (1983), *Black Marxism: The Making of the Black Radical Tradition*, Chapel Hill, NC: U of North Carolina Press.
Cox, R. (2016), 'Cleaning Up: Gender, Race and Dirty Work at Home', in C. Lewe, N. Oxen, and T. Bielefeld Othold (eds), *Müll, Interdisziplinäre Perspektiven auf das Übrig-Geliebene*, 97–116, Germany: Transcript.
Cox, R. (2020), '#Cleanergate: Domestic Workers and the Intimate Geographies of Lockdown', *Geography Directions RGS-IBG*, June 8.
Delgado, R. and J. Stefancic (2017), *Critical Race Theory: An Introduction*, New York: NYU Press.
Dini, R. (2021a), *'All-Electric' Narratives: Time-Saving Appliances and Domesticity in American Literature*, 1945–2021, New York: Bloomsbury.
Dini, R. (2021b), '*Into the Blue Again: Academic Dissolution, Postmillennial Remnants, and Sarah Wasserman's The Death of Things*, Ancillary Review of Books, 6 October.
Dulap, L. (2011), *Knowing Their Place: Domestic Service in Twentieth-century Britain*, Oxford: Oxford University Press.
Fairy (2020), 'For an Effortless Clean', 19 November. https://www.youtube.com/watch?v=3aCComoT2TU.

Finish and National Geographic (2021), 'Triarchy'; 'Emily Tianshi'; 'Matika Wilbur', 11 May. https://www.youtube.com/watch?v=L7RzXNSs2rU;https://www.youtube.com/watch?v=IKWXIQZICv8;https://www.youtube.com/watch?v=JHW5r4XacBo.

Gao, Z. (2021), 'Sinophobia during the Covid-19 Pandemic: Identity, Belonging, and International Politics', *Integrative Psychological and Behavioral Science*, 4 October.

Gray, A. (2021), 'Consumer Brands to Protect Ad Budgets even as Other Costs Spiral', *Financial Times*, 22 August.

Hahm, H. C., et. al. (2021), 'Experiences of COVID-19-Related Anti-Asian Discrimination and Affective Reactions in a Multiple Race Sample of U.S. Young Adults', *BMC Public Health*, 21: 1563.

Hoy, S. E. (1995), *Chasing Dirt: The American Pursuit of Cleanliness*, Oxford: Oxford University Press.

Human Rights Watch (2021), '"Years Don't Wait for Them": Increased Inequalities in Children's Right to Education Due to the Covid-19 Pandemic', 17 May.

Jaquette Ray, S. (2013), *The Ecological Other: Environmental Exclusion in American Culture*, Tucson: U of Arizona Press.

Kelly, A. (2018), 'The Housewives of White Supremacy', *New York Times*, 1 June.

Klein, N. (1999), *No Logo: Taking Aim at the Brand Bullies*, New York: Picador.

Lohmann, L. (1993), 'Green Orientalism', *The Ecologist*, 1 November, 202–4.

Lungumbu, S. and A. Butterly (2020), 'Coronavirus and Gender: More Chores for Women Set Back Gains in Equality', *BBC*, 26 November.

McCann Erickson for Dettol (2021), 'Dettol Tru Clean'; 'House Proud'; 'For Your Electronics', https://www.youtube.com/watch?v=6TeO_xYB9jw;https://www.youtube.com/watch?v=hvLqpQ0aOU0;https://www.youtube.com/watch?v=flTANbXTX2s.

McClintock, A. (1994), 'Soft-Soaping Empire: Commodity Racism and Imperial Advertising', in G. Robertson et. al. (eds), *Travellers' Tales*, 506–18, London: Routledge.

MullenLowe for Persil (2020), 'Home Is Good', April. https://www.katandej.com/persil-home-is-good.

Neuhaus, J. (2011), *Housewives and Housework in American Advertising*, New York and Basingstoke: Palgrave Macmillan.

Parker, K., J. Horowitz and R. Minkin (2020), 'How the Coronavirus Has – and Hasn't – Changed the Way Americans Work', *Pew Research Center*, 9 December.

Rothenberg, T. Y. (2007), *Presenting America's World: Strategies of Innocence in National Geographic Magazine*, 1888–945, London: Routledge.

Shankar, S. (2012), 'Creating Model Consumers: Producing Ethnicity, Race, and Class in Asian American Advertising', *American Ethnologist*, 39(3): 578–91.

Shankar, S. (2019), 'Nothing Sells Like Whiteness: Race, Ontology, and American Advertising', *American Anthropologist, Special Section: Anthropology of White Supremacy*, 122(1): 112–19.

Shove, E. (2003), *Comfort, Cleanliness and Convenience: The Social Organization of Normality*, Oxford: Berg.

Strasser, S. (1982), *Never Done: A History of American Housework*, New York: Henry Holt.

Vogels, E. A. (2020), '59 Per Cent of US Parents with Low Incomes Say Their Children May Face Digital Obstacles in Schoolwork', *Pew Research Centre*, 10 September.

Warren, T., C. Lyonette and Women's Budget Group (2020), 'Are We All in This Together? Working-Class Women Are Carrying the Work Burden of the Pandemic', *LSE Blog*, 12 November.

Zehle, S. (2002), 'Notes on Cross-Border Environmental Justice Education,' in J. Adamson, M.M. Evans, and R. Stein (eds), *The Environmental Justice Reader: Politics, Poetics, and Pedagogy*, 331–49, Tucson: University of Arizona Press.

15

Uncanny on display

Musée Dom-Ino. A virtual museum of domesticity in lockdown

Nina Bassoli and Roberto Gigliotti

As recently stated by Mirko Zardini commenting on the current global crisis due to the pandemic: crises surprise us, but they never come unexpectedly; and even if they do not usually bring with them new ideas and solutions, they do, however, force us to change our priorities and accelerate ongoing processes (Zardini 2020). The Covid-19 emergency, which officially began in Italy in March 2020, on the exact same day as our course of Interior and Exhibit Design, pointed out some of the most dramatic contradictions of our contemporary world, revealing them to our eyes, as if we were watching them on a cinema screen. The course, held by Roberto Gigliotti, Davide T. Ferrando and Nina Bassoli, offered to art, visual communication and product design students, is usually focused on elementary exercises on space, allowing students used to deal with spatial issues inserting objects in a given space to approach the experience of space in a way that we could define more 'architectural'. Unfortunately, due to Covid-19 restrictions, the course moved abruptly to the online teaching platform, and our performative form of teaching, usually based on a physical approach to the third dimension, was suddenly flattened to a two-dimensional screen. The communication of space was inverted, and the students started letting us into their homes through the interfaces of their laptops. Their private interiors were publicly shared through a guided process of observing, re-reading, deconstructing, re-writing. The transformation – *design* as project – is a short deviation from the description – *design* as drawing. Looking, listening, describing, representing, drawing, designing, transforming, inhabiting: all these actions overlapped now in the same place.

While crises never come unexpectedly, they do act as triggers for a series of accelerations. As Byung-Chul Han pointed out, the most radical change in the transition from the industrial to the digital age lies in the home–work relationship (Han 2017). If in the nineteenth and twentieth centuries, machines enslaved workers and employees in the workplace, nowadays digital devices are producing new constraints. In fact, thanks to their mobility, digital devices are able to transform any place into a place for work and any time into a time for work. At this rate, Han continues, this great flexibility has broken down the separation between the place of work and the place of non-work, so that we can no longer separate it. Our productive duties have become perpetual, and the apparent freedom of mobility has turned into the obligation to work anytime and anywhere. So we asked ourselves, what happens when this separation is drastically, ostensibly, cancelled due to confinement measures? We decided to ask the students to draw their daily habits on different scales.

The first exercise, *Small Pleasure of Life*, was inspired by a series of sketches by Alison and Peter Smithson edited in their *Changing the Art of Inhabitation*. The Smithsons' drawings represent everyday domestic situations able to produce pleasure, such as 'to work or write at a creeper bordered window' or 'to see the sunlight spread across the floor'.

We asked the students to repeat the Smithson's exercise by drawing at least five pleasant situations related to the experience of their domestic space. Our aim was to start by working on the love of home focusing on comfort, on the pleasantness of the familiar and on the beauty of the daily and ordinary. We suggested that they pay particular attention to the optical, acoustic, olfactory and tactile conditions of the chosen spaces, in order to promote a sensory – non-abstract – approach to space. Doors ('Abandon all hope, ye who enter here', in the words of Nicolaï Martini), windows ('useful for listening to Covid-19 flash mobs', again for NM) and balconies ('where eating spaghetti on the tiny table', for Sara Tebaldi) seem to be the most significant objects as well as fresh air, sunlight, plants, domestic animals and any other element linked to nature. The students used descriptions such as: 'Looking out of the window at the neighbours' clothes lying in the sun and blowing in the wind; being back in the room after changing the air and having the impression of being in a totally new space' (Sara Tebaldi); 'tasting the fresh air in this quarantine period' (Nensi Dafa); 'seeing my plants hit by the sun as I walk through the corridor' (Stefanie Andergassen); 'neighbour's cats when they meow while I am resting' (Giulia Olivieri); 'being able to hear the sounds

FIGURE 15.1 *Roberto Bartolacci*, Small pleasures of life, *2020. Courtesy of Roberto Bartolacci.*

of nature even inside the home' (Sofia Piffer). In addition to the obsession with air and sun, some first concerns began to make their way into the drawings. The shape of objects, ergonomic issues and sedentary problems have never seemed so important for such young people. 'The curvature of the armrest is perfect for stretching your back', writes Andrea Maffei, stretching out over the sofa; 'I am very unproductive and spend hours playing Play Station: my posture has already deteriorated', 'my quarantine housemates thank the windows for existing otherwise the stench would be lethal' (NM); 'The only way to spend time with friends in these quarantine days: computers and video games' (Giovanni Matteotti). In a student's sketch, the separation between the place of rest and the place of work is only represented by the posture of his own body, which, pivoting on a swivel chair, move from the desk to the bed. 'Moving from the "at work" position to the "drinking tea, resting, phoning, thinking of how to", in short, to the "pause" position, in one fell swoop of the kidneys (i.e. turning the chair 90°, using the bed as a footrest and the table as an armrest, and vice versa)' reads the caption of Roberto Bartolacci's drawing (Figure 15.1). On closer inspection, these simple, ironic comic strips made by bored twenty-year-old students can reveal the much deeper implications of an overlap between the spaces of life and the spaces of work.

In this regard, Paul Preciado explains in an insightful way the not only physical, but psychological and political implications of the confinement of bodies, with reference to Foucault's thesis on immunity and control and expands them to the concrete case of the pandemic (Preciado 2020).

> One of the fundamental biopolitical changes in pharmacopornographic techniques characterizing the Covid-19 crisis is that the domestic space, and not traditional institutions of social confinement and normalization (hospital, factory, prison, school, etc.), now appears as the new center of production,

consumption, and political control. The home is no longer only the place where the body is confined, as was the case under plague management. The private residence has now become the center of the economy of tele-consumption and tele-production, but also the surveillance pod.

(Preciado 2020: 81)

In fact, like in the worst Freudian nightmares where bosses, professors, teachers pour into the bedroom (Willbern 1979), we professors – as person and as institutions – are working where the students live. The moment work enters a space, it ceases to be private and becomes part of the social, productive, economic sphere; no longer intimate but subject to power dynamics. Furthermore, with the confinement measures, the encroachment of the private into the public has taken a clearer form: the two spheres finally overlap perfectly and can be understood within a precisely measurable perimeter.

As a second exercise, we invited the students to measure this perimeter, mapping the space through their own movements repeated on different days. We were in the third week of lockdown. The small pleasures of the first exercise, pleasant because perceived as rare moments of peace in the daily frenzy, began to become annoying, tedious and cloying. The repetition of daily actions saturates the available space, crashes against the walls while the outside presses on the windows but cannot be reached. In Asia Maria Andreolli's exercise, the circles representing the time spent stationary in a point, multiply and expand within the walls of the flat (Figure 15.2). The image recalls Alberto Savinio's famous *Annunciation*, painted in 1932 as part of the series of surrealist portraits with bird heads and preserved in the Casa Boschi Di Stefano Museum in Milan. A pelican Virgin Mary is sitting in the corner of the room, while an enormous face with classical lines presses lopsided on the window, too big to enter the room like the mystery of which he is the bearer, too big for Mary to understand. In a similar suspended and unbearable atmosphere, the students' plans show how the landscape, the city and the whole outer life are squeezed out of their haunting houses.

When did the flat become so small? When did the comforting domestic walls become so threatening and oppressive? As many scholars pointed out in recent months (Agamben 2020; Bianchetti 2020; D'Eramo 2020; Nicolin 2020; Zardini 2020, 2021; Žižek S. 2020), the themes of the *unhomely* and the *uncanny*, argued by Antony Vidler, are back in the limelight during the lockdown (Vidler 1992). Vidler identifies the origin of this feeling historically in the insecurity of the bourgeoisie at the end of the eighteenth century, when this social class had become rich and educated too quickly, 'suddenly' finding itself in an unprecedented position and not feeling completely 'at home'. Following Vidler's argumentation, it is here that the 'peculiar unstable nature

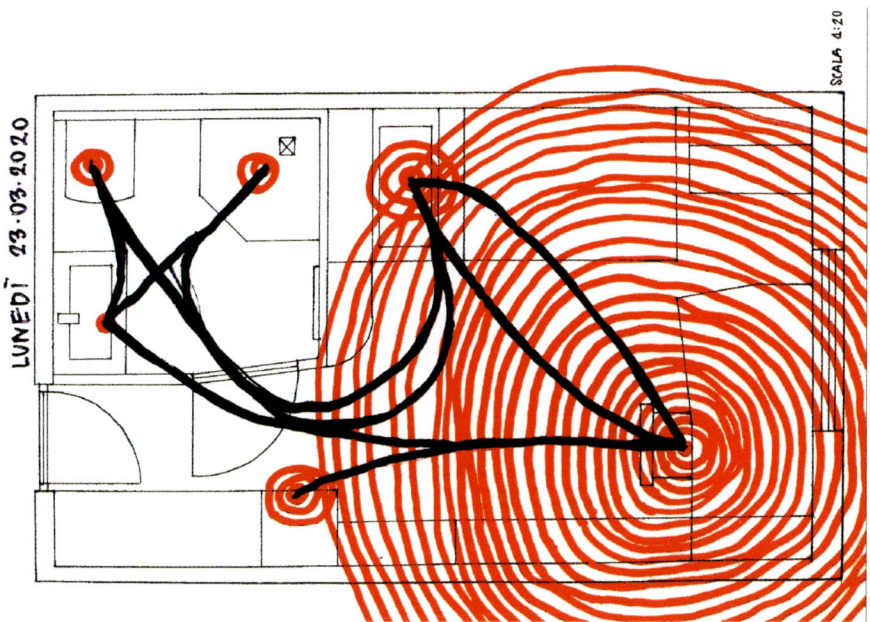

FIGURE 15.2 *Asia Maria Andreolli*, Stuck in the domestic landscape. 750 minutes at the desk, *2020. Courtesy of Asia Maria Andreolli.*

of "house and home"' (Vidler 1992: 7) arises, curiously simultaneous with what Charles Rice identifies as *The Emergence of the Interior*, not only as a physical space but also as an image (Rice 2006).

For different reasons but with a similar lack of self-confidence, the students neither felt represented nor perfectly belonging to their own homes. They often still live at their parents' places in tiny childhood bedrooms, or they recently moved into crowded shared flats or anonymous student halls. While during a regular student's life, they construct their identity through a continuous movement in and out of domestic walls, finding recognition in the gazes of others, suddenly the lockdown is freezing their movement, their spatial perception, their sense of belonging.

As a third task, we asked the students to first find narrative themes for their own confinement and then to choose some objects and the more significant spaces of their places, in order to rearrange them according to this narrative. The themes emerging in their work constantly echo Vidler's essay: transparencies, dust, voyeurism, mechanization of technological devices are among the most recurrent themes, unknowingly close to those dealt with in *The Architectural Uncanny*. Think for instance to chapters as *Transparency*, *Buried Alive*, *Dark Space*, *Oneirism*, *Homes for Cyborgs*, but also to essays related to Vidler's theses as *The Split Wall: Domestic Voyeurism* by Beatriz

Colomina, held in the volume *Sexuality and Space* (1992). In the students' works, the issues of transparency and reflections are central. The transparency of windows is instinctively questioned as an unstable device of freedom and oppression. Luisa Heindl named her exhibition *The Breach: Transparency, Intimacy and Privacy*. Based on rearranging objects with glass panels so that they interact with their own reflection, she explains: 'In general, the physical transparent border surrounding a space helps to define that space. It helps to put an end and a beginning to a spatial entity. However, a transparent border also frames the inside space. When the area within the space appears to be a domestic space, the glass walls frame our personal life like a museum exhibit.' In Nensi Dafa's exhibition *I See You*, not only the 'literal and phenomenal transparency' are questioned from a physical point of view, as Colin Rowe and Robert Slutzky did in 1963, but also a layer of surveillance is added though cameras that make the exhibition both interactive and disturbing.

Moreover, in many exercises household appliances take an active role in student's projects. The lights and switch indicators deform the space as do their noises. Anghelina Coslet's show, titled *The Speaking House*, for example, is a map of the sounds emitted by objects into the house: the coffee machine, the kettle, the washing machine, the clock and the ceiling fan are the protagonists. For his *Bossa (Casa) Nova*, Nicolaï Martini composes an obsessive piece of music with the sounds emitted by household appliances and, later in the course, reassembles them to create mechanized robots capable of producing controlled sounds (Figure 15.3). 'Our machines are disturbingly lively, and we ourselves frighteningly inert', recalls Vidler, quoting Donna Haraway's *Cyborg Manifesto* (Vidler 1992: 148). Further on, Vidler proposes a 'mutual mechanization' between inhabitant and object and refers to the concept of the ready-made as investigated by Diller and Scofidio in their installation for the Capp Street Project gallery in San Francisco in 1987. In the installation, just as in the analyses by our students, the domestic environment is deconstructed beyond its functions and 'domestic objects are now set free to map their own space of instrumentality; human agency is supplied by surrogate objects, themselves prostheses of objects in their dangerous extensions' (Vidler 1992: 161).

At this stage in the course, we realized that although we were asking students to follow this ready-made, we were inviting them in fact to disappropriate their homes, to withdraw their domestic functions and to transform them into exhibition galleries. By proposing a change of programme in their domestic environments, we were enabling the students to free themselves from the fear of 'not feeling like owners in their own home' and to retrace, as authors, the system of relationships inside their houses.

Through a series of specific exercises, the home space and character were exacerbated: architectural elements got amplified and re-shaped, while

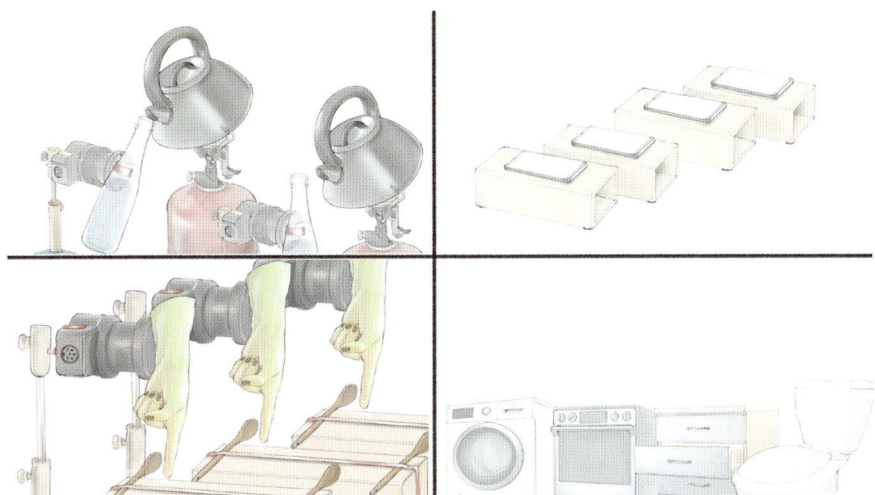

FIGURE 15.3 *Nicolaï Martini*, Bossa (Casa) Nova, *2020. Courtesy of Free University of Bozen-Bolzano.*

characteristic objects were re-arranged in the shape of an exhibition that produced completely new and untypical sensations in those very spaces. The curation of an exhibition is related to a process of abstraction and this offered the students the possibility of freeing themselves from functional constraints, an 'escape door', since 'estrangement from the world is a moment of art' as argued by Theodor Adorno referring to Freud's essay on *Das Unheimliche* in his *Aesthetic Theory* (Vidler 1992: 8).

It may be helpful in this regard to recall two striking case studies that have made this idea of estranging from the world as a moment of art a significant artistic statement (Otero and Axel 2018). The first is the well-known case of Hugh Hefner's life, who without leaving his home (or even his bed) directed and produced the US magazine *Playboy* for almost forty years. Hefner's round bed – 'at once his desk, his office as editor-in-chief of the magazine, a photographic set, a television studio and a place for sexual encounters', as Preciado described it in a recent text about the lockdown – was a kind of prophecy of what is happening to all of us, albeit in a more modest and less spectacular way, first with the spread of telework and later more especially during the lockdown months (Preciado 2020: 84). Far from being an act of reticence, his voluntary segregation was a gesture with an enormous communicative charge that anticipated not only a certain way of living in the home, but also its complete permeability to the media and the definitive melting of public and private life. The images of the interior, filmed, among other things, with a 24/24 CCTV system, ended up being published in turn on the pages of the magazine and thanks to a constant multimedia connection with the other rooms of the Mansion and the outside world, Hefner was able to make this situation of reclusion an extraordinary spectacle.

The second case is the Bed-in for Peace, a performance by John Lennon and Yoko Ono during their honeymoon in 1969. From March 25 to 31 in room 902 of the Hilton International Hotel in Amsterdam, they decided to stay in bed from 9.00 am to 9.00 pm inviting journalists and press for interviews and documentation. Beatriz Colomina analysed the performance with these words: 'John and Yoko were undermining the normal understanding of what is work, what is private, what is protest, and what is an event. The bed had taken over from the street as the site of protest. They invited the world's press into their room, treating the bed as a work-space'. As Yoko put it: 'Instead of writing a play about it, we just started to do it in real life – so the whole world is a theater actually. I mean, the Hilton was the stage. Life as art for two performers for whom there is no longer a backstage' (Colomina 2018: 194).

Similarly, in our course experiment, each flat became a stage where objects and actions – as in every 'exhibitionary' act – were re-signified following a specific narrative. They were in a word: showing. Indeed, in some reading of Foucault's thesis, museums themselves have been interpreted as 'institutions of confinement' (Bennett 1988; Bergdoll 1987). Tony Bennett describes the transition from the enjoyment of art and science in privileged private places to the gradual sharing of knowledge with the public through the establishment of museums. Bennett refers to Foucault who described the formation of a disciplinary society that stretches from the enclosed disciplines, a sort of social 'quarantine' (in those exact words!), to an indefinitely generalizable mechanism of 'panopticism', a society that is 'one not of spectacle, but of surveillance' (Bennett 1988: 77). 'In a society in which the principal elements are no longer the community and public life, but, on the one hand, private individuals and, on the other, the state, relations can be regulated only in a form that is the exact reverse of the spectacle' (Foucault 1977: 216f). However, it is Bennett himself who points out that Foucault underestimated the possibilities of new and mass media in the spectacularization or 'the tendency for society itself – in its constituent parts and as a whole – to be rendered as a spectacle' (Bennett 1988: 78). Indeed, in the task that we gave to the students, and maybe even more in a present characterized by the pervasive presence of social media and the spectacularization of private life, the echo of the shift from the 'theatre' to the 'penitentiary' is still present and the exhibition retires in the interiors of private homes where we were secluded due to anti-Covid measures.

As a final act, we decided to exit from the 'carceral archipelago' (Bennett 1988: 80) we were confined to in an attempt to move towards an – albeit abstract – social recomposition: towards the idea of sharing. Once each flat had been stretched, deformed and set up in order to become a personal, thematic gallery, we proceeded with the method of the *cadavre exquis*, producing a collage of all the apartments, creating a sort of Museum of Domesticity in Lockdown (Figure 15.4). Le Corbusier's famous project Maison Dom-Ino, 1914, often regarded as the origin of modernism and functionalism, is provocatively cited here to invert the terms of efficiency and function, but to borrow the same character of 'manifesto'. Referring to the industry-based constructive system, but reversing his idea of functionalism, we called it 'Musée Dom-Ino'. Here, the inefficiency of these new aggregates of spaces – spatial *machines celibataire* – underlines, once again, the definitive end of the functionalist view in the exploration of domestic spaces. This is what it looks like: huge corridors that lead nowhere, mundane but labyrinthine rooms, the changing shrill sounds of wood floors, the dominance of cleaning devices in a time dominated by sanitation, and the secret life of the dust hidden under furniture and carpets as an act of resistance. The loss of meaning in the original function of the selected objects that became exhibits enables a more complex understanding of these things, and an even better perception of those original meanings.

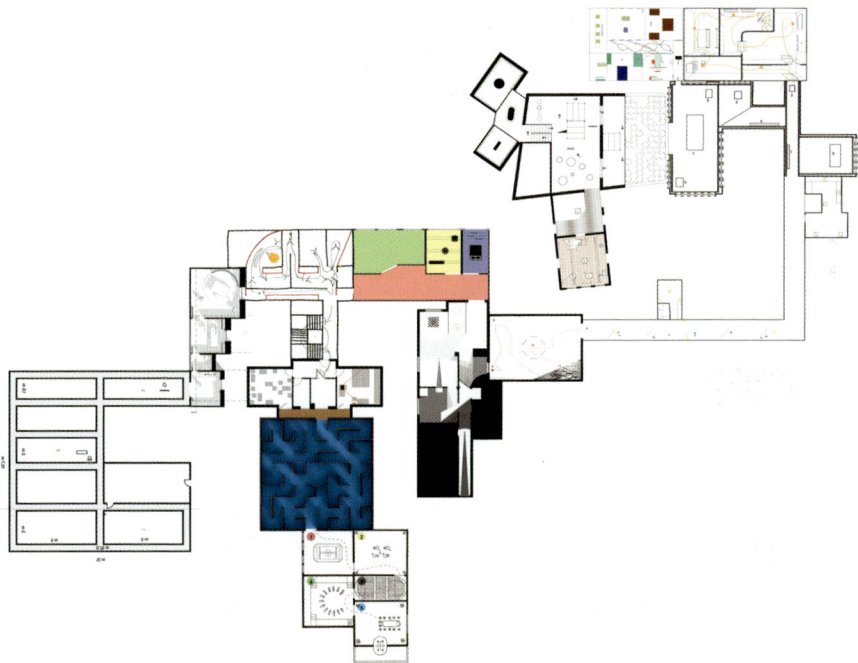

FIGURE 15.4 *Nina Bassoli, Davide Tommaso Ferrando, Roberto Gigliotti*, Museé Dom-Ino, *2020. Courtesy of Free University of Bozen-Bolzano.*

Beyond being a didactic experiment, the 'Musée Dom-Ino' has forced us to reconsider the consolidated understanding of interior spaces and shifted our attention to the observation of behaviours, feelings and perceptions within the domestic space. Above all, the exercise revealed the anachronistic idea of an interior intended as a merely functional space. But even more than that, it showed once again how the action of exhibiting is always a critical operation, capable of reopening the meanings of things we thought were established.

References

Agamben, G. (2020), *A che punto siamo? L'epidemia come politica*, Macerata: Quodlibet.
Bassoli, N., ed. (2020), *Lockdown Architecture*, Milano: Editoriale Lotus.
Benjamin, W. (1978), 'Louis-Philippe, or the Interior', in Peter Demetz (ed.), *Reflections: Essays, Aphorisms, Autobiographical Writings*, New York: Schoken Books.
Bennett, T. (1988), 'The Exhibitionary Complex', *New Formations*, 4(Spring I): 73–102.
Bergdoll, B. (1987), 'The Architecture of Isolation: M.-R. Penchaud's Quarantine Hospital in the Mediterranean', *AA Files*, Spring, (14): 3–13.
Bianchetti, C. (2020), *Corpi tra spazio e progetto*, Sesto San Giovanni, Milan: Mimesis Edizioni.
Beatriz Colomina (2018), 'The 24/7 Bed', Marina Otero Verzier and Nick Axel (eds.), *Work, Body, Leisure*, Catalog of the Dutch Pavilion at the 16th International Architecture Exhibition of La Biennale di Venezia, Rotterdam: Het Nieuwe Instituut and Berlin: Hatje Cantz, 189–204.
D'eramo, M. (2020), 'The Philosopher's Epidemic', *New Left Review*, 122, March–April 2020.
Foucault, M. (1975), *Surveiller et punir: Naissance de la prison*, Paris: Gallimard (*Discipline and Punish: The Birth of the Prison*, Allen Lane, London, 1977).
Han, B.-C. (2017), *In the Swarm: Digital Prospects*, Cambridge, MA: MIT Press.
Haraway, D. (1985), 'A Manifesto for Cyborg: Science, Technology, and Socialist Feminism in the 1980s', *Socialist Review*, 80: 65–108.
Nicolin, P. (2020), *Architettura e Pandemia*, Milano: Skira.
Otero, Verzier M. and N. AXEL, eds (2018), *Work, Body, Leisure*, Berlin: Hatje Cantz Verlag Gmbh.
Preciado, P. B. (2020), 'Learning from the Virus', *Art Forum International*, 58(9), May/June: 76–85.
Rice, C. (2006), *The Emergence of the Interior: Architecture, Modernity, Domesticity*, London: Routledge.
Rowe, C. and R. Slutzky (1963), 'Transparency: Literal and Phenomenal', *Perspecta*, 8: 45–54.
Vidler, A. (1992), *The Architectural Uncanny: Essays in the Modern Unhomely*, Cambridge, MA: MIT Press.

Willbern, D. (1979), 'Freud and the Inter-Penetration of Dreams', *Diacritics*, 9(1): 98–110.
Zardini, M. and F. Doglio, eds (2021), *Dopo le crisi. 1973, 2001, 2008, 2020*, Siracusa: LetteraVentidue.
Žižek, S. (2020), *Virus: Catastrofe e solidarietà*, Milano: Ponte alle Grazie.

SECTION FOUR

Collecting the interior in the era of Covid-19

16

Changing scenes: Image-making from parlour to screen

Patrick Lee Lucas

In March 2020, with the looming global health pandemic due to the rise of Covid-19, technology in hand, on laps and perched on desks made possible the view of curated and not-so-curated living rooms, dining rooms, great rooms, dens, family rooms, bedrooms, porches and home offices. These hybrid public/private spaces within the home became windows through which others could see the lives of individuals across the spectrum of the population throughout the globe, connecting producers of the images to business, education and community settings. Through digital interfaces such as Zoom, Microsoft Teams, Google Meet and FaceTime, these projections provide significant visual evidence of the extension of identity-making in the United States that began in domestic spaces more than 300 years ago. By exploring the visual images in each of these spaces through time, the contemporary practice of curation comes into sharp focus along a continuum of such endeavours rather than singled out as a unique moment in time.

Spaces for public performance

In projected images of the Zoom room and other digital portals, the visual narratives that unfold provide self-curated displays that allow individuals to externalize themselves as 'material manifestations of their personal identities' (McKellar and Sparke 2004: 73) and consequently blur the public/private boundaries of their most intimate spaces, what Lois Weinthal (2011) labels as spaces for 'public performance' distinguished from 'private chambers'. Moreover, the visual sharing of rooms online conflates the positions of consumers and producers, further challenging boundaries that were disintegrating prior to the pandemic on social media platforms. Because we order the world in which we live by gazing at it and making sense of it through visual data (Foucault 1975), we increasingly obscure distinctions between representation and reality. With many circulating images, 'the clear-cut distinctions between home and away – a place one visits or curates outside of everyday life' exist with 'incredible fluidity of multiple signs and electronic images' (Lash and Urry 1993: 259). We thus exist in mediated and physical worlds as we consume visually.

Before the days of Zoom during the pandemic, social media helped shape the digital realm of public performance and images of self outside our analogue lives. From the first decades of the twentieth century, on to platforms such as *MySpace*, *Facebook*, *Pinterest* and *Instagram*, millions of users poured visual content, alongside text, for followers to view and consume. These social media sites and tools provide streams of highly curated visual data yet to be mined for content analysis. Though some scholarly interest has been directed to social media, no one has yet looked beyond the main subjects to the silent performances of and in the backgrounds of the displayed images.

In more general terms, scholars have investigated motives for documentation and belonging in media forms such as *Instagram* and how the taking of selfies and 'other images and icons that we use to express ourselves, such as the photos we choose to share' find their way to social media (Rettberg 2017: 429). As exploration of ideal and real selves presented online, Green (2013) characterized that 'we consider our profiles to be presentations of who we are' where those constructed identities of 'the real and ideal selves intersect; and the ideal self is at least partially actualised', representing an ideal identity rather than a real one. Chen (2011) speculated about the importance of connection that resulted from entering into visual and written conversations online through these forms of social media, noting that: 'the more the person gratifies a need for an informal sense of camaraderie, called connection, with other users', what Benedict Anderson defined as 'imagined communities' thirty years before.

Cultural anthropologist Erving Goffman provided the conceptual foundations for these later analyses of social media. Goffman (1959) articulated a view that every person attempts to control or guide impressions of others by altering settings, manners and appearances. In his work, Goffman used the metaphor of acting with onstage actors presenting themselves to the audience where backstage, hidden from audience view, actors can be themselves and drop societal roles and identities. Goffman based his own work on that of anthropologist Gregory Bateson, who described frameworks for encounter to 'construct a general statement regarding the structure, or form, of experiences individuals have at any moment of their social life' (Fine and Manning 2003: 35).

The reality of the twenty-first-century identity-making project actually has deep roots in the visual and material culture of previous centuries. Before examining the themes of curation, success and credibility in the Zoom room in the last portion of this chapter, I consider the longer view of three centuries of identity formation in a review of scholarship with examples of houses from the United States beginning with its colonial foundations, in the years of the Early Republic, through the Victorian era and then to the ubiquitous house forms of the twentieth century. This strong continuity of identity-making conveyed through visual images and material goods in the domestic interior – whether physical or digital – unites these practices through time across class. By the same token, spaces and how people curated them also provide lenses to examine any of these lines of inquiry in order to see distinctions. This delicate balance of belonging and individuality sewn in the American project from its beginnings and, perhaps, in this century more than any other, can be used to help us understand both the commonalities we share and the differences that make that examination most interesting.

Collecting identities in the mediated home

As the eighteenth century unfolded, middle-class homeowners in the United States (as well as other places in the Western world) increasingly collected artefacts from around the globe. They displayed them for others to see in the entertainment rooms of their increasingly large houses, bringing the world to the home in rooms for gathering, eating, singing, sitting, conversing and more. As aspiring actors, homeowners and visitors alike performed on these curated interior stages populated by furnishings and decorative arts to provide comfort and symbolically confer gentility (Garrett 1990; Larkin 1988) through the creation of discrete social spaces as outward signs of civility (Gowans 1964). Production and consumption frameworks, those 'stages of communication from manufacturer to seller to homeowner to visitor' linked 'aesthetics to construction, function, cost, and technology' (Ettema 1981: 233) as the meanings ascribed to artefacts shifted across time (Bourdieu 1984). These frameworks represented continuous processes through which people 'simultaneously impose[d] meaning on and read meaning from material culture, and by extension the rest of their surrounding material and social world' (Purser 1992: 105).

Within the rooms for public performance in the domestic interior, images served as keys to transmit identity from owner to visitor. In the decades of the nineteenth century, as before, framed portraits and scene paintings and, increasingly less expensive lithographs and prints, adorned the walls of interior spaces along with visually rich scenic textiles and wallpapers (Bushman 1993). Alongside these depictions of everyday life, chinaware for use and display added visually to the interior with a wide variety of domestic and foreign scenes, including exotic scenes of Asia, Africa and South America. As house owners used these images to memorialize life experiences – both imagined and real – they simultaneously revealed their projected ideals with 'furnishings that embodied the social ideals of material prosperity, love, rest, permanence, and individual liberty' (Bray 1992: 43), representations they put into the world. Genre painter John Krimmel captures a glimpse of middle-class life in the Early Republic in *The Quilting Frolic* (1813), including the presence of period material and visual culture (Figure 16.1).

Throughout the nineteenth century, many homeowners had access to household manuals and treatises on architecture as well as periodicals with

FIGURE 16.1 *The Quilting Frolic, John Lewis Krimmel, Philadelphia, Pennsylvania, United States, 1813, Oil on canvas, 1953.0178.002 A, B, Museum purchase, Courtesy of Winterthur Museum.*

further suggestions for living, both made ever more available through advances in printing. The taste-makers who wrote and illustrated these volumes deeply influenced homeowners and designers alike as to the kind of material goods and their appropriate distribution within a genteel household. Together these media sources helped create and maintain a robust culture of consumerism across the decades.

As social values changed in the last quarter of nineteenth century and exponentially so in the first quarter of the twentieth century, so too did domestic interiors. Less formalistic parlours and halls yielded to more informal living rooms and 'a new theory of aesthetics that stressed practicality and simplicity, efficiency and craftsmanship' (Clark 1986: 132). Moreover, with the advent of photography, an ever-greater number of visual images could be readily produced and distributed to domestic interiors. Like their eighteenth- and nineteenth-century counterparts, residents in the bungalows of the 1920s continued to convey a sense of who they were to others through their collections and, specifically, through the images collected as evidence of worldliness and gentility. They continued to buy consumer goods made ever more available through mail-order catalogues and the advent of a

FIGURE 16.2 *Wallace Nutting. At the Fender, ca. 1904. Wallace Nutting, Public domain, via Wikimedia Commons.*

department store consumer framework, what Paul Cherington described as the democratization of things. As a contemporary visual example, minister turned photographer Wallace Nutting (1861–1941) produced hand-coloured highly curated, and largely fictional Colonial Revival images that shaped American sensibilities about the use of appropriate material and visual objects to populate parlours at the turn of the twentieth century drawing on the nation's Colonial past (Figure 16.2).

By the mid-twentieth century, collecting visual images and material culture continued apace, with owners and designers taking advantage of consumer networks in ever increasing numbers to meet the pent up post-Second World War consumer demand. While design magazines such as *House Beautiful* provided a location for easily attained and copied floor plans and design issues, television provided a particularly salient visual source for ideas of the home, an increasingly dominant media form with deep influence at the mid-twentieth century and beyond. From the 1950s to the end of the twentieth century and into the twenty-first, one only had to turn on the television to bring the viewer to the residences on shows ranging from the modest suburban middle-class home on *The Adventures of Ozzie and Harriet* (1952–66) all the way through the stylish urban townhouse on *The Cosby Show* (1984–92) and the cluster of suburban residences on *Modern Family*, Throughout the seventy years of television featuring residential interior spaces, all manner of material and visual culture appeared on screen influencing, both consciously and subconsciously, the viewers of the American family home. Add a picture window or other large openings to the twentieth-century living space and suddenly homeowners provided snapshots of domesticity easily viewed from the street, further blurring private and public distinctions (Marling 1996; Spigel 2001).

In the last decades of the twentieth century, homeowners and builders alike turned to an 'all in' approach to house design, with impact on the domestic interior and the visual images and material culture within. On suburban tracts of land and unfettered by historical precedent – or perhaps calling on it – individuals constructed ever larger dwellings with free-wheeling forms and features. The all-inclusive great room (combining living, dining and kitchen spaces interconnected with one another) became the place not only for family living but also public performance. In this space family members and visitors alike experienced much of the same activities as their forebears in a single space, reversing the trend of single use rooms so carefully set apart in the nineteenth-century Victorian home.

As print media declined in the latter twentieth century and the first quarter of the twenty-first, consumers tuned in on desktop computers, smart phones, and tablets to purchase and equip their home with the latest furnishings, gadgets and decorative items. Beginning in the late twentieth century and certainly cemented as a pattern in the twenty-first, goods arriving from across the world found their way to domestic spaces from online ordering. Like before, these consumer patterns resulted in spaces for collecting and curating made easy by the economic-cultural complex of digital shopping. One aspect of image making within this larger context of consumer goods, the images and roomscapes projected through websites on digital portals helped to shape the sensibilities of individuals as they projected identities to not only stand out from but fit within the 'imagined communities' they created by 'keeping up with the Joneses'.

By the arrival of the world wide web in the opening decades of the twenty-first century, consumers continued to demand products but then, more than ever, commercial concerns generated consumer demand, driven by ever increasingly sophisticated algorithms and data mining. Companies responded in kind by dangling all manner of domestic consumer products made available with the click of a mouse. With these advancing technologies, the ability to track users and their consumer habits significantly advanced the evolution of identity-making across the space of several hundred years. Further blurred public/private boundaries resulted from the introduction of these electronic portals and projections, coexisting with earlier media forms as the changing and interwoven scenes of everyday life (Weinthal 2011). Which brings us back to the Zoom room.

Self-curation in the Zoom room

With the widespread use of Zoom during the pandemic, the questions and approaches to self-representation and intentionality through curation take on additional meaning – in a live stream sort of way – as people intentionally and unintentionally share the backgrounds of homes and offices with others. Before the Zoom 'blur out' feature roll out in February 2021, the highly personal signs and symbols of humanity took centre stage in a very public manner, continuing a long tradition of sharing markers – material culture and visual artefacts in the form of decorative arts and furnishings – as a shorthand language to tell others who we are and who we aspire to be. These acts of sharing that began in the parlours of the eighteenth-century middle-class home are far from complete. As social media, and specifically the Zoom room, offers opportunities for self-curation of identity through image making, twenty-first-century citizens, like their counterparts in the centuries before, continue to shape what others perceive of their place in society in the digital space of a computer screen or a handheld digital device. Where people in American domestic spaces with public performances in previous centuries brought the world to their homes, Zoom roomers project images of the domestic interior to the world through a digital interface, as in the case of the author's Zoom room itself (Figure 16.3). Though this topic is ripe for exploration, the purpose of this particular chapter, an exploration of the connections and commonalities from predecessor interiors in the eighteenth to the twentieth centuries, benefits from three quick examples of Zoom rooms from the present day.

A response from a designer and a social media influencer to the Zoom room environment and the self-curation that occurs there provide evidence that suggests the need for curating the backgrounds that individuals project. Designer Patrick Ediger indicates the importance of good lighting and a carefully selected series of artefacts that tell a cohesive story. Ediger (www.patrickediger.com) advises that 'your space should tell a story about you. After all, it's your home, and we need to embrace our humanity now more than ever! Select decor that's inviting and shows who you are: memorabilia and books you love, art that speaks to you, your favorite colors, and fresh flowers, live plants, or a lit candle'. He offers recommendations about eliminating distractions from competing elements including the final bit of guidance to 'look at your space onscreen and adjust accordingly'. Echoing the curation of nearly three centuries, Ediger's advice points to the self-curated displays that have informed the public performances in homes physically and now digitally.

FIGURE 16.3 *The author's own room, with its background from a 1902 Colonial Revival House. Screen capture by author, 2021.*

Twitter provides a particularly pertinent source for the fleeting glimpse of domestic interior backgrounds. Since April 2020, Claude Taylor's *Twitter* feed, @ratemyskyperoom rates Zoom backgrounds on a ten-point scale with hilarious quips and ratings. With more than 33,600 tweets in a year's time, Taylor's 408,600+ followers merited enough interest that he and a co-author are compiling a handbook for more successful backgrounds and a 'best of' publication chronicling the range of rooms and their ratings. Taylor's commentary speaks volumes about people and the images they project in the quest to manifest identities, connecting his twenty-first-century observations to the remarks offered by advice givers and taste-makers across three centuries of the American domestic dwelling. His Twitter feed, particularly, frames the American domestic interior as a backdrop that helps to explain who is on screen by encapsulating their values in pithy prose for entertainment. Beyond the cultural commentary that Taylor provides, his chronicle links to and expands the authors, homeowners and designers who join across three centuries of identity-making and sharing regardless of the medium.

Finally, amid the Covid-19 pandemic, an unknown user generated a new *Twitter* feed *@BCredibility* (https://twitter.com/BCredibility) with the tagline 'what you say is not as important as the bookcase behind you'. Not unlike Taylor's room ratings, the anonymous author, with 115,800+ followers, characterizes the quality of the books in view (or lack thereof), linking to aspects of individual personalities featured. For example, the account included a screen shot of actor Tom Hanks from 7 July 2020 and the writer noted: 'Tom Hanks doesn't need to do anything except exist but is humble enough to seek bookcases for support. He offers his reality and his dreams with politics, baseball, and space exploration but the question is what's in the case. It's our heart, of course. We gave it to Tom long ago' (*@BCredibility*). Conflating pop culture references and generalizations of the actor, the Twitter feed's unknown author participates in the same kind of cultural exchange that has always taken place in American domestic interiors, though the medium has changed to an online interface – as seen in the example of Angela Davis in front of a bookcase amid the pandemic in June 2020 (Figure 16.4). Though bordering on parody, this Twitter account speaks to an examination of the material objects that many people generally associate with an intellectual elite. Books, in this instance, represent a centuries-old visual and material object that convey certain assumptions and characteristics of their owners. Significantly, blogger Kylie Walters (https://medium.com/print-and-screen/bookcase-credibility-screened-465b7ba39c1) speculates from her own examination of the *@BCredibility Twitter* account big questions about making and consuming images online:

> I wonder about this ritual alignment with books, and how it may be changing as Covid-19 spurs relationships with technologies to transform. Has the

screen been training us to broadcast ourselves all along? Has alignment with the print book come, increasingly, to be a badge of analog in a digital world? What does this badge do and say? How does the video call prompt class/property performance?

As Walters notes, these complex questions continue to shape contemporary curatorial practices by homeowners and designers to shape our understandings of who we are, a practice that has extended for over three centuries in the American domestic interior.

Far from these three more intentional and highly curated digital spaces, thousands of individuals show up to the Zoom room (and other digital portals)

FIGURE 16.4 *The anonymous author of Bookcase Credibility provides pithy reviews of the bookcases that appear in the Twitter feed. Here activist Angela Davis appears, as featured on 19 June 2020.*

often unintentionally, or perhaps subconsciously, revealing projected images that encapsulate both the owner's own aspirations, hopes, and dreams and the perceptions the viewers have of these individuals while viewing them. This intertwining of domestic space and the images of domesticity (where public 'stops' and private 'starts') gives us the mechanism for role-play in the changing scenes of the theatres of everyday life we manifest online, images worth exploring as we continue to chronicle who we are and what we hope.

References

Bourdieu, P. (1984), *Distinction: A Social Critique of the Judgement of Taste*, London: Routledge.
Bray, M. (1992), 'The Power of Home,' *Gateway Heritage*, 12: 43.
Bushman, R. A. (1993), *The Refinement of America: Persons, Houses, Cities*, New York: Vintage.
Chen, G. M. (2011), 'Tweet This: A Uses and Gratifications Perspective on How Active Twitter Use Gratifies a Need to Connect with Others,' *Computers in Human Behavior*, 27(2): 755–62.
Clark, C. E., Jr. (1986), *The American Family Home, 1800–1960*, Chapel Hill: University of North Carolina Press.
Ettema, M. J. (1981), 'Technological Innovation and Design Economics in Furniture Manufacture,' *Winterthur Portfolio,* 16(2/3): 197–224.
Fine, G. A. and P. Manning (2003), 'Chapter 2. Erving Goffman', in G. Ritzer (ed.), *The Blackwell Companion to Major Contemporary Social Theorists*, 34–62, New York: Wiley.
Foucault, M. (1975), *Discipline and Punish: The Birth of the Prison*, New York: Vintage Books.
Garrett, E. D. (1990), *At Home: The American Family, 1750–1870*, New York: Abrams.
Goffman, E. (1959), *The Presentation of Self in Everyday Life*, New York: Anchor.
Gowans, A. (1964), *Images of American Living: Four Centuries of Architecture and Furniture as Cultural Expression*, New York: Lippincott.
Green, R. K. (2013), *The Social Media Effect: Are You Really Who You Portray Online?* https://www.huffpost.com/entry/the-social-media-effect-a_b_3721029 (Viewed 15 October 2021).
Larkin, J. (1988), *The Reshaping of Everyday Life: 1790–1840*, New York: Harper.
Lash, S. and J. Urry (1993), *Economies of Signs and Space*, London: SAGE Publications.
Marling, K. A. (1996), *As Seen on TV: The Visual Culture of Everyday Life in the 1950s*, Cambridge: Harvard University Press.
McKellar, S. and P. Sparke, eds (2004), *Interior Design and Identity*, Manchester: Manchester University Press.

Purser, M. (1992), 'Consumption as Communication in Nineteenth-Century Paradise Valley, Nevada,' *Historical Archaeology*, 26: 105–16.

Rettberg, J. W. (2017), 'Self-Representation and Social Media', in J. Burgess, et al. (eds), *SAGE Handbook of Social Media*, 429–33, Chapter 23, Thousand Oaks: SAGE Publications.

Spigel, L. (2001), *Welcome to the Dream House: Popular Media and Post-War Suburbs*, Durham: Duke University Press.

Weinthal, L. (2011), *Toward a New Interior: An Anthology of Interior Design Theory*, New York: Princeton Architectural Press.

17

Shelter in Place Gallery: Exhibiting contemporary art and creating community in a pandemic

Michelle Millar Fisher, Eben Haines and Courtney Harris

Introduction

This chapter explores how a miniature gallery-within-a-home, Shelter in Place Gallery, created in Boston at the start of the global coronavirus pandemic, played with received expectations around the intersections of contemporary art, the home, health and representations of interiors. The chapter will also contextualize this project within the history of miniature interiors as places of escape, imagination and resistance.

Introducing Shelter in Place Gallery

As soon as the Covid-19 lockdown started in March 2020, Boston-based artist Eben Haines dusted off a scale model of a contemporary art gallery that he had begun the previous year and that had been lying fallow in his studio. Together with his then-partner and now-wife, Delaney Dameron, Haines decided to create a space where contemporary artists could show their work at a moment of crisis in the art world and in the larger global landscape. Together, they created a basic website platform for the project (www.shelterinplacegallery.com) and – crucially – an Instagram handle (@shelterinplacegallery). They then made an open call over social media to other Boston-based artists who wanted a place to show their work despite social distancing measures. And so was born the Shelter in Place Gallery, which quickly amassed a large, dedicated online following on Instagram as well as international press interest (Di Liscia 2020; Kambhampaty 2020).

One of the only interior visual art spaces of any kind that was 'open' in a moment of near-global closure of similar institutions – it also gave Haines and Dameron something to focus on during lockdown – necessary given that Haines, who usually worked at the Museum of Fine Arts (MFA), Boston, as a designer for exhibitions, was furloughed for over five months as the MFA's operations slowed. In Haines's own words, the gallery initially began as a 'kind of a rainy-day project to plan artworks that I didn't have the money or space to produce at scale'. When lockdowns went into effect, for reasons of convenience and safety and also to relieve the financial burden of a studio outside the home, Haines moved the model into his small Boston apartment, along with the rest of his studio contents. It was something 'to keep my hands busy', a need that Haines and Dameron quickly realized that many other artists were also experiencing. Making miniature work suddenly became an avenue – previously unconsidered but now much more attractive and feasible – for artists with less space, time and material resources. Paradoxically, these constraints also allowed them to experiment and dream of large-scale works for which these same resources might never be available.

Haines and Dameron have over the last eighteen months staged more than eighty exhibitions featuring nearly a hundred artists across media, drawing interest from across the world. The first exhibition featured Haines's parents, Gail English and Andrew Haines, and an open invitation to artists to direct message the gallery on Instagram to propose miniature artworks for exhibition. Once accepted and slotted into the programme, artists were invited to drop off their work on Haines's front doorstep at a prearranged time for a safe, contactless handover. Every single artwork exhibited at the miniature gallery is created as an original work using the media that would be employed if the artwork was life size.

Crafting the interior

The project itself was a palimpsest of interiors. The gallery was initially set up in Haines and Dameron's living room on a workbench, its perfectly crafted internal walls, floor and windows at odds with the messy blue painter's tape

FIGURE 17.1 *Shelter in Place gallery, seen from exterior in the artists' living room. Photo courtesy of Eben Haines.*

and irregularly cut foam core board that made up its exterior. Roughly twenty inches high by thirty long, the set up was large enough to displace the gallery co-founders from a significant portion of their available living space. Shelter in Place (Figure 17.1) was made from a mixture of materials Haines had at hand in his studio: foamcore, matboard, acrylic and latex paint, balsa wood for the floor, baseboards, beams, plexiglass for the windows, adhesive backed vinyl on windows, as well as scraps from the paper Haines used within the MFA design studio and had salvaged for personal use.

Perhaps the most spellbinding application of these materials are the miniature gallery desk and chair, mini-Mac computer and the exquisitely realistic small-scale packing, crating and shipping materials the artist created to augment his illusory interior. Indeed, some of the exhibiting artists took Haines's furnishings as a challenge and created their own miniature packaging materials for transporting their works, relishing the opportunity to create miniature crates, pallets and forklifts to add to the illusion of the functionality of a full-scale gallery (Figure 17.2).

Many online viewers do not immediately recognize the installation as a model, instead engaging as if the gallery were housed in a building of human scale. For its co-founders, the gallery was both a personal response to being

FIGURE 17.2 *'Another show down as another show arrives! Miles Jaffe's crates are acclimatizing in the gallery as we break for coffee and eat our wheaties. Gonna be some heavy lifting, thank god he provided dollies!' Photo courtesy of Eben Haines.*

confined in their own home, and a way to support artists suddenly cut off from means to share and sell their work. In Haines's words, it is 'a rejection of the "white cube" space – it's a weird deceit – where you know that it's all fake, but at the same time it feels a lot more authentic than a lot of art experiences that people are having right now'. It is, in their eyes, more an artist's studio than an art gallery. In this sense, in its refusal of aesthetics that commonly signal contemporaneity in presentations of fine art, as well as because of its site in a domestic interior, Shelter in Place has precedent in exhibitions that have occurred in residential spaces. Such exhibitions range widely and are not always well documented precisely because of their more makeshift nature. They include guerrilla presentations created by art students in their own apartments, as well as more established and well-known instances like the legendary at-home salons held by the artist Louise Bourgeois (Chiaverina 2019).

The first Instagram post introducing the project to a public audience was made on 27 March 2020, with a simple welcome, a note on the one to twelve scale (one inch to one foot), and an invitation for artists to 'go big' with their proposals. The image (shot, as all of them are, on Haines's iPhone) posted above the text showed a gallery interior with a high, beamed ceiling; patinated walls and a large, framed artwork (by Haines himself) in the centre of the space (Figure 17.3). Light streamed in from the windows and cast shadows across the painted wooden floor. Though the very first gallery text highlighted the miniature nature of the space, it was immediately complicated by the perspectival trickery of the accompanying image. This reciprocal relationship between text and image has continued throughout the project, with the words of each post, as critical to the illusion as the images. These texts point to an obvious and extensive familiarity with the operations of museum galleries, and poke fun at some of the common experiences and frustrations of artists and arts administrators in such spaces.[1]

FIGURE 17.3 *The first post on @shelterinplacegallery Instagram. Photo courtesy of Eben Haines.*

This politicizes the interior in a specific and important way, a small space providing an outsized commentary not only in its subversion of the aesthetics of display but upending the ways in which artists and audiences gain access to spaces of display, and the labour that underwrites such work. Haines and Dameron are direct and deliberate in this aspect of their project:

> We joke about how many people it takes to make these shows happen with such rapidity, from the sweating (and unionised) art handlers working overtime, to our registrars pacing on the loading dock and pulling their hair out over late trucks. Even though it is really just Delaney and I doing things here, I hope these jokes address some of the massive inequities and toxic practices inherent in galleries and museums. The major difference here being that this work is done in benefit to the community, as opposed to padding the bottom line of some major institution. Rarely does an institution mention the people, many of whom are artists themselves, that make the art world run. As a longtime museum worker, I know that those institutions rarely pay their workforce in a way that acknowledges their dedication and skill, either.

The gallery co-founders filled their weekly exhibition schedule with artists and group shows that addressed many urgent and sensitive social and political issues that are globally and locally relevant. Thanks to a small grant from the City of Boston, they were able to pay artists small stipends for shipping and materials to make showing with the gallery more accessible.

Contextualizing miniatures

Miniaturization is not new but rather a constant within art and design histories. At key moments in Western history, artists and collectors have turned to miniaturization as a way to negotiate major societal shifts and the changing shape of their world. Miniatures derive their meaning and scale by comparison with their full-size or 'parent' objects. As the 'parent' world has changed over the past 500 years miniaturization has changed in kind. The rapid expansion – or, in the case of the current pandemic the *contraction* – of worlds prompts artists to find new ways to be creative in the face of challenges not only to their art making but also to their livelihoods.

If we think of the seventeenth century and its concomitant wave of colonial exploration, we might argue that an explosion of the scope and size of the world around oneself prompted a turn inwards and a yearning for things of smaller, tangible scale. Miniatures were one way to place one's body in relation to the expanding world around it, and artists explored this phenomenon by shrinking down the world. Consider an object like the terrestrial globe compass

FIGURE 17.4 *Terrestrial globe compass, around 1675–1685 in Dieppe, France, engraved ivory. Gift of the heirs of Bettina Looram de Rothschild (2015.109a-b). Photograph © Museum of Fine Arts, Boston.*

(2015: 109a–b) (Figure 17.4), which at just two and a quarter inches in diameter fits neatly into the palm of one's hand. It is engraved all over with foliage, as well as equinoctial, tropical, Arctic and Antarctic circles, zodiac symbols and the months of the year. This globe teeters between a decorative and a useful object. The halves separate to reveal a fitted interior containing a brass compass with folding gnomon (the projecting piece on a sundial that shows the time by the position of its shadow). The other half contains a printed compass directional chart. The miniature object begs the question of whether it was ever used for a practical purpose, or simply collected and admired by a wealthy, worldly individual as part of a collector's cabinet of curiosities (*wunderkammer*).

Over three centuries later a similar trend for miniaturization was precipitated by another moment of increasing globalization. This time, it was wrought by the migration of the internet into our pockets in the form of smartphones (which themselves became increasingly small in this period). Ron Ho's work, *TV Guide* from 1992 (2006: 251) (Figure 17.5), is a playful exploitation of wearable fashion that conjures an interior setting. This elaborate necklace, surely too delicate to be worn, combines elements of Ho's Chinese American heritage. Ho's scene of a television placed on a Chinese altar table, complete

FIGURE 17.5 *Ron Ho (American, 1936–2017), TV Guide, 1992, silver, patinated copper, polymer clay; silk cord. The Daphne Farago Collection, 2006.251. Reproduced with permission. Photograph © Museum of Fine Arts, Boston.*

with offerings of silver fruit, red candles and thin incense sticks in silver and copper vessels, is laden with metaphor and connotation that traverses geographic and cultural boundaries even as its scale does the reverse. In an ever-expanding world, which prioritizes globalism, grandeur, spectacle and immersive experiences, miniature objects and interiors, like those of the Shelter in Place Gallery, can catch us off guard, stop us in our tracks and force a different frame of mind.

Collecting Shelter in Place Gallery

The Shelter in Place Gallery was acquired into the permanent collection of the MFA, Boston, in June 2020. Due to pandemic-related delays, it only came on site at the Museum in December of that year and so it continued to operate in Haines's and Dameron's apartment until that date. The gallery interior was materially changed in small but significant ways at this juncture of it passing from the domestic space into the museum collection. Critically, due to his role as a museum employee working directly at the interface of exhibition design, Haines had a sense for which materials might be conservationally preferred. He collaborated with woodworker and glass artist Zachary Herrmann, to design a more robust shell to encase the gallery interior, and the roof now lifts off in one piece and is held in place by gravity. The opening at the front now has the option to install a plexiglass protecting sheet if there is not a plexiglass case available. The co-founders built a 2.0 version which they now use in their home, maintaining their Instagram presence, and so the gallery's exhibition programme has been uninterrupted by the acquisition. The original gallery is now on display as part of a collection-based exhibition, *New Light: Encounters and Connections*, as the city of Boston, like so many others, reawakens after a year and a half of lockdown with audiences now ready to see art in the 'real' world.

In one sense, the deceit of scale that had been an integral part of Shelter in Place's essence on Instagram was broken upon its entry into the analogue gallery space of the Museum. In another, it leant a fitting context to works long in the Museum's collection, and that had languished in storage. In *New Light*, the Shelter in Place model houses works from the MFA's holdings by French nineteenth century-potter Auguste Delaherche. He produced miniature vases in a variety of shapes and sizes as a way of testing different glaze colours and patterns before applying the glazes to larger 'full-size' vessels. The artist must have considered these miniature vases as works of art in their own right, as each is marked on the underside with his initials and a model number. Seen in the context of Shelter in Place, the vases take on monumental qualities, and their quality of execution – both in the potting of the shapes as well as the glaze mixtures – is apparent.

Now on display for a much more intimate encounter in the MFA's gallery (Figure 17.6), one important outcome of this presentation's success with in-real-life audiences is that it opens wide the possibilities for displaying not just miniatures – of which the MFA has strong holdings – by living artists but also historical works like those of Delaherche. It asks us to consider how a museum setting can change based on how a viewer encounters it. In a pointed and inescapable manner, the Shelter in Place Gallery presentation, shows the way that miniature art works and interiors require deceit. They must fool us, and we must allow ourselves to be fooled. How far can a miniature take its viewers before the trick falls down and it fails? Though these questions can only be answered subjectively by individual encounters with these works, anecdotally observing encounters with Shelter in Place, in the MFA's gallery hammers home how happily deceived viewers online were in comparison to those in the museum who had to work harder to build the illusion.

From its inception, the Shelter in Place project was a deliberate riposte to the often clinical and inaccessible interior of the museum or gallery interior. This stereotypical encounter was deliberately unsettled through the scale of the miniature, where even if the viewer did not immediately understand the

FIGURE 17.6 *Eben Haines's 'Shelter in Place Gallery' on view in the exhibition New Light: Encounters and Connections at the Museum of Fine Arts, Boston, 28 July 2021. Photograph © Museum of Fine Arts, Boston.*

work, it was hard not to be curious about it. One can choose whether to be fully immersed, or see things from a bird's eye view, taking it all in at once. Per Haines:

> Knowing that a sculpture is the size of a fist, and that the room is an illusion, includes people in the joke and seems to make them look more closely. They notice the room itself, and the way the objects seem to engage and live in the space, instead of just scanning the wall. In this way, exhibitions that tackle really big and difficult ideas don't seem as overwhelming.

Haines's hope was that Shelter in Place could make art more approachable to people, especially contemporary art, a genre often seen as impenetrable to those not inside an art world bubble. His gallery was, unlike most US museums, totally free to 'enter' when it was online, something reversed entirely, by its entry into the MFA where admission varies but is around $25 for many visitors.

The interior he and Dameron created is in many ways in direct opposition to the museum model in which it is now displayed, though it is far from being assimilated into this space. Haines reflects, 'The relationships fostered by Shelter in Place within the art world grew exponentially as more traditional and well-resourced infrastructures shrunk all around us, framing art not as a commercial product, but a community project.' The gallery is not a place to 'see and be seen' or to secure exhibitions because of who an artist knows. Instead, it is about creating art regardless of an artist's physical or socioeconomic situation. The gallery founders reflected that one of the most rewarding aspects of their project was that they still got to see ambitious and challenging new works in person every day despite being confined to their own home. In their estimation, the innovative and imaginative work made and the rapidity with which audiences embraced Shelter in Place despite the closure of mainstream art world venues demonstrated that museums and mega galleries are unable to substantively react to crisis or benefit their audience when they need it most. Instead, artist-run collaboratives and alternative spaces that show and promote this work will be the sites to seed unadulterated and expansive visions of the world around us and to collect and acknowledge the pain and the triumphs of our communities.

Conclusion

A provocative analogue means to engage and support contemporary artists that meet the digital in its form of presentation and dissemination, the Shelter in Place Gallery is a historical maker of this most recent moment of upheaval as well as a convincing artistic response to it. For many people, work and home were by necessity merged during the lockdown. The creation of Shelter in Place brought artistic practice into the home. When the outside world offered uncertainty and few opportunities, the dis/comfort of the home, took on more importance and an outsized role. Artists clearly responded – and continue to respond to – the call for miniature works.

In the early period of the pandemic artists faced many overlapping challenges: gallery space was inaccessible, materials were hard to come by due to shortages, commercial sales had all but halted, and while time may have seemed endless to some people stuck at home, increased elder and childcare responsibilities may have made finding the time difficult. This was often overlayed with anxiety over the health crisis, and sadness and anger in the face of the civil unrest in response to endemic police brutality. Shelter in Place Gallery offered low opportunity costs to art making and participation in the gallery's programming. Artists could simply mail or hand-deliver their works and the exhibitions were mounted quickly and efficiently. As Haines notes, 'I think one of the best things about the gallery is that it lowers the stakes so much when it comes to making big, impressive works of art, and doing ambitious things that people normally can't do.'

While gardens, sculpture parks and outdoor installations allow art to be presented outside of the museum's walls, the physical walls of the museum are still so often a limiting factor for the display of art. The online dissemination and subsequent acquisition into a permanent museum collection of Shelter in Place gallery represent another boundary traversed. It generates more wall space within the museum's exhibition space, both literally in that there are four more walls on which to hang art, but also conceptually in its commitment to accessibility which was written into the acquisition notes and artist questionnaire. In the inaugural installation at the MFA, Boston, there are five works on view that, at scale, are between two and three feet in height – and more, on their platform. At full-size, they would take up nearly a quarter of the gallery space allocated for the entire exhibition *New Light*. Instead, they're shown within a two–times three foot space and brought out of storage for the first time in decades.

Acknowledgments

All direct quotes from Eben Haines used throughout this chapter were collected during multiple conversations with the artist over the course of the last eighteen months as we prepared to acquire his work into the MFA's collection and then to present it as part of a collection-based exhibition at the museum.

Note

1. For example, references to art handlers being overworked and undercompensated. In a true breaking of the fourth wall, when Haines and Dameron were married in September 2020, they posted a picture of themselves at their nuptials and made a joke about needing to inform the SIP Human Resources department.

References

Chiaverina, John (2019), 'Three Bedrooms, One Bathroom and an Art Gallery', Arts and Letters, *New York Times*, 18 March. https://www.nytimes.com/2019/03/18/t-magazine/new-york-apartment-art-galleries.html

Di Liscia, Valentina (2020), 'A Miniature Gallery Mounts Tiny Artworks, with Big Results', *Hyperallergic*, 5 May. https://hyperallergic.com/561859/shelter-in-place/

Kambhampaty, Anna Purna (2020), 'The Pandemic Closed Art Galleries' Doors. But Who Said a Gallery Needs Four Walls and a Ceiling?' *Time Magazine*, 11 June. https://time.com/5851312/pandemic-art-galleries/

18

The Domestic Body

Stefania Napolitano

Learning through architecture

The Domestic Body is a workshop conceived as part of the educational programme of MAXXI – the National Museum of 21st Century Arts, located in a building designed by Zaha Hadid – which took place during the Italian lockdown of spring 2020.[1] The aim was to observe and analyse the metamorphosis that has been occurring in our relationship with the domestic interior during the Covid-19 pandemic. The Education Department of MAXXI was established before the museum opened in 2010, and since then the learning activities it has supported have aimed to provide visitors with the tools to read and interpret both the building's architectural language and the surrounding urban landscape. This institution, in fact, is not only a museum devoted to the conservation and the exhibition of modern and contemporary artistic heritage but also acts as a place where to learn *from* and *through* art, design and architecture. Zaha Hadid's building taught us not only how architecture is shaped by the human body but also how it may affect and inform our bodies and their movements, thus showing, the importance of both a multisensory and a kinaesthetic perception of space.

#stayathome _ Living spaces as 'contested terrains' of the outside world

Faced with the first wave of the Covid-19 pandemic in Italy from February 2020 onwards and the subsequent *#stayathome* policy, MAXXI decided to move forward with its research on education through the built environment (even if deprived of the physical relation with the museum's space) and as a means of engaging the public, to make domestic interior the focus of its activities. The domestic interior, like every other space, has a relationship with the social, hierarchical, organizational and productive systems of different historical moments. Living spaces can be considered one of the *contested terrains* of class, ethnicity, power or gender relations and confrontations, as they model, determine or simply reflect relationships between and among genders; adults and children; the public and private realms; and the interior and the exterior (Fiorino 2019: XXI). So, providing its virtual public with simple instruments through which to observe their own physical (and mental) behaviours, MAXXI Education set out to show them how space and architecture could become a common language with which to share enriching experiences, even that of the lockdown, however bewildering it was.

The domestic interior has always reflected a relationship between the socio-economic situation outside and the spatial organization inside. For example, the renewed economic prosperity and the exponential demographic growth that occurred in post-war middle-class America led to an easier way of living and a less gendered segregation of interior space. As Imma Fiorino notes,

> the open plan allowed the components of the same family to live together without any reclusion – like women in the kitchen or children in the playroom – and the *living room* become to all effects the *family room*; thus satisfying the new expectations of *companionate marriage* but also translating, in the other hand, the reduction of privacy and the increasing responsibility of the maternal figure.
>
> (Fiorino 2019: 224)

As an exponent of a new design freedom in Italy, Gio Ponti developed a similar concept describing the so-called casa all'italiana (Italian house), not just as a 'machine for living in' but as a renewed approach to interior design which focus on the Italian word 'conforto' (comfort/solace). Ponti argued that domestic interiors did not simply respond to dweller's needs but imagined a house 'giving us with architecture a measure for our own thoughts, a health for our habits, a meaning for our life and finally a communication with nature' (Ponti 1957: 106–8).

The fluidity of our contemporary nomadic lifestyle has dissolved the boundaries of the house into the urban landscape, expanding domestic space into a series of 'external rooms' such as cafés, bistros or restaurants which replace the traditional conviviality of the domestic kitchen. Recent phenomena, such as changes in work habits, have already forced room-mates, or members of the same family, to re-absorb those 'rooms' back into the house, and to find new ways of sharing domestic spaces by designing multiple routes in order to avoid potential clashes or facilitate moments of greater conviviality. The lockdown has pushed this trend to its limits, obliging us to fulfil all our daily functions inside restricted spaces.

During a brainstorming session, the MAXXI Education team tried to analyse all these phenomena in the light of the lessons learnt from the numerous exhibitions hosted at the museum during its ten years of life. The almost hallucinatory daily repetitive activities experienced by the team during lockdown highlighted an urgent question: If 'we are the space we inhabit', how are we and our homes reacting to the experience of lockdown? How are the **domestic bodies** we have been inhabiting for so long?

Soon after, the MAXXI Education team started to look for a graphic visualization of our physical and mental experiences that was clear enough to become a decoding system of space behaviour which suggested an experimental learning activity in order to provide many members of its public (ranging broadly across categories such as age, culture, class, income, sexual orientation, etc.) with effective instruments to represent, analyse and understand the multiple changes in the uses of their domestic interiors throughout the first lockdown, from 8 March to 18 May 2020. Born as an online do-it-yourself workshop, *The Domestic Body* collected all responses in a database through which the museum aims to structure a deeper research programme.

The body as a narrative medium

While MAXXI Education methodology is based on the kinaesthetic perception of architecture, *The Domestic Body* follows a different route: namely it invites people to use mapping techniques with which to talk about their physical experiences, thereby seeing the domestic space as a narrative medium. As researchers and members of MAXXI Education staff, we started by trying to represent our homes in a very simple but effective way in order to use this synthetic representation as a means of hosting further reflection about the natural displacement of daily activities and movements in our domestic interior. Inspired by Bernard Tschumi's *Manhattan Transcripts* – 'Architecture is not simply about space and form, but also about event, actions and what happens in space' (Tschumi 1994: 7–12) – and by Stan Allen's theory about *fields* (Allen 1997: 24–31) we gradually arrived at the final version of this workshop.

Reflecting on the *time* (both in terms of quantity and intensity) devoted to certain activities in relation to the locations within the domestic *space*s in which we carried them out led us to map our use of the domestic interior through a graphic visualization method surprisingly close to the *motion studies* inspired by F. W. Taylor's Principles of Scientific Management. Following figures from the past, such as Margarete Schütte-Lihotsky and Sigrun Bülow-Hübe, we focused on static and dynamic functional diagrams to help us understand what space could tell us about our personal lockdown experiences.

In the tutorial uploaded on the museum's YouTube channel, the participants are first asked to make a synthetic representation of their domestic interiors using simple geometric forms and a few items of furniture to connote the different spaces. This is followed by a series of quick exercises of 'space anatomy' which led the online audience to an actual mapping of the time and space devoted to *eating*, *sleeping*, *working* and *caring* (leisure). We ask the audience to choose four different versions of the same items (such as cereals, vegetables, building toys or multicolour post-its) (Figure 18.1a, b, c). Placing different elements in different amounts according to the kind of activity and to the intensity or frequency with which it was carried out before the lockdown, the participants can easily obtain a graphic visualization of their customary pre-quarantine use of domestic space (Figure 18.1a). The participants were asked to create three different maps – pre-lockdown, lockdown and post-lockdown period – to visualize how their habits have changed during lockdown and to understand how unanticipated practices may have reshaped, or could still reshape their daily environments, sometimes reconfiguring it completely.

In order to make this happen, the MAXXI Education team posed a series of questions to the public. They focused on the type of activity in order to understand which activities suddenly invaded the domestic interior, even ones never carried out before at home. The daily *preferential pattern* instinctively or programmatically followed – a sequence of different activities in the same room or a functional diversification of the same room achieved by dividing it into different areas; and any other trends that were detected (Figure 18.1b).

The participants were asked to trace the trajectories followed during the day which enabled them to move from one place/corner/room of the house to another in order to carry out different activities. The dynamic diagrams that emerged immediately revealed the preferential path followed by the participant in their daily routine, thus showing how and where they focused their energy and time (Figure 18.1c). In my own case, for example, my preferential route was clearly from my workstation (the desk in my bedroom) to the kitchen, from the kitchen to the dining table and from there back to my workstation, tracing a clear triangle, the vertices of which represent the most important activities which are connected by the sides as movement vectors. As time went by, I started feeling the need to diversify my working landscape, using the desk in my bedroom only during the morning and moving to the dining table during the

THE DOMESTIC BODY

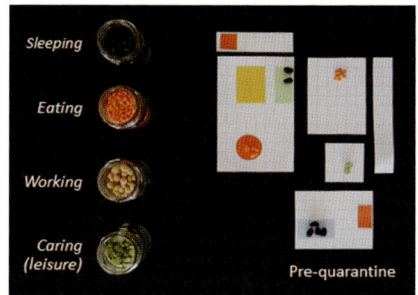
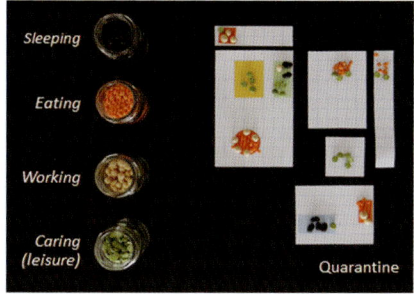
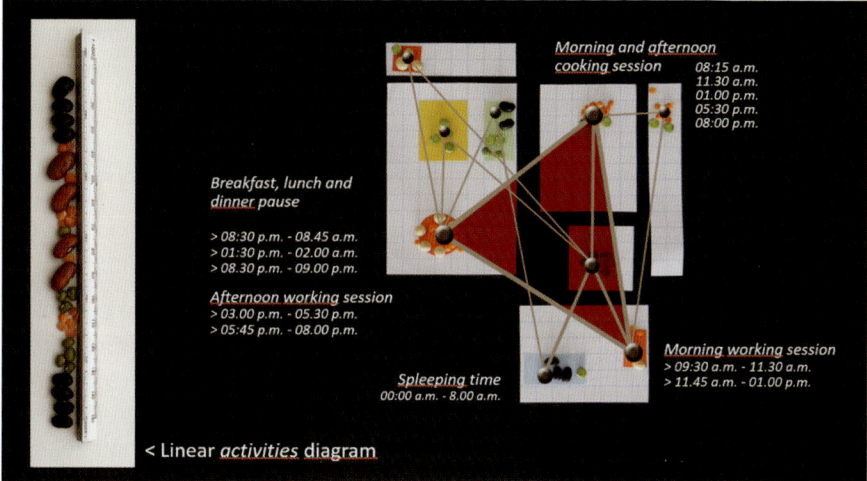

FIGURE 18.1a, b, c *Still from the tutorial of* The Domestic Body *workshop: Pre-quarantine map, quarantine map and dynamic diagram. Courtesy Fondazione MAXXI. Credits Gianfranco Fortuna.*

afternoon, always paying attention not to sit in the same position where I ate my meals, as if changing perspective could enrich my visual horizon during the day!

Finally, the participants were asked to focus on their personal *Mq_uarantena* (a krasis between the Italian unit of measurement *Mq* = 'square metre' and the word *quarantena* = 'quarantine'), and to take a picture of it and showing the absolute truth of their *domestic bodies* or realizing a staged composition of tools, furniture and daily objects whose utility or beauty has been discovered, rediscovered or reinvented. This last step was conceived because, as Shirley Ardner notes, 'The "theatre of action" to some extent determines the action. The environment imposes certain restraints on our mobility, and, in turn, our perceptions of space are shaped by our own capacity to move about … So: *behaviour and space are mutually dependent*' (Ardner 1993/2000: 113).

Work, labour and leisure: The unconscious gender of domestic space

The MAXXI Education team received a wealth of material from virtual visitors spread all over the country and abroad. Although they were very varied in their backgrounds, they all monitored the same phenomenon: the evolution of our domestic behaviour following the different phases of isolation we had experienced. Analysing this material, the team discovered how domestic interiors created in the 1920s or the 1950s, exhibited in the museum, supported current models of living (even unintentionally): on the one hand, the abolition of any functional fixed destination to grant absolute freedom of movement referred back to the traditional Japanese house or the dystopian provocative propositions of Superstudio; on the other hand, the opposite trend of the ergonomic optimization of space, to obtain the highest efficiency with the minimum effort, reminded us of the Nakagin Capsule Tower, a masterpiece of Japanese Metabolist prefabrication.

The concentration of activities normally undertaken outside but now supported within the domestic interior is clearly illustrated in the mappings of a Milanese heterosexual couple with a newborn child (Figure 18.2a, b). They demonstrate a rational distribution of the various activities – from *work* to a deep diversification of the concept of *leisure* (playing and learning with the child, personal care, home-cleaning, fitness routines, reading or relaxing) – which were undertaken in specific rooms or corners of the interior in order to optimize the use of time and energy.

FIGURE 18.2 *Contribution to* The Domestic Body *workshop from a Milanese heterosexual couple with a newborn child: Pre-quarantine and quarantine maps. Courtesy of Fondazione MAXXI.*

In the case of a Parisian couple of young heterosexual professionals, smart working invaded the domestic interior (which was much smaller than the Milanese couple's apartment), leading each person to choose a preferred location – in order not to bother the other – *her* in the living room, *him* in the bedroom (Figure 18.3a, b). We observed that a modern living room was much more likely to be open to interruption than a bedroom, and, as a result, this space allocation allowed the man to enjoy the room with the least likelihood of interruption. This led us to reflect on the conscious and unconscious gendering of space.

In both examples the participants remarked that, before the lockdown, the amount of time spent at home was only a small part of their daily life, thus allowing a single use of every space. The need to use the domestic interior for both living and working generated a functional diversification of every room, and at the same time clear divisions in the use of space were emphasized in the dynamic diagrams of the daily movements of each individual: Riccardo's preferential path was from his working station in the bedroom to the leisure moments spent on the sofa in the living room; whereas Valentina tended to bounce from the table to the sofa inside the same room. These arrangements created the necessity for a new phenomenon in their daily routine – *isolation* – to allow for a breathing space from constant intimacy. All the professional couples, in fact, registered a sudden necessity for some *dispositif* (from the French word meaning 'devices' or 'solutions') of reciprocal isolation. They included pieces of physical equipment – such as screens, panels, mobile furniture – and digital devices such as noise-cancelling headphones or any other kind of isolation solution, even simply turning their backs on each other when they were obliged to work in the same space.

The paradigm shift in use of the domestic interior during the lockdown has been evident in the rehabilitation of almost forgotten archetypes such as the *perimeter* of the house – a filter between inside and outside – between domestic microcosms and urban landscape, the *threshold* (doors, sliding doors, windows or panels), *light* and *roots* (in the gravitational sense of the relationship with the surrounding environment). Our reading of the collected mappings confirmed, for example, the rediscovered importance of the *door* as the only true device of separation and privacy. Therefore, the rare, and increasingly precious, spaces still equipped with doors, like bathrooms and some kitchens, became out of necessity phone booths or conference rooms. Also, *windows* and *French doors* gained incredible importance, not only because they let in fresh air (outside>inside) but also as projection screens for extra-domestic wanderings (inside>outside) and/or as analogic devices for rediscovered social interaction (inside><outside). This reminded us of Beatriz Colomina's observation that 'The etymology of the word window reveals that it combines *wind* with *eye* (ventilation and light in Le Corbusier's terms). […] an element of the outside and an aspect of innerness' (Colomina 1997: 121).

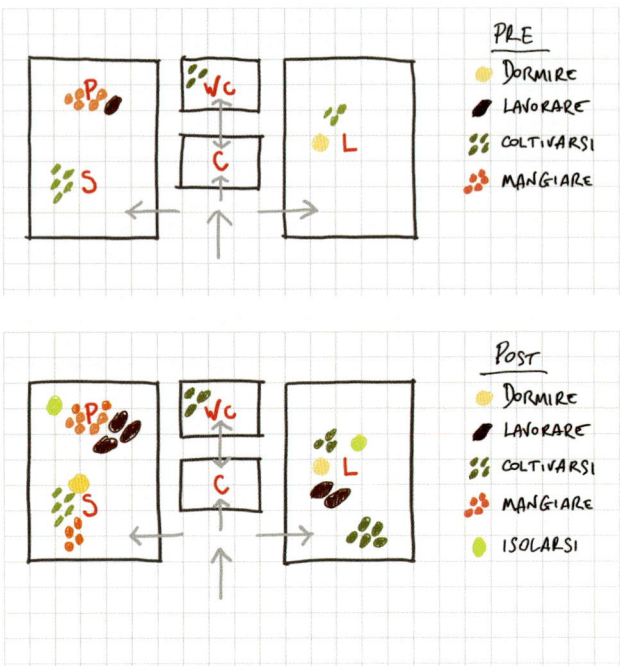

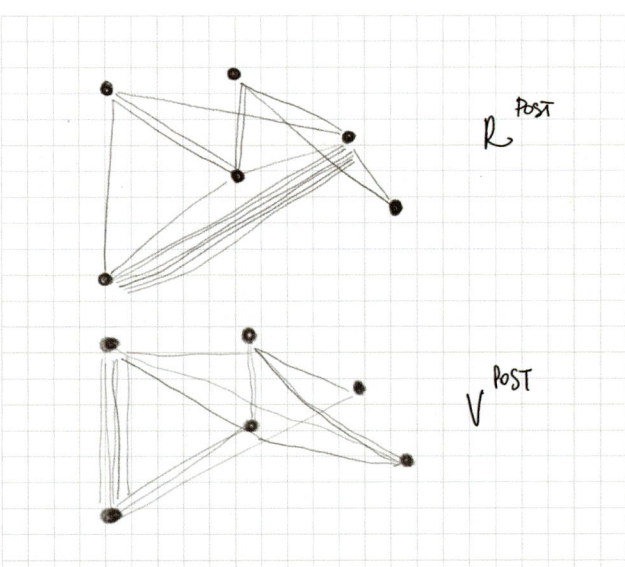

FIGURE 18.3a, b *Contribution to* The Domestic Body *workshop from a Parisian couple of young heterosexual professionals: Pre-quarantine and quarantine maps; individual dynamic diagrams. Courtesy of Fondazione MAXXI.*

In the early twentieth century, clear divisions were established between private and public spaces and within the spaces of the domestic interior. According to Walter Benjamin the very contrast between private space (*l'intérieur*) and working space (*le comptoir*) was the most obvious sign of the development of modern capitalism (Benjamin 1955: 153). Of course, this theory took in consideration only the *paid work* of the career men and not the *home (unpaid) labour* of the family housekeeper (traditionally a woman, the wife). At the same time the domestic interior was designed according to functional principles. The most prominent example of this approach was the Frankfurt Kitchen, commissioned by a housing committee in 1926 to avoid the return to the working-class multi-use 'living kitchen' (Wohnküche), thus obtaining, as a result, a true machine for cooking (Arbeitsküche or 'working kitchen'). The second half of the twentieth century, on the contrary, saw the dilution of this functional approach to designing the domestic interior. Marianna Janowicz notes, 'The walls have fallen away and the boundaries between kitchen and living room – and by extension between labour and leisure – blurred' (Janowicz 2022: 6). For many working women this paradox has been always evident, even amplified by the proliferation of the open-plan kitchen celebrating an alleged leisurely togetherness. During the lockdown, the sudden absorption of more working tasks inside the house created a strange short-circuit that made many men finally aware of the amount of domestic work undertaken by women before the pandemic (whether they had previously worked outside the domestic space or not), while many women could not find any solution to the continuity between 'ordinary' work (often referred to as 'work work') and domestic work, including child care, cooking, cleaning and house management. So what many women (more than men) experienced during the lockdown was a total collapse of spatial and mental boundaries between work, labour, leisure and rest, all compressed into one single time-space dimension, while man only had a taste of it working at home.

The post-confinement return to ratio or the homecoming to the outside

Compared to the examples of families and couples, the case of a single professional – Filippo – allows us to observe and analyse different phenomena: the explosion of work within the domestic interior during the lockdown is followed by a drastic contraction of this activity in the post-lockdown phase (Figure 18.4a, b). This is concentrated in three essential locations: those of the desk, the chair and the kitchen table (Figure 18.4c).

The majority of single people, both living alone or in cohabitation, recorded an initial concentration of *working* tasks (which the greatest amount of time was devoted to) in one or two locations, then a rapid degeneration into an undifferentiated sprawl all over the domestic interior, and finally a sort of sudden absorption of all the exceeding locations. Looking at Filippo's third map (Figure 18.4c), in fact, the comparison between the lockdown phase and the ensuing 'no man's land' where we have been living since its end (we are officially free to do everything but still waiting for new restriction measures at any moment) demonstrates a rationalization of his habits (see Figure 18.4a, b, c).

His work activity has been reducing its tendency to spiral, while his eating pauses have been re-located entirely to the kitchen, and his leisure activities returned to a more rationalized rhythm. The third dynamic diagram appears cleaner, perhaps because of a renewed balance in his relationship with the domestic interior: It is no longer perceived as a suffocating prison. Emanuele Coccia remarked in his *Filosofia della Casa* that the experience of lockdown obliged us to live home from the inside while we used to enter it from the outside (Coccia 2021: 16). During lockdown we experienced a process of re-appropriation of our domestic interiors, a process close to the original meanings of the word *oikeiosiss* – 'appropriation' – in the sense of making something our own while making ourselves appropriate to that something; 'dependency' in the sense of making something similar to ourselves while

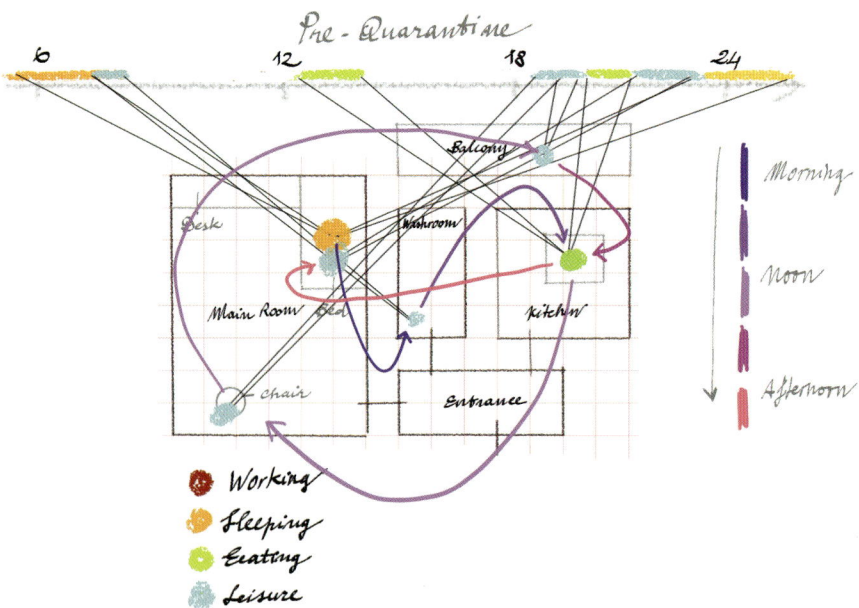

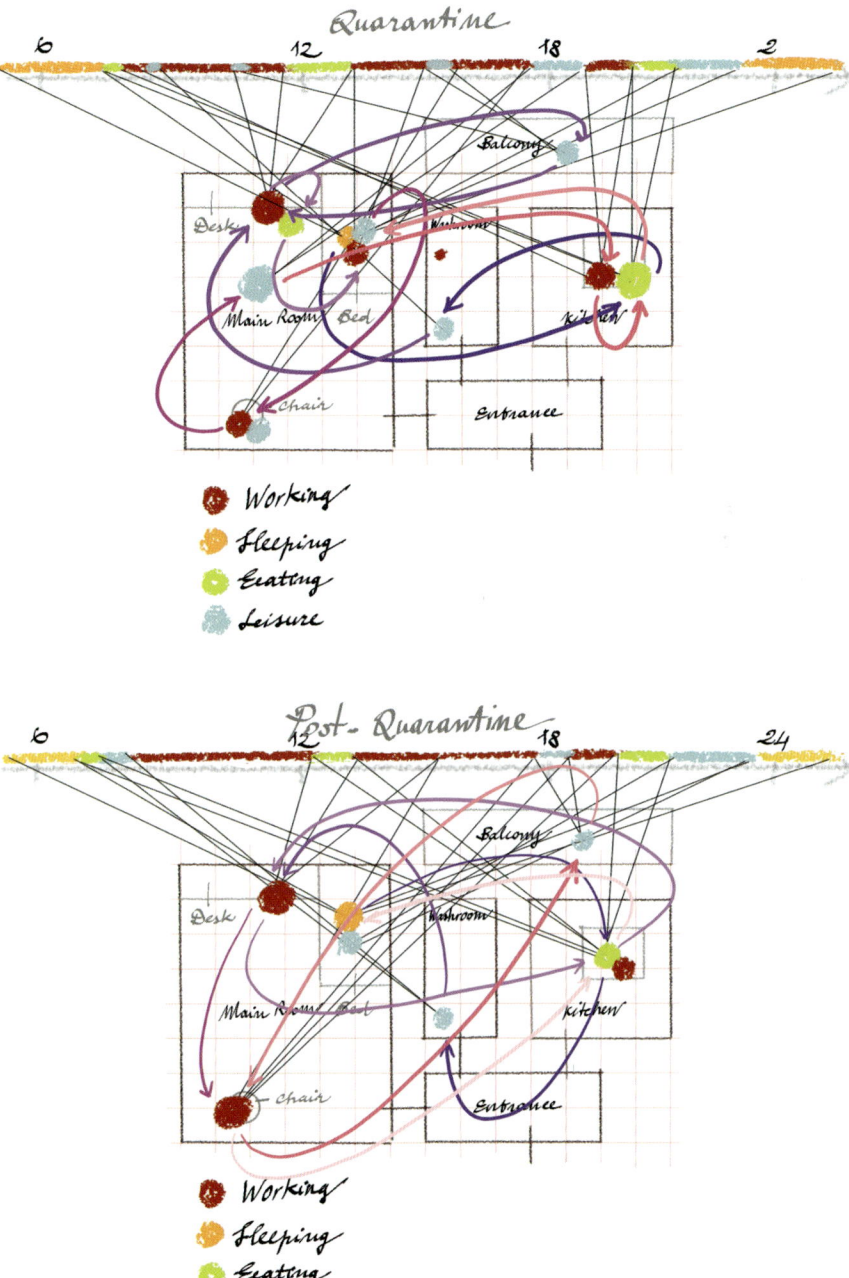

FIGURE 18.4a, b, c *Filippo's contribution to* The Domestic Body *workshop: Pre-quarantine, quarantine, and post-quarantine maps. Courtesy of Fondazione MAXXI.*

making ourselves similar to that something; and 'domestication' in the sense of building intimacy between our own and what is surrounding us, thus creating intimacy both as consciousness and care (Coccia 2021: 18).

One of our main observations associated with the concept of appropriation is the rediscovered richness of domestic leisure. The data analysis indicates towards the 'maximization' (quantitative) and the 'optimization' (qualitative) of leisure time. This prompted us to reflect on the nature of non-work time and on the qualification of the consumption of leisure time (Savorra 2017: 42). In order to maximize efficiency and optimize work time many apps have been developed in deep connection with the multiple new forms of non-work time, for example, time in which to speed up the process of buying groceries from the supermarket or remembering to take pauses when relaxing. Many people, mostly young single professionals, remarked not only on their constant search for optimization but also on a profound sense of alienation and exhaustion, which many researchers blamed on the dangerous tendency to apply the same productive criteria to both work and not-work time.

On the occasion of the 13th Milan Triennale, *The Triennale of Leisure Time* (1964), the corridor of captions organized by Massimo Vignelli warned of the danger posed in industrial civilization: 'free time could be organised by the same centres of power that controlled work time so that finally having fun had to mean being "integrated"' (Savorra 2017: 125). The extreme, and sometimes unconscious, consequence of this 'integration' of leisure and pleasure to the same productive standards is that *leisure* and *labour* collapse into the same time-space continuum, feeding a sense of alienation and frustration. This intensified during the lockdown as both leisure and labour were pursued very often through the same device, the computer.

However, many participants mentioned, inside the *leisure* category, activities often overlooked such as cooking, in a very performative sense, or almost forgotten activities such as bread making. The rediscovered importance of these making rituals was a direct consequence of the necessity to punctuate the continuum of time. As Byung-Chul Han notes, 'Rituals are in the *time* what home is in the *space*. They make time *habitable*, almost *walkable* like a home' (Byung-Chul Han 2021: 12). In a moment where every day could have been just an alienating repetition of the previous one, or a frustrating premonition of the following, the re-evaluation of rituals helped to mentally and physically map daily routines, escaping the passive repetition, to build something gradual, conscious and intense, thus *habitable* and *stable*.

Considerations and legacy of the project

The open-ended structure of *The Domestic Body* workshop enabled us (and hopefully will continue to lead us) to collect a series of case studies useful for tracing the continuing evolution of contemporary life. We are always trying to unlearn old spatial codes of the domestic interior and to define a new design alphabet – if not an architectural language – in order to better express and understand our true needs. The MAXXI Education team was concerned that asking people to share personal, delicate and potentially traumatic experiences would focus their attention less on space perception than on autobiographical narratives. But even in the most personal testimonies we found a valuable contribution to our study. The online version of this workshop (also selected as part of the 2021 Grand Tour of Palazzo Grassi) enabled us to reach a wider public thus expanding our research basin to completely different urban realities (such as Venice) and helping us to retrieve common trends notwithstanding huge anthropological and ethnographical diversity.

Note

1   For an overview of MAXXI's educational activities, see https://www.maxxi.art/educazione/ Io capisco solo l'arte antica. Educare, apprendere e interpretare al MAXXI, curated by Sofia Bilotta, Lida Branchesi, Walter Curzi, Edizioni MAXXI, Roma, 2018.

References

Allen, S. (1997), 'From Objects to Field', *Architectural Design*, 67: 5–6, Maggio-giugno1997, 24–31).
Ardner, S. (1993), 'The Partition of Space', J. Rendell, B. Penner and I. Borden (eds) (2000), *Gender, Space and Architecture*, 112–17, London: Routledge.
Benjamin, W. (1955), *Schirften*, Suhrkamp, Frankfurt am Main, 153.
Coccia, E. (2021), *Filisofia della casa. Lo spazio domestico e la felicità*, Torino: Einaudi, Stile libero Extra.
Colomina, B. (1997), *Sexuality and Space*, Princeton Papers on Architecture.
Fiorino, I. (2019), *La cucina. Storia culturale di un luogo domestico*, Turin, Einaudi: Einaudi.
Han, B.-Ch. (2021), *La scomparsa dei riti, Una topologia del presente*, Milan: Nottetempo, Milano, 12.

Janowicz, M. (2022), 'Kitchen Debate: Where Labour and Leisure Collide', In Kitchen + AR House: The Architectural Review Issue 1487, December 2021/January 2022.
Ponti, Gio (1957), 'Antica casa all'italiana', in Gio Ponti (ed.), *Amate l'architettura*, 106–8, Genova: Vitali e Ghianda.
Savorra, M. (2017), 'Intersections between Art, Communication and Design. The Triennale of Leisure Time', *Casabella*, 872(4): 40–56.
Tschumi, B. (1994), *The Manhattan Transcripts*, London: Academy Editions, 7–12.
Il corpo domestico, see https://www.maxxi.art/programmi-educativi/il-corpo-domestico

19

Interior Archipelago – postcards from our islands

Lois Weinthal, Patrick Macklin, Wen Liang and Alice Huang

The interior has never been given such attention as it has during Covid-19 as waves of lockdowns in the pandemic turned the gaze inwards. Near-sighted views of interior spaces have been magnified drawing into focus areas often gone unnoticed. New genres of interiors have formed within our environments, both physical and virtual, and the pandemic made us look inside like we never have before. Boundaries between interior, exterior and virtual were blended and influenced our thresholds into private and public spaces.

At a global scale, boundary lines delineating countries are represented as lines on a map, but, in reality, they are conceptual as the ground surface is continuous. At the scale of the interior, boundary lines are represented as walls and thresholds but are often underrecognized as having equivalency in meaning as global boundaries. Covid-19 redefined the conventions of boundaries at personal and global scales in addition to the virtual realm which brought forward new thresholds. As boundary lines between countries were closed, interior walls and thresholds emerged from latency and came to the foreground as stay-at-home orders meant spending more time inside. Familiar rooms were reassessed for new potential and rearranged to toggle between work and life or take on new quarantine quarters before being fully integrated into the interior. Walls emerged not just as micro boundary lines between rooms but as buffers between individuals and neighbours. Even closer, facemasks represented intimate boundaries that screen-off friends and families not in one's immediate bubble drawing into question where thresholds begin and end. Globally, lockdowns across regions brought intense and heightened senses of interiority – and not by one's own will, rather, from the need to keep oneself, family, friends, neighbours, co-workers and citizens safe. These altered interiors gained more visibility through everyday documentation as home, work and school overlapped, putting private interior envelopes on display as physical and virtual interiors merged.

The practice of interior design uses orthographic drawings such as floor plans, elevations and sections to convey spatial configurations that include furniture, objects, occupants and atmospheric conditions. Complementing these with greater spatiality and dimension are renderings, diagrams, collage, video, laser scans, and other experimental tools and mediums, the interior provides a more immersive view. These alternative forms of representation, coupled with a heightened sense of interiority, allow experimental views of interiors to transcend two-dimensional boundaries of orthographic projection. As software programmes brought people together for everyday events, representation became broader as views opened up to domestic interiors through digital lenses. These views became dynamic as time and the unexpected entered into one's camera. Coming into focus were views of interiors that were curated with plants, furniture and wall hangings, or un-curated as family members and pets made unexpected guest appearances. Sometimes the view was highly controlled through virtual backgrounds that would give way to digital glitches as ghost like appearances of body parts unravelled the inner working of artificial intelligence in competing for the camera's attention away from the face.

This dynamic collection of interior views and experiences provided the impetus for this project as a desire to record how everyday activities was affected during the pandemic. The limitations on travelling outside meant more activity was happening inside. Representation helped fill these voids and became the start of a collection of postcard-sized works acting as souvenirs during the pandemic for an international collaboration titled *Interior Archipelago – Postcards from Our Islands*. This collection reflects the domestic setting emphasizing interior moments, encounters online, shared experiences and desires missing from the everyday. Contributions showed how latent areas of the interior came to the foreground, such as mini-quarantine spaces at the entry of homes, areas carved out to accommodate new workspaces, a yoga mat on the floor, masks drying on lines and the rearrangement of furniture to make sub-rooms. These representations of the confined interior also reveal the desire for having space to oneself when constantly surrounded by others, or the need to have others around when constantly alone. The interior is not only defined by size, measurement, view, sound, smell and so on, but by the frequency of absence.

This context prompted a collaborative project between three interior design communities consisting of students, faculty and staff from The Glasgow School of Art in Scotland and Singapore (GSa); the School of Interior Design at Toronto Metropolitan University, Canada (TMU), and the Academy of Art and Design at Tsinghua University (AADTHU) in Beijing, China. The invitation sought to collect visual representations of views looking in and out of interiors, along with daily routines and disruptions to elicit details previously unnoticed. Individual moments of interiority gave hints to locations across the thirteen-hour time span. The framework used to collect these views was the dimension of a postcard with the option to include a brief narrative as is often found on the back side of a postcard. This framework was selected as the medium for this project because postcards allow a simple object to carry significant meaning and representation expressing time and location. As the gaze turned inwards, the postcard images revealed interruptions to daily routines, and with it, the ability to travel at will as journeys became limited from room to room. A website became the repository for these images creating a hub for international community engagement and shared interior views across the three interior design programmes. The website – *Interior Archipelago* – was launched in December 2020, just as the second wave of Covid-19 and the Delta variant was emerging. As postcard images were received, the website was updated along with narratives that accompanied the submissions, transforming the website into a shared digital album. Standard themes and categories traditionally used with postcard collecting did not represent this collection, rather, a multitude of themes appeared in a hybrid of reality, fiction, reflection and desire.

Postcards

Postcards reflect time and place and endure as souvenirs and objects of desire. Postcards were a starting point for this project since they represent travel, landmarks and narratives, all made possible by the ability to traverse borders both near and far. These characteristics were halted as travel restrictions were put in place at the start of the pandemic. As travel quickly declined, virtual forms of communication quickly increased, and an opportunity for sharing virtual postcards became evident. The standard postcard format was selected for this project because of its recognizable shape and framework with an image on one side and text on the other, making it conducive to translate into the digital realm.

A postcard is immediately identifiable in a pile of mail as it is slightly taller and more rigid than a standard number 10 envelope, yet the image and written message make it unique where no two are alike. This 'Principle of No-Two-Alike' is what Brenda Danet and Tamar Katriel identify in collecting as a 'tendency to seek out items that are the-same-but-different' (Danet and Katriel 1994: 227). The collection of postcards for *Interior Archipelago* aligns with the 'Principle of No-Two-Alike'. As no two interiors are alike, no two postcards are alike as the digital format allowed each to be uniquely customized. The pivot to digital was a way to give contributors freedom to work across all mediums and support the outcome of virtual sharing. This shift can be seen as a continuation of how postcard production has evolved over time to reflect updates to fabrication methods that include physical paper stock to finishing methods. In one example reaching back to the 1940s, linen-finished cards were commonly touched up to enhance features. These touched-up views pushed postcards into the realm of fantasy, where airbrush techniques removed unwanted shadows and distractions, and scenery was enhanced with the addition of dramatic clouds or sunsets (Baeder 1982: 20). This 'element of make-believe or fantasy, is present in many aspects of collecting' which Danet and Katriel term 'as-ifness', where collections have an ability to transport oneself to another time and place (Danet and Katriel 1994: 223). The liberty to alter images and to enter into the realm of fantasy is evident in the collection of postcards for *Interior Archipelago* as a means of expressing desires limited by the pandemic.

Images transport viewers to other times and places, 'as-if' the pandemic was not a limitation. Danet and Katriel refer to Susan Stewart's writing on collectables to convey the objects reframing to create new worlds. Stewart writes,

> The collection is a form of art as play, a form involving the reframing of objects within a world of attention and manipulation of context. Like other forms of art, its function is not the restoration of context of origin, but rather the creation of a new context, a context standing in a metaphorical, rather than a contiguous relation to the world of everyday life.
>
> (Stewart 1993: 151–2)

The postcard submissions for *Interior Archipelago* shifted the everyday pre-made, mass-produced postcard into the digital realm where contributors could document their existing world or create new worlds using digital tools not limited by location, time or gravity. New views to interiors and beyond were created prompted by the pandemic, where limitations informed the creative process. Referring to Stewart's quote, new contexts were created using the pandemic as a re-envisioning of the everyday made evident in the postcards.

Collections

Designing the display of collectibles requires bringing the collection to the foreground, while the method of display takes a background supporting role. Methods of display outside of museums and galleries include Kunstschrank, collector's cabinets, cabinet of curiosity, vitrines, photo albums and scrapbooks. More recently, the emergence of non-fungible tokens (NFTs) as artwork heightened the digital realm during the pandemic as an alternative form of display outside of traditional physical formats (Thaddeus-Johns 2021). The *Interior Archipelago* website housed the postcard images where contributors and visitors could openly access the collection. Submission requirements allowed for each contributor to share up to five images with a format size of A6 postcard 148 x 105 mm, 300 dpi, in portrait or landscape. Prompts were provided with the submission requirements to elicit imagery that could be virtual, physical, sequential, encounters, meeting places, rooms and the body to name a few. In addition to the images, contributors were asked to provide their affiliated school location, name and brief description of their imagery if they desired.

Over a four-month period, the postcard collection grew from fifty to a hundred and on to 300. The website, as a digital photo album, allowed our three design communities to share images from travels within the domestic realm and immediate surroundings, reflecting the real and surreal. Students in China could capture a moment of an interior from another student in Scotland, while a student in Canada could view an interior moment from a student in China. Submissions represented a variety of creative methods, ranging from black and white photography to textiles, collage, 3D scanning and still animation. Accompanying descriptions provided moments of reflection on the contributor's gaze. At times, these descriptions moved into personal narratives revealing desires and confinement invoked by the pandemic, such as the following narrative by Ruilin Luo, a student at AADTHU:

> This group of photos shows the scene of my mom and me visiting grandma [and] grandpa during the epidemic. At that time, I had just returned home from a certain risk area. In order to protect each other, we simplified the usual visiting ceremony. We didn't enter the door, didn't speak, and used simple and short body language to convey emotions. The different personalities of grandma and grandfather are also reflected in these body movements. They are trying their best to shorten the distance between us. The carpet representing safe access has also become a measure of our distance. No matter what form relatives get together, emotions can be conveyed.

Changes made to visiting family and friends emerged as one of many pandemic-related themes in the postcard collection. Seen as a whole, the collection uses the interior as the starting point to reveal how Covid-19 caused ordinary activities that take place on the interior to change or be suspended. Visuals and brief narratives offered insight into these newfound complexities.

Pandemic interior-scapes

Contributions prompted contributors to look inwards at rooms, objects, routines and experiences that altered work, school and leisure. Views took the form of quiet moments in a kitchen with early morning sun, laundry hanging on a balcony to dry and fantasy-like imagery that reminded viewers of disruptions to the norm. Within these views, items specific to Covid-19 could be found such as masks, hand sanitizer and gloves. Shared sentiments came to the foreground across contributions, helping gain a multicultural understanding of interiority by virtually travelling through one another's postcards. Recurring themes appeared across images, and while one theme does not take precedent over another, the collection can be viewed through three primary topics: State of being, spatial configurations and representation.

State of being can be understood through one's physical and psychological well-being. These were made evident in postcard images where a single figure is the focus, often in moments of contemplation (Figure 19.1). Other times, quiet moments were highlighted by everyday acts typically unnoticed, but now the focus, such as washing fruits and vegetables in a kitchen sink. The sentiment, *Wish You Were Here*, often embedded in travel narratives was expressed as the main focus of a postcard, drawing attention to the desire to travel now halted by the pandemic.

Spatial configurations brought the interior to the foreground and included interior envelopes as a container for life inside and atmospheric conditions. This included heightened views through thresholds from one room to another, and from inside to outside, as lockdowns and stay-at-home orders redefined the gaze. Intimate moments are revealed such as a cat looking out a window, neighbouring apartments across a courtyard, a sliver of light in a staircase, exterior light illuminating everyday objects such as a coffee pot and a balcony with masks hanging to dry (Figure 19.2).

The previous examples are made possible through different forms of representation. Images were generated with traditional methods such as photography and collage, while other images (Figure 19.3) were highly rendered through digital technology using 3D scanning and software programmes to produce altered realities. Standard drawing methods, such

INTERIOR ARCHIPELAGO – POSTCARD FROM OUR ISLANDS 253

FIGURE 19.1a, b, c, d *top left: Liu Meiming (AADTHU), One Day; bottom left: Joanna Rosado (GSA), The table- my universe centre; top right: Ruixue Wang, (AADTHU); bottom right: Daniela Nicole Ellero (TMU).*

as floor plans, provided a base upon which site-specific information could be mapped, such as travel from room to room throughout the day or as a base for redrawing in a textile weave. Familiar objects continued to be found in images, such as masks hanging to dry, hand sanitizer and quarantine quarters. Supporting these representations were varying lengths of narratives, similar to the writing on the back of a postcard. One contributor gave visualization to these activities taking place on the interior, noting: 'People practice swimming at home using skateboards, TV movements or visual effects on chairs or beds to simulate swimming pools,' shared by BeiJia Li at AADTU. One example summarized many sentiments with: 'The outbreak of coronavirus changed my lifestyle. Washing hands became a daily ceremony of "worship", and masks

FIGURE 19.2a, b, c, d *top left: Spatial Configurations, Jiao Zha (AADTHU); bottom left: Dennis Lum, (GSA); top right: Alice Huang, (TMU), Ritual Artifacts: Laundry; bottom right: Linghang Cai, (AADTHU).*

became the decoration of handle' as noted by Ying Chang at the Glasgow School of Art. Everyday activities that were normally done as second nature, such as washing hands, were re-evaluated through this new lens, transforming the act into a heightened ritual.

Reflections on the near past

Throughout the pandemic, normal routines of work and life were interrupted and this collaborative project sought to bring a community of creatives together to fill gaps of time spent indoors through making. Each participating

INTERIOR ARCHIPELAGO – POSTCARD FROM OUR ISLANDS

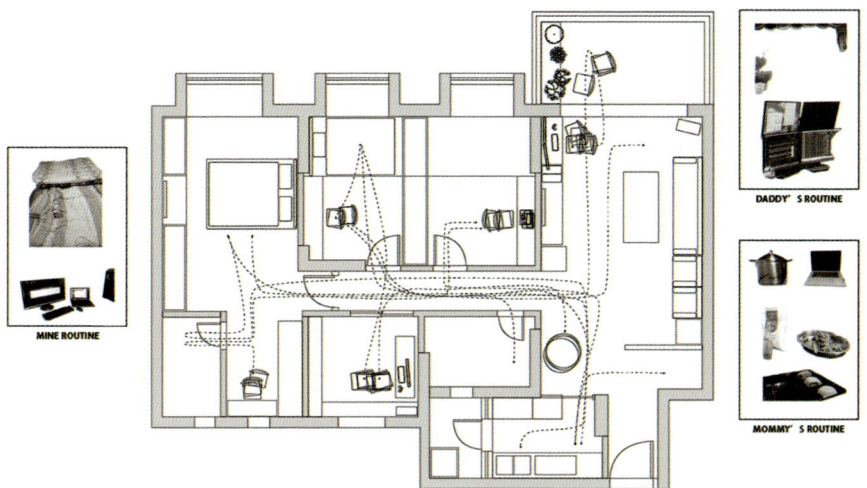

FIGURE 19.3a, b, c, d *top: Representation, Shuxin Yin (AADTHU); middle left: David Ross (GSA); middle right: Paul Armand Georgescu (GSA); bottom: Xuefei Chen (AADTHU).*

design programme was in a different phase of the pandemic when *Interior Archipelago* initially began in fall 2020. The Glasgow School of Art and the Interior Design programme at Toronto Metropolitan University were in the first phases of lockdown, while the Academy of Art and Design at Tsinghua University was emerging from the first lockdown and reopening, allowing everyone to see each other in person with masks. The postcard contributions reflected these variations where some postcards were constructed during phases of lockdown, while others were constructed post-lockdown. Some were generated at the speed of a photograph, others over the course of a day or two. Not only did personal life and work change during the pandemic, but a shift in the representation of interiors and the documentation of daily life.

In autumn 2021, the AADTHU took the project out of the virtual repository and started printing the postcard images so students, faculty and staff could see them in the school every day (Figure 19.4). Onlookers viewed the collection together in person, which prompted comments between one another, such as the following:

To see inside the homes of others. After all, rarely do we get to see another person's bedroom, toy collections, cats or dogs at home, etc.

To hold the postcard in your hand. The paper used to print is very similar to postcards, they are just like a real postcard. When you hold one in your hand, you have a compulsion to send it out. I can't help but choose my favorites when I am in front of them.

The images gave onlookers peeks into what other people's homes looked like, allowing for a comparison among the three communities. This insight also acted as a form of reflection and what one does in their revised daily routes, such as overheard of one student saying to another at the AADTHU exhibition: 'I should have done something like that when I was in lockdown.'

These reflections have asked us to rethink our relationship between the physical and digital in interior design, not just in the making of postcard images, but in the everyday and how they shape the experience of interiors. The pivot to virtual platforms for work and school led to new virtual backgrounds inserted as digital wallpapers. Off-screen, interiors were curated and altered to support more time spent indoors. This led to the resurgence of hand-craft and time-consuming activities less present in daily pre-pandemic life, such as sewing, knitting, pickling and bread baking. The postcard collection in *Interior Archipelago* documents these everyday activities and acts as a record of this time. Even the act of seeing the postcards in person brought a sense of slowness, giving onlookers time to absorb the imagery as opposed to the quickness of scrolling through a website. For now, only the AADTHU has had a physical in-person exhibition. At the time of this writing, we are

FIGURE 19.4a, b, c *Images of the Exhibition of* Interior Archipelago *at Academy of Art and Design, Tsinghua University. Photographs by Wen Liang.*

moving through another phase of a variant, Omicron, and like the images and narratives in the postcards, the project also responds to daily changes where virtual viewing is the norm. This project continues as a record of this time bringing a community together virtually when needed and slowly migrates to in-person when allowed.

References

Baeder, J. (1982), *Gas, Food and Lodging*, New York: Abbeville Press.

Danet, B. and T. Katriel (1994), 'No Two Alike: Play and Aesthetics in Collecting', in S. M. Pearce (ed.), *Interpreting Objects and Collections*, 221–39, London: Routledge.

Stewart, S. (1993), *On Longing: Narratives of the Miniature, the Gigantic, the Souvenir, the Collection*, Durham: Duke University Press.

Thaddeus-Johns, J. (2021), *What Are NFTs, Anyway? One Just Sold for $69 Million*, New York Times. https://www.nytimes.com/2021/03/11/arts/design/what-is-an-nft.html

20

Stay Home – rapid response collecting project at the Museum of the Home

Danielle Patten

The Museum of the Home is based in Hoxton, East London. We reveal stories of home life, past, present and future, sparking empathy, debate and understanding. The concept of home has the power to connect people: it is universally relevant and simultaneously deeply personal. Our vision is to inspire everyone to explore the meaning of home through our exhibitions, displays, programming and online content. We reveal objects, artworks, images and testimonies from behind closed doors to encourage and challenge different ways of thinking about domestic life today.

When the UK government sent out the mandate to 'Stay at Home' on 23 March 2020, the museum was compelled to record this once in a lifetime shift in our home lives. The museum's vision is to reveal and rethink the ways we live, to enable us to live better together. We wanted to put this into practice when the coronavirus pandemic took hold, and so we embarked upon the Stay Home project. Stay Home is a rapid response digital collecting project, started in direct response to the coronavirus lockdown. We sought to document how coronavirus has reshaped the way we live and explore the uncertain future of home life.

This was the first time the museum had launched a collecting project as an immediate response to societal changes as they happened and will therefore inform the future of rapid response collecting model for the Museum of the Home. We wanted to record people's experiences as they were happening, so it was important to get the call out to action to the public as soon as possible.

We were able to jump into action almost immediately due to our pre-existing Documenting Homes archive which we used as a blueprint for Stay Home.

The Documenting Homes collection records people's everyday experiences of home. It allows people to share photographs and testimony about their past and present homes, recording home life dating back to the early 1900s. The archive brings to light hidden or overlooked stories of home and enhances our understanding of it. We have been collecting in this way since 2007, and the collection has been used to enhance galleries and exhibitions, and has also been utilized by researchers and artists. Documenting Homes is constantly expanding and includes a wide range of people's stories of home, told in their own words. It currently contains over 8,000 items. However, the museum's focus has been to further diversify the collection so that it is more reflective of the demographic and experiences of people across the UK, and to give a voice to those who have previously been underrepresented within the museum's collections and displays.

The Stay Home collection builds on our existing Documenting Homes collection, bringing to life the themes of the museum and representing our ambition to collect a breadth of materials showing the diversity of today's society while recording the impact of historical events like the coronavirus pandemic on our lives and living spaces.

The collecting process

The Stay Home project asks people to share their experiences of lockdown and the pandemic by answering seven questions and submitting photographs, videos or voice recordings. People also have the option to submit lockdown diaries to record daily changes and struggles. Questions were devised to be as open as possible, but to make people feel comfortable answering, we provided some prompts for the open-ended questions. The main questions were as follows:

1. Please describe your home; include information like where you live, the type of property, whether it is where you usually live, if you live alone or with anyone else, if so who?
2. In what ways has the coronavirus pandemic changed the way you use your home?
3. How do you feel about your home? How have these feelings changed?
4. How does staying at home affect your relationships?
5. What do you appreciate most about your home? What do you find frustrating?

STAY HOME – RAPID RESPONSE COLLECTING PROJECT

6 How has lockdown changed your habits or routines at home? What do you have more or less time for? Have you done anything new?

7 How is your sense of home affected by your neighbours or those living nearby?

Participants were able to submit their responses to these questions, or submit audio or video responses. We wanted to make the process as accessible as possible to ensure that a wide range of participants would take part. We consulted with people from the museum's community who had access requirements, to make the form as usable as possible and did several stages of user testing.

This was the first time the museum had used a form embedded in our website. The easy-to-share format allowed us to reach many more people than we had previously. A means of reaching people easily and quickly was especially important as the channels we would usually use, such as youth groups, community centres and health services, were closed or were diverting their resources towards the crisis.

Perhaps due to the anonymity of the online form provided, people have responded candidly in their submissions, revealing their struggles and the ways they have adapted to the new 'normal'. They have shared how they have learned new skills, made new connections, but also struggled with the isolation

FIGURE 20.1 *Lahiru's family exercising in their living room, 2020. Courtesy of the Museum of the Home.*

and economic hardships caused by the pandemic. The project has given us a compelling insight into the role of home during the pandemic – how it has been a sanctuary for some and a place of isolation for others (Figure 20.1).

> *My sofa is now the shape of me, as if we are merging into one. The silence is deafening.* – Alex

> *Life has been turned on its head by the pandemic and lockdown. Our home has now turned into the multi-functional centre of our lives. We work, cook, exercise, play, hang out with friends and relatives (virtually) all in the same space. Our relationships have got stronger. We have had time to spend properly with one another without rushing off here and there.* – Lahiru

Experiences from the collection

While the pandemic has been a challenging time for people, it has also been a chance for some to rebalance their lives, learn new hobbies and reconnect with loved ones.

Some people who took part in the project have shared some of the positive effects the pandemic has had on their home lives.

Since April 2020, people from across the UK, and further, have contributed over 500 submissions. Through these questionnaires, photographs, oral recordings and diaries, we have been recording the varied and changing impact of coronavirus on homes. Together the material creates a picture of the dynamics of home life during the pandemic, how we related to each other, how home spaces evolved and how neighbourhoods, local communities and digital platforms were drawn upon to help people stay connected when other support systems were inaccessible.

Chantelle, who lives with her two daughters in a flat in London, shared how she has struggled with the lack of space in her home, and being cut off from friends and family, but how she developed painting as a creative outlet and used it to transform her home into a space of artistic expression (Figure 20.2):

> *I have rediscovered my talents – my front room looks like an art gallery/ photoshoot room. It's made me realise how much my confidence has grown over the years looking at my work. It's feeling very artsy right now where as I changed from that years ago to being a mum. I painted a wall mural which was a big risk but it happened and I'm proud of it.*

For others, the lockdown was transformative for behaviours as well as spaces. Mrs B lives with her husband and two children in Leicestershire. The family

FIGURE 20.2 *Chantelle painting her mural, 2020. Courtesy of the Museum of the Home.*

have used the pandemic to learn life skills and adapt their time to reshape their experiences in their homes:

> *We love our home, it is our safe place but realise it's the people in it that are far more important. My son is severely autistic, he has taken some time to adjust. Our home is now his classroom. He has learnt to bake, to clean and to develop lots of life skills. He would run and hide from the vacuum and the electric mixer because of the noise, it caused us so many problems. But now part of his new routine he bakes cupcakes every day (using an electric mixer) and he helps me vacuum both massive positives to come out of the pandemic.*

Karl, a student living in a shared house, told us that during the lockdown he relied on his housemates to help with the feeling of isolation and the hardship of being separated from his partner:

> *It has changed our mental health and we are all laughing to avoid crying. We treat our home differently now, before the crisis we wouldn't dream*

of smoking weed inside the house but now we are smoking everyday. My boyfriend is in the Netherlands and due to border lockdown we are separated until this is all over. We love each other very much so we miss each other dearly and feel a part of our soul is missing. The relationship inside the house is of friendship, everybody is trying to make sure every member of the household is holding up as well as can be. We are all suffering in isolation but there is solidarity to that.

The feelings of isolation that Karl mentions surface in many of the submissions. Like Karl, people commented on how they changed their use of domestic spaces, and the behaviours within them, to find new ways to stay connected. Unsurprisingly, one of the most common strands that came out in the material was the impact of not being able to see loved ones, and how in some cases the absence has changed how people feel about their homes. Gareth emotionally describes how the absence of loved ones, particularly his grandchildren, had dramatically changed his sense of home and how he feels in his domestic spaces: 'The grandchildren have moved to their Dads (they are normally here seven nights in fourteen). The absence of the grandchildren echoes everywhere. We sometimes sit in their rooms sending love and hugs.'

It is not just the absence of family that has impacted people's sense of home but also people's wider networks, communities and neighbourhoods. The pandemic has changed our perceived idea of home and re-established boundaries and thresholds of home community and neighbourhoods (MacNeill 2021: 32). The shift to home working, home schooling and even medical appointments from home has blurred the private and public and changed how people perceive their home spaces.

Of course, the impact of the pandemic did not hit people equally. Young people, migrants, low-income households and those who rely on the care of others outside of the home were particularly vulnerable (Byrne 2020: 352). The diversity of experiences submitted to the collection has highlighted the inaccuracy of the often-used line, 'we are all in this together'. While some flourished under the restrictions and new way of living, others struggled or were unable to adapt (Sobande 2020: 1035).

Christine describes how the lack of contact with her networks had a negative impact on her well-being: 'I am single. Have no close family, but normally volunteer and so all that has come to a stop as I am 70. I miss serving others and hugging people. I can't meet with anyone at the moment, and this is detrimental to my wellbeing. I miss so much being with people.'

Alex (age 5) describes very sweetly the situation many people are feeling of spending more time with close family but missing a wider social circle: 'We spend more time together. It is good spending more time with my brother. I miss my best friend Jake.'

Many people have relished unexpected moments of coming together, such as the weekly 'Clap for Carers', an event taking place on Thursdays in the UK during lockdown when people stepped out of their homes or stood at their windows to applaud NHS workers. People have shared how the weekly ritual was a way to connect with neighbours; participant Onjali commented that 'my street is full of families from all walks of life – English, Chinese, Somali, Pakistani, Indian, Bengali, Turkish, Nigerian, Kenyan, Polish, French. The recent Thursday night "Clap for the NHS and Key Workers" events have been lovely in bringing us together.' For others, the weekly event has been a way to mark the passing of time. Participant G describes how her son born shortly before the lockdown 'has spent half of his life hearing us clap for key workers each week'. The supposed coming together of people led many in the media to draw comparison to a wartime spirit of camaraderie and unity in the goal to fight, in this case, an invisible enemy (Pettitt 2021: 2). There have been criticisms of how this rhetoric has been politicized, and how it excludes the experiences of marginalized groups (Figure 20.3).

For many, these relationships, and connections beyond the home, with neighbours and local communities, have been an essential lifeline. Julie

FIGURE 20.3 *G holding her son to the window behind a sign saying thank you to all key workers. 2020. Courtesy of the Museum of the Home.*

lives alone in a maisonette in east London, she caught the virus in the spring and relied upon her neighbour support to get her through her illness: 'I had coronavirus symptoms and my neighbour Raju left me home-made south Asian meals, and items of food, newspapers and magazines during my convalescent. Other friends from nearby dropped off food and goodies too. Others called and/or sent text messages.' Others like Jake, who lives on a council estate in London, have taken it upon themselves to provide care for those in need, 'during lockdown we've been organising food parcels for vulnerable residents who have slipped through the net. We make a point of speaking to people on the street. It was already a friendly road. It has become more so.'

The lockdown also caused a shift in community relationships, some of which were hostile before the pandemic began. Clair lives alone in a home she has lived in for her whole life, she is transgender and has had conflict with hostile neighbours in the past:

More remarkable is the change that's come over my other neighbour the one who organised that police raid on my house amongst other things ... three weeks ago during the 8pm clapping session he talked to me quite normally as if the past 18 years had never occurred. I was speechless, surprised, as if the past between us never happened. Last week he even waved to me as he drove past and it now my village feels like a good place to live.

Boundaries and thresholds within the home have also shifted as people have been forced to reshape their lives to be centred on their homes. People showed how they reused once overlooked spaces, rooms or furniture and cherished outside spaces available to them. As participant, Daughter no. 1, described: 'Our home has become messier! Because of the new animal arrivals and the three of us spending all our time in the garden we've found our indoor and outdoor spaces have begun to merge, which is not always a good thing when you find a chicken on the sofa!' However, some households needed to create new thresholds within the home to keep family members safe. Anna has found her home divided when her husband, a surgeon, had to work throughout the height of the pandemic. The family zoned off their basement with a sign, 'Do not enter the basement, always ask mum first'. Anna recalls: 'When the covid crisis struck my husband decided to move down to the basement and socially distance himself from the rest of us because I have moderate asthma. His work is extremely dangerous.'

Considerations and the legacy of the project

When starting the project, we were conscious that many of the submissions may prompt people to revisit potentially upsetting and traumatic experiences, so we had to carefully consider the risk in asking people to share them with us. We drew upon the wealth of material available around conducting ethical contemporary collecting such as Museum Association's guideline to collecting ethically, sustainably and responsibly during a crisis. To ensure that we were supporting those who needed it we provided details of someone at the museum they could contact if they had wanted any further information or if they needed assistance. We also give participants the option to withdraw their material at any time.

As the project has progressed, we have contacted all participants who took part to make sure they are comfortable with how their stories are being used. We remain in contact with participants, contacting them with regular updates on the project and to encourage further engagement. Through this process, we are building relationships with participants and hope that they will continue to engage with us in future. We hope that taking part in the project can also help people process events and feel connected in a troubling time. As we move the project forward, building long-lasting and meaningful relationships with participants is crucial. We want to ensure that they feel that they have been involved in something relevant and useful. Meg, a participant said: 'I've lived in Dalston for more than a decade so having to do something with your Museum means a lot to me! I'm so proud of myself to do something meaningful!'

We hope this collection will inform a new understanding of home. Each submission provides a snapshot of experiences during the pandemic and together they build a picture of how our homes have dramatically shifted and been reimagined. Within the museum it has been used in our newly redeveloped Home Galleries, which look at the variety of ways we make and experience home and questions some of the assumptions around the idea of home.

What next?

The museum, in partnership with Queen Mary University London (QMUL), National Museums Liverpool, Royal Geographical Society, University of Liverpool and Birkbeck University, has been funded by the Arts & Humanities Research Council to look at how the pandemic has changed our experiences and understanding of home. Through this collaboration, Stay Home Stories, we are exploring how factors such as type of housing, work or education status, age, gender, faith and ethnicity has impacted on people, and what insights the Stay Home material can provide about future relationships to home.

To disseminate the research and findings of the Stay Home Stories project we commissioned artist Alaa Alsaraji to produce an artwork, *Our Home Our Stories*, at the Museum of the Home. The artwork draws on the Stay Home material and responds to how the instruction to 'Stay Home' has prompted

FIGURE 20.4 *Our Home Our Stories display by Alaa Alsaraji, 2021. Courtesy of the Museum of the Home.*

people to adopt their own rituals of care within lockdowns. Through her creative practice Alsaraji aims to explore themes, such as belonging and reimagining space and community. In the display, Alsaraji invites audiences to debate, share, write, draw and connect within the artwork, to help create an understanding of how we can build compassionate homes together. Alsaraji weaves people's experiences during the Coronavirus pandemic into the fabric of the display to build a picture how the role of homes has changed (Figure 20.4).

Conclusion

Stay Home is helping the museum to achieve its purpose which is to be a living, breathing resource that responds, adapts and reflects the changing ways that society, communities and individuals are relating to home in the broadest sense of the word. As time moves on from the initial lockdown, and as we navigate what the 'new normal' looks and feels like, Stay Home will allow us to be reactive to the changing needs of our visitors, participants and our immediate community.

The focus of the museum and Stay Home Stories project is to understand the multiple experiences of the lockdown through the material. How we represent and display inequality as a museum and how we discuss this as a society. In the context of the Stay Home Collection, we want to actively think about how we include and understand the stories of people from racialized, gendered and classed backgrounds. Therefore, a collaborative practice is crucial to how we engage with the Stay Home Collection. We continue to work with project participants, academic researchers, creative practitioners as well as museum workers that want to inspire different meanings and representations of home and challenge established notions of home life during the coronavirus pandemic.

Acknowledgements

The Stay Home project is funded by the Esmee Fairbairn Collections Fund and Arts and Humanities Research Council (AHRC) as part of the UK Research and Innovation rapid response to Covid-19. All the material related to the Stay Home rapid response collecting project at the Museum of the Home, including the quotes and images used in this chapter, can be found at https://stayhomestories.co.uk.

References

Byrne, M. (2020), 'Stay Home: Reflections on the Meaning of Home and the Covid-19 Pandemic', *Irish Journal of Sociology*, 28(3): 351–5.

MacNeill, A. (2021), *The Changing Boundaries of Home during COVID-19*, MSc diss., Leiden: Leiden University. https://hdl.handle.net/1887/3217269

Pettitt, J., ed. (2021), *Covid-19, the Second World War, and the Idea of Britishness*, Oxford, UK: Peter Lang.

Sobande, F. (2020), '"We're All in This Together": Commodified Notions of Connection, Care and Community in Brand Responses to COVID-19', *European Journal of Cultural Studies*, 23(6), December: 1033–7.

Index

Abel, Lothar
   Das gesunde, behagliche und billige Wohnen (Healthy, Comfortable and Inexpensive Living) 36
   no rules approach 37
The Academy of Art and Design at Tsinghua University (AADTHU) in Beijing, China 249, 251, 253–7
Adorno, Theodor 201
The Adventures of Ozzie and Harriet (1952–66) television show 214
advertising campaigns for cleaning products (British and US) 182
   #cleaninfluencers 190
   Dettol (Reckitt Benckiser) 183–6
   diversity 182, 185–6
   environmental crisis 187–9
   Finish
      digital short stories 187, 190
      #SkipTheRinse 187–90
   Green Orientalism 184, 190
   Join the Millions 188
   model minority 184, 189
   National Geographic 183, 187–90
   Persil (Unilever) 183–6
   Proctor & Gamble 182, 186–90
   racism/racialized themes 184–6, 188–90
   #tradwives 187, 190
   visual/aural vocabulary 184, 187, 189
   white baby mascot (Fairy) 186–8
aesthetic experiences of staying at home 75–6
   expectations about objects 84
   material changes/adjustments/reorganization 77–82
   rechoreographing 83
   re-materialization 82–4
Africa/African 133, 135, 212
air purification 2–3, 37, 42. *See also* houseplants
alienation 63, 127–8, 133–4, 136, 164, 244
Allen, Stan, fields 235
Alsaraji, Alaa, *Our Home Our Stories* 268–9
amateur dance 15–17
Anderson, Benedict, imagined communities 210, 215
animism 187
anti-Asian racism 182, 184. *See also* race/racism
appropriation, spatial 4, 62, 65, 67, 70, 92–3, 104, 109, 242, 244
architecture/architectural 38–9, 55, 76, 90–2, 95–6, 97 n.1, 101–4, 108–10, 113, 115–17, 122–3, 156, 167, 170, 177, 195, 200, 212, 233–5, 245
Ardner, Shirley 237
artefacts 83–4, 159, 211, 215–16
arts-for-wellness programme 63–4
arts therapy programme for children 4
Asia/Asians 135, 183–5, 212
Asian Americans 184, 188
Australia 2, 5–6, 114, 123, 128
   Flemington and North Melbourne towers, Melbourne 6, 128, 134–6
Austria 2
   Austrian Association for Housing Reform and Housing Hygiene 40
   Vienna (*see* Vienna, Austria)
autonomy 66, 88, 90, 94, 97

INDEX

Bachelard, Gaston 62, 127, 156–7
Bangladesh 5, 129, 134, 136
    Cox's Bazar 6, 128–31, 135
Bartke, Raphael 171
Bartolacci, Roberto, Small pleasures of life 197
Bateson, Gregory 211
Baudelaire, Charles 7
Bed-in for Peace (Lennon and Yoko) 202
Belgian National Broadcasting Institute (NIR/INR) 14–15, 21
Belgium 2–3, 13, 16
    economic crisis in (1930s) 14–15
    lay movement choirs in 16
    radio fitness classes (see Daan, Lea [1906–95])
    socio-theatrical mass events 15–16
Benjamin, Walter 241
Bennett, Tony 202
BEST (Advice Bureau for Interior Design and Housing Hygiene of the Austrian Association for Housing Reform) 40
#BlackLivesMatter protests 182, 184
body culture movement 3, 14–15, 36, 103
Bourgeois, Louise 224
The Breach: Transparency, Intimacy and Privacy exhibition (Heindl) 200
British domestic hygiene reforms 51
British National Archives 151 n.2
Bülow-Hübe, Sigrun 236
bungalows, residents in (1920s) 213
Burke, Enda 162–3
    Homebound with My Parents series 163

Campbell, Joseph 68
Capp Street Project gallery, San Francisco 200
Catholic/Catholicism 16, 149–50, 151 n.7, 163. See also Protestant
Chen, Gina Masullo 210
Cherington, Paul 214
childcare 1, 37, 89, 175, 182–3, 231
children, spaces for
    case study 63–4
    EPR wellness programme (objectives of) 61–2, 64
    create 65–8
    explore 68–9
    methods 64–5
    reduce 69
    fictional space/narratives 62, 68
    imagination (representation) 62
    mental-health (over-crowded housing during lockdown) 63
    play spaces for 62
    reverie (daydreaming) 62, 69
    scenographic spaceship 66–7, 69, 71
    space helmet (astronaut's costume) 67–9
    telehealth programme 4, 61, 64, 67, 70
child therapy model. See arts therapy programme for children
China 2, 5
    architects during pandemic in 101–2
    architecture studio office (drawing) 105, 109
    drawing domesticity 108–10
    growing home 104–8
    living by interface (drawing) 107
    minimal dormitory room 103–4, 109
    tale of two apartments (drawing) 106, 109
    Chinese American 227
cholera 2, 51–2
Chollet, Mona, *Chez-soi* 87
chronic illness 3, 129, 134
class 3, 8, 18, 38–40, 198, 211, 234–5. See also gender/gendered space; race/racism
#cleanergate 181
cleanliness 8, 148–9, 191
Coccia, Emanuele, *Filosofia della Casa* 242
cohabitation 92, 242
Colombia 2, 27
    El Mochuelo museum, Montes de María region 115, 117
    restorative and transitional justice 114–15
    Truth Commission (case study of Alejandra Gutiérrez Gómez) 6, 113–17

INDEX

architecture of 115–17
   in Bogotà (design by *DUCON Disenos y espacios productivos*) 115–16, 118–19
   caseta/kiosk 113–14, 116–17, 121, 123
   cuarto (place of work) 114, 118, 120–3
   gendered space of alternative justice 120–2
   Peace Accord 115
   public interior into private room 119–20
   shift to working from home 118–20
   spatial tools of reconciliation 122–3
   vernacular traditions 113
Colomina, Beatriz 239
   analysis of Bed-in for Peace (John and Yoko) 202
   The Split Wall: Domestic Voyeurism 199–200
comfort/cosiness 3–4, 8, 15, 35–8, 40, 43–4, 51, 65, 67, 93, 131, 175, 188, 196, 198, 211, 231, 234
commercial spaces 2
commodity/commodification 177
communal space 67, 104, 109, 118, 129, 134
communication 9, 22, 27, 64–5, 101, 104, 109, 173, 190, 195, 211, 234, 250
   radio as mass medium 14–15 (*see also* radio)
   spatial relationships 65
   technology 13–14, 26
confined spaces 1, 4, 7, 51, 88, 134, 155, 174, 176, 202, 224, 231, 248
   well-being in 40–4
confinement 7, 38, 62–6, 71, 159, 196–9, 202, 251
Confucian/Confucianism 4, 57
   well-being and hygienic homes 50–2
consumer goods/consumerism 184, 186, 213, 215
The Cosby Show television show (1984–92) 214

Coslet, Anghelina, *The Speaking House* show 200
Cox, Rosie 191 n.1
Croft, Thomas 161
Crombez, Thomas 15
curation of exhibition 8, 201, 209–11
   self-curation (in Zoom room) 209, 215–19
cyber metamorphosis 177
cyberspace 26, 31, 33

Daan, Lea (1906–95), radio fitness classes (1935–1940) 3–4, 13–15, 20
   Body Culture and Amateur Dance 17
   and body movement (to music) 13, 15–19, 22
   Collection City of Antwerp 17–18
   cover for Wie Turnt er mee… met het N.I.R? programme brochure 19
   dance-sound-word 17
   female gymnast in action (programme brochure) 20–1
   icosahedron 16
   vs. Woestyn 18–20
Dafa, Nensi, *I See You* exhibition 200
Dameron, Delaney 221–2, 226, 228, 230, 232 n.1
dance-based fitness class. *See* Zumba fitness class
Danet, Brenda 250
Davis, Angela 217–18
Davis, H., *Living Over the Store: Architecture and local urban life* 102
de Chirico, Giorgio 156
Dec-net IKEA 170. *See also* IKEA
de-individualized space 104
de Jongh, Eddy 147
Delaherche, Auguste 229
Delgado, R. 182
de Muynck, Gust 15
Dettol (Reckitt Benckiser), campaigns of 183–6
Dicker-Brandeis, Friedl 40
digital interfaces 209, 216
digital shopping/online ordering 215
digital spaces 61, 157, 215, 218

digital technology 101, 196, 252
  and IKEA 170–3, 177
  and privacy 107–8
digitization 177
disciplinary society 202
diversification 236, 238–9
diversity 8, 30, 102, 169, 182, 185, 245, 260, 264
domestic instability 5, 155
domestic interiors 2, 4, 8–9, 13, 36, 50, 61, 114, 122, 150, 155, 161–2, 174–5, 177, 211–18, 224, 233–5, 237–9, 241, 248
domesticity 2, 7–8, 88, 101–2, 108–10, 120, 151 n.1, 167, 181, 189–90, 214, 219
domestic spaces 3–4, 6–8, 15, 22, 24, 33, 49, 65–6, 68, 70, 97, 101–2, 104, 109, 118, 129, 157, 160, 162, 164, 167–8, 171, 177, 178 n.3, 196, 200, 203–4, 209, 215, 219, 228, 234–7
  as narrative medium 235–7
  unconscious gender of 238–41
domestic violence against women 50
Dovey, Kim 76, 83
dramatherapy, EPR model of 61–2, 64
Dutch paintings of plague patients 7, 141–2, 149–50, 151 n.1. *See also* plague/plague patients
  broom and liminal objects 146–50, 151 n.6
  Death at Ramshorst, 1660 (Gesina ter Borch) 144
  Pest Victims in a Pest House, 1682 (van der Schuer) 142
  The Sick Child, 1664–66 (Metsu) 142
  A Sick Woman and a Weeping Maidservant, 1657–59 (Metsu) 142
  The Slaughtered Pig, 1670 (ten Oever) 143, 145
  The Slippers, 1658 (van Hoogstraten) 145–50
  symbolic paintings (letters) 146–7, 151 n.2
  vanitas objects 144, 146, 149–50
  Woman Reading a Letter (Gerard ter Borch) 147, 149

e-commerce 171–2
Ediger, Patrick 216
Billy Ehn 76
Eidan, Nihon Jutaku 53–4
elementary exercises on space 195
  design as project/drawing 196
  domestic space
    continuous movement in (Asia Maria Andreolli) 198–9
    drawing of pleasant situations 196–7
    narrative themes for confinement 199–200
  Smithson's exercise 196
Embodiment-Projection-Role (EPR) model of dramatherapy 61–2, 64
Exploration in Space programme 64–6, 68
emotions/emotional behaviours 7, 16, 26, 33, 39, 62–3, 66, 69–70, 117, 119, 121, 127, 175, 251, 264
empathy 38, 119–20, 123, 190
empty spaces 155–6, 164
English, Gail 222
entertainment 5, 172, 211, 217
ethnicity 76, 184, 234, 268
Europe 14–16, 27, 135. *See also specific countries*
  body culture movement in 14
  European Modern Movement 15
  refugee arrivals to 131
Evans, Robin 109
exhibitions/exhibition galleries 8, 36, 40–1, 113, 161, 200–2, 222, 224, 226, 229–33, 235, 256–7, 259–60. *See also specific exhibitions*
Exploration in Space programme 64–6, 68

face masks/masking 49, 150–1, 247
  Wearing on 161
Fahd, Cherine, *The Conversation* 156
Feigned letter rack (*ca.* 1655) 151 n.7
feminine independence. *See* independence for women (workspace)
femininity 82, 119, 184

Feng Lu 107
Fiorino, Imma 234
fitness classes (online courses) 2, 13
  dance-based (see Zumba fitness class)
  in-person classes 26–8, 31
  radio fitness classes (see Daan, Lea (1906–95))
  spaces for home gym 18, 20–1
Fletcher, John 62
flexible spatial art (*Raumkunst*) 37
Foucault, Michel 197, 202
France 2, 38, 49, 63, 97 n.1, 129, 227
  The National Institute for Statistics and Economic Studies 63
Franits, Wayne 141
Frank, Josef 4–8, 37–8, 40
free body culture (*Freikörperkultur*) movements 36
Freud, Sigmund 156, 198
  Das Unheimliche in his *Aesthetic Theory* 201
  Imago 38
Fujii, Koji, *The Japanese Dwelling-House* 52
functionalism 203
functional space theory 54, 204
furniture/furnishings 1, 8, 15, 22, 26, 36–7, 39–40, 47, 77–8, 81, 83–4, 92, 95, 103, 116, 163, 168–72, 170, 174, 177, 203, 211–12, 214–15, 223, 236–7, 239, 248, 266. See also IKEA

gender/gendered space 3, 6, 8, 37–40. See also class; race/racism
  of alternative justice 120–2
  gender-domination 6, 66, 87–8
  gendered production of space 119
  inequalities 37, 87, 91
genre paintings 146–8
Germany 15–16, 36–7, 49
  Berlin 16, 28
Getty Museum 162
Giddens, Anthony 47
The Glasgow School of Art in Scotland/Singapore 10, 249, 254, 256

Goffman, Erving 210
graphic visualization 235–7
Grayson's Art Club television programme 157
Greek Islands 129, 131, 133, 136
Green Orientalism 184, 190
Green, Kay 210
green spaces 36, 40, 50
Gross, Fritz 41–2
  Einwohnraum (single multi-use room for living, dining, working, and sleeping) 42
gym/gymnasia 1, 3, 13, 15–17, 20, 27–9
  radio gym classes 17–18, 20
  spaces for home gym 20–1
gymnastics 13, 18

Hadid, Zaha 233
Hahn, Lotta 167
Han, Byung-Chul 196, 244
Hand, Martin 83
Hanks, Tom 217
healthcare 61, 101, 129
Hefner, Hugh, reticence 201–2
Heindl, Luisa, *The Breach: Transparency, Intimacy and Privacy* 200
Herbert, Martin 161
Herrmann, Zachary 229
Hofmann, Else 40
Holland 149
Hollis, Edward 157
Holliss, Frances, *Beyond Live/Work: The architecture of home-based work* 102
home-based workers, independent 87–8, 101–2
home economics 36–7, 39
homelessness 6, 49, 136
homeowners 211–14, 217–18
home territory 102–4, 106–9
Ho, Ron, *TV Guide* 227–8
Hoste, Huib 20
House Beautiful magazine 214
houseplants 37, 41–3. See also air purification
humanity/humanitarian 129, 171, 177, 215–16
human-non-human relations 7

human subject 155, 157–8, 184
hybrid interiors 83
hygiene/hygienic homes 2, 4, 15, 36–7, 47–8, 181
    Mclintock on 191 n.1
    and well-being (Confucian thought) 50–2, 57

ideal self/identity 210
identity-making
    collecting identities in mediated home 211–15
    public performance, spaces for 209–11
    self-curation in Zoom room 215–19
Igo, Sarah, *The Known Citizen: A History of Privacy in Modern America* 31
IKANO Bostad 170
IKEA 5, 7, 76, 78, 83, 167–8
    backstage for 1974/75 catalogue 169
    The Big Home Reboot report 178 n.3
    click & collect service 171
    Dec-net IKEA 170
    Democratic Design 167
    design by fiction 167, 176–8
    with digitalization 170–3, 177
    home communication project 168
    IKEA Historical Archives (IHA) 178 n.1
    The IKEA Home research project 178 n.1
    IKEA Media Content Center (IMCC) 170
    ikéa-nytt brochure 168
    IKEA questionnaire, 1955 173
    Instagram posts (Instagrammable home) 168–9, 173–5, 177, 178 n.2
    laptop table 78
    Life at Home reports 170, 175–6, 178 n.3
    living room working space 79
    Marketing & Communication department (IMC) 170
    Place app 170–1
    #RipartiamoDaCasa (Let's re-start from home) 173

social distancing 172–3
video-call helpline 172, 176–7
YouTube clips 172–4, 177
imagination (representation) 62, 65, 67, 104, 169, 177
imagined communities 210, 215
immigrants 181, 191 n.1
independence for women (workspace) 87–8, 185
    border-objects (thick boundary) 94–5
    domestication of independence 89–90, 95–6 to autonomy 90
    financial 89
    gendered specification of spaces 91–2
    home-based workers 88–9, 101–2
    inhabited spaces 5, 92, 95–6
    unstable boundaries 92–4
    workrooms 91–3
Indigenous people/traditions 114, 189–90
influenza epidemic (1918–19) 36, 128
informal space 113
inhabitants/inhabitation 1–2, 5–6, 42–3, 63, 89–90, 92, 95–6, 102, 105, 108–9, 129, 131–4, 156, 162–3, 168, 200, 235
InnenDekoration, psychology and dwelling 4, 38
Instagram 9, 161, 173, 210
    IKEA's posts on (Instagrammable home) 168–9, 173–5, 177, 178 n.2
    @shelterinplacegallery 222, 224–5, 229
    @tussenkunstenquarantaine (Dutch user) 162
Interior and Exhibit Design course 195
Interior Archipelago – Postcards from Our Islands 248–50
    collections 251–2, 256
    exhibition images at AADTHU 257
    pandemic interior-scapes 252–4
    Principle of No-Two-Alike (Danet and Katriel) 250
    representation forms 252–3, 255
    spatial configurations 252, 254
    state of being 252–3
    submission requirements 249–51

interiority 3, 10, 148–9, 248–9, 252
interior-scapes 9, 252–4
intermediate space 149
internet 26–7, 64, 155, 157, 159, 183, 227
intimate space 26, 82, 101, 108, 119, 156–7, 160, 210, 239, 244
I See You exhibition (Dafa) 200
Italy 2, 7, 168, 174, 178 n.3, 195, 233–4
    casa all'italiana (Italian house), Ponti 234

Japan 2, 4
    cholera epidemic in 51–2
    Cultural Lifestyle 52
    domestic violence against women 50
    Healthy Housing Competition 52–3, 57
    housing (*see* Japanese housing)
    Hygiene Bureau (1876) 51
    Japanese housing survey (2019) 49
    Japanese Society of Lifeology survey 48–9
    The League for the Improvement of Living 52
    Nakagin Capsule Tower 238
    pandemic guidelines 48–9
    Tokyo 48
Japanese housing 4
    51C model home 55
    airtight homes 55
    contemporary housing 47
    Great Kanto Earthquake (1923) 48, 53
    and hardships 49–50
    health/hygienic living/well-being 48–52, 57–8
    historical dwelling (by Morse) 51
    n+LDK housing 55–6
    post-second world war 55
    rental homes size 49
    sanitation and public housing planning 53–5
    small homes/apartments 47, 49–50, 54–5
    tatami-floored rooms 52, 55, 57
    vernacular design 56
    Western-style 52

Jentsch, Ernst 156
Jooss, Kurt 14, 16

Kaare Nielsen, Henrik 84
Kaibara, Ekiken, *Youjou-kun* (*Youjou theory*) 51, 57
Kamprad, Ingvar 168
Katriel, Tamar 250
Klein, Alexander, functional space theory 54
Klein, Naomi, *No Logo: Taking Aim at the Brand Bullies* 188
Kobayashi, Yotaro 55
Kon, Wajiro 48, 53
Krimmel, John Lewis, *The Quilting Frolic* 212
Kristofferson, Sara 177

Laban, Rudolf von 14, 17
    Choreutics 16
    Laban system 15–16
Le Corbusier 239
    Maison Dom-Ino project (1914) 203
Legge di Bilancio 2021 172
Lerner, Adam 119
Lewis, Clive Staples, *The Lion the Witch and the Wardrobe* 62, 68
Lichtblau, Ernst 40–1
liminal objects 146–50
liminal space 62, 67, 70
Lincoln, Sara, *Justin, from the Outside In* 162
living spaces 2, 35, 47, 55, 61–2, 103, 168, 214, 223
    as contested terrains 233–5
Lockdown exhibition, Maureen Paley gallery, London 161
lockdown (quarantine) 1–2, 4, 6, 8–10, 13, 35, 49, 63–4, 76, 87–8, 104, 128–9, 131–2, 134–5, 141, 155–64, 171–2, 174, 181–3, 198–9, 201, 222, 229, 233, 235, 241, 247–8, 256, 259. See also portrait/photographic portraiture; quarantine at home
Löfgren, Orvar 76
Lohmann, Larry, Green Orientalism 19, 184

Lopez, Ana 116–17
Löwitsch, Franz 38
  spatial value (*Raumwert*) 39
Lundgren, Gillis 168
Luo, Ruilin 251

Maffei, Andrea 197
Maison Dom-Ino project, 1914 (Le Corbusier) 8, 203–4
Mapes, Richard 157
Marcus, Clare Cooper, *House as a Mirror of Self: Exploring the deeper meaning of home* 102
marginalized groups 129, 136, 265
Marley, Bob 186–7
Martin, Enthed 170
Martini, Nicolaï, Bossa (Casa) Nova 200–1
Mask Masked sculpture 161
Massey, Doreen 104
material culture 211, 214–15
material goods 211, 213
materiality/material artefacts 77, 79, 82–4, 93, 164
MAXXI, the National Museum of 21st Century Arts 9, 233
  brainstorming session 235
  The Domestic Body workshop 233, 235–7
    considerations and legacy 245
    Milanese heterosexual couple with newborn 238
    Parisian couple of young heterosexual professionals 239–40
    single professional (Filippo) 241–4
  domestic space
    as narrative medium 235–7
    unconscious gender of 238–41
  educational activities of 245 n.1
  Education Department of 233–5, 237–8, 245
  graphic visualization 235–6
  #stayathome policy 233–5
Mclintock, Anne 191 n.1
mediation 75–6, 167–70
mental health 2, 51, 61, 63–4, 119, 132–5

Metsu, Gabriel
  The Sick Child (1664–66) 142
  A Sick Woman and a Weeping Maidservant (1657–59) 142
middle class 32, 181–3, 189, 211–12, 214–15, 234
  in Early Republic (painting) 212
  house/homeowners in the United States 211–15
The Middle East 27, 135
migrants/migrant camps. *See* refugee camps
miniature gallery/miniaturization 9, 221–3, 226–9. *See also* Shelter in Place Gallery
minimal dormitory room 103–4, 109
minorities/minority group 181, 184
Modern Interiors Research Centre (MIRC) 1–2
Monks, Fran 159–60, 163
  Sally by 159
Morse, Edward S., *View of dwelling from garden, Tokio* 51
multi-functional spaces 55, 102
municipal housing programmes 15, 36, 40
Musée Dom-Ino project. *See* Maison Dom-Ino project
Museum of Domesticity in Lockdown 203
Museum of Fine Arts (MFA), Boston 222–3, 228–32
The Museum of the Home, Hoxton, East London 9, 259
  Clap for Carers event 265
  community relationships 266
  considerations and legacy 267
  Documenting Homes archive 260
  experiences of lockdown (questionnaire) 260–6
  Home Galleries 267
  Our Home Our Stories (Alsaraji) 268–9
  partnerships 267
  Stay Home Collection 269
  Stay Home project/Stay Home Stories project 259–60, 268–9
  vision of 259

National Geographic 183, 187–90
National Health Service (NHS) 157, 160
The National Institute for Statistics and Economic Studies, France 63
national radio network 13–15
Nemet Pier, Lyliane 63, 65–6
neoliberal/neoliberalism 88–90, 92, 96, 169, 171, 177, 184
neologism 62, 70
The Netherlands 16, 38, 143
  Amsterdam 28, 146, 202
Nilsson, Daniel 76
  Hemmakontor (home offices) 5, 80–1, 84
Nishiyama, Uzo
  food-sleep separation 55
  sketch of his small dwelling (1930s) 54
  sketch of typical n+LDK dwelling (1970s) 56
non-fungible tokens (NFTs) 251
Nutting, Wallace, *At the Fender* 213–14

Oczko, Pjotr 148, 151 n.5
  View into a Hallway (*ca.* 1662) 151 n.4
oikeiosiss. *See* appropriation, spatial
Omi, Shigeru, new lifestyles (Atarashii Seikatsu Yoshiki) slogan 57
Ortiz, Verónica 115
Oscar, Sara, *The Conversation* 156
overcrowded housing 62–3, 70, 128–31. *See also* refugee camps
Oxfam International 130

panopticism 202
Pantzar, Mika 76
Parr, Martin, *Autoportrait* 160
paternalism 55, 57
patriarchal society 87, 89, 91–2, 96
Patron of the National Portrait Gallery 161
Pattaroni, Luca, Domotopy: At home in a world in motion project 97 n.1
peace/peaceful 14, 38, 51, 116, 150, 174, 198

Pearson de González, Annette 116
Persil (Unilever) 183–6
pestkruis 143, 147
physical proximity 120, 173
physical space 62, 104, 107–9, 119–20, 123, 168, 199, 247
plague/plague patients 7, 141–3, 149–50. *See also* Dutch paintings of plague patients
Plischke, Ernst 42
  Das Blumenfenster (design for windowsill garden) 43
political economy 169, 177, 184
Ponti, Gio, casa all'italiana (Italian house) 234
pop culture 217
popular media 87, 181, 184
portrait/photographic portraiture 155–6, 164, 212
  anonymous spaces 159
  Autoportrait (Parr) 160
  Burke's 162–3
  Egg Head (Sewell) 160
  environment 159
  face mask/masking 161
  familiar/unfamiliar spaces 155–8, 161, 164
  framed 212
  of Harriet Durkin (nurse with PPE) 161
  Hold Still community project 161–2
  Justin, from the Outside In (Lincoln) 162
  middle-class family 160
  Monks on 159–60, 163
  occupational 161
  Portraits for NHS Heroes 161
  self-portraits 28, 155, 157, 160–1
  social connection/group identity, role of 161
  Sontag on 158
  symbolism in Renaissance portraits 157–8
  Tesco Value Dad (Burke) 163
  West on 158
  Zoutman on 160
Povey, Thomas 151 n.4
Prague Castle Picture Gallery 151 n.7
Preciado, Paul 197–8, 201

pre-recorded workouts 27
privacy 25, 31, 33, 41, 47, 94, 106–7, 120, 122, 127, 131, 239
　lack of 4, 6, 26, 63, 66, 132
　and technology 107–8
private space 9, 30–3, 50–1, 57, 66, 77, 82–3, 90, 92, 94, 101–2, 106–7, 113, 119, 123, 131–2, 143, 195, 198, 202, 209, 241, 247. *See also* public space
Proctor & Gamble 182
　Fairy Liquid soap 186–90
Protestant 150, 151 n.7. *See also* Catholic/Catholicism
psychic self 62
psychoanalysis 38–9
psychology 37–9, 62
psychoscenography 4, 62, 69–70
public performance, spaces for 209–12, 214–16
public space 50, 68, 77, 82–3, 101–2, 110, 129, 132, 155–6, 164, 198, 209, 241, 247. *See also* private space
Puerta, Carlos 115
purpose-built museums 113, 117, 123

qi (Ki) 51
quarantine at home 76, 130, 136, 157, 164, 196–7, 202, 237–8, 240, 243, 247, 253. *See also* lockdown (quarantine)

race/racism 3, 8, 182, 184, 187. *See also* class; gender/gendered space
radio
　fitness classes (1935–1940), Daan's (*see* Daan, Lea (1906–95))
　home listeners 3–4, 14, 18–19
　as mass modernizing medium 14–15
　women audience 15, 18, 20
Rahman, Farhana 134
ready-made concept 200
rechoreographing process of home 83
reconciliation process 114, 117, 122–3
refugee camps 5–6, 127
　Camp-22 131
　Cox's Bazar, Bangladesh 6, 128, 130–1, 135

everyday life in (during Covid-19) 129–30
Flemington and North Melbourne towers, Melbourne 6, 128, 134–6
insecurity of migrants in 127
interview with women in 134
Kara Tepe, Greece 131
makeshift shelters 128–30
Moria and Mavrovouni (women's camp), Lesbos, Greece 6, 128, 131–5
physical instability 130–2, 136
Rohingya refugees 130, 134
scapegoats 133–4, 136
sweltering greenhouses 133
Syrian refugee 133
vaccination campaign 133
restorative justice 114–15, 122–3. *See also* transitional justice
reverie (daydreaming) 62, 69
Rice, Charles, *The Emergence of the Interior* 199
Richter, Christian, *Abandoned* 156
Robert, Christophe 63
Rowe, Colin 200
Royal Meteorological Institute 15
Russia 16

sanctuary, home as 3, 178 n.3, 262
Savinio, Alberto, *Annunciation* 198
scenographic/scenography 61–2, 64, 66–7, 168, 172
　therapeutic 70
The School of Interior Design at Toronto Metropolitan University, Canada 249, 256
Second Life online platform 26
second-wave feminism 91
Seits, Irina 177
self-employment 89
semi-contaminated zone 104
semi-directed interviews 87, 97 n.1
semi-private aesthetics 77
semi-public space 77, 82
Sendak, Maurice, *Where the Wild Things Are* 68
seventeenth-century paintings 141, 145, 150, 151 n.3
Sewell, Mike, *Egg Head* 160

INDEX

sexual harassment/violence 31, 114, 123, 130
Shankar, Shalini 182, 191 n.1
  racial naturalisation 184
Shelter in Place Gallery 221–2, 231–2
  crafting interior 222–6
  living room (from exterior) 223
  and MFA 228–31
  miniatures 226–8
  New Light: Encounters and Connections exhibition 229–30, 232
  packaging materials for transport 223–4
  @shelterinplacegallery (first Instagram post) 222, 224–5, 229
  terrestrial globe compass (ca. 1675–1685), Dieppe, France 227
  www.shelterinplacegallery.com 222
Shove, Elizabeth 83
Shutte-Lihotzki, Margarete 236
Slutzky, Robert 200
smallpox 51, 134
Smithson, Peter, *Changing the Art of Inhabitation* 196
Sobotka, Walter 40
social boundaries 28, 31
social distancing 13, 30–1, 129–31, 155–6, 160, 171–3, 222
social media 7, 26, 92, 160, 168, 170, 172–3, 202, 210, 215–16, 222. *See also specific companies*
social relations 57, 84, 104, 109, 117
Social Sciences and Humanities Research Council of Canada (SSHRC) 123
solidarity 30, 160–1
Sontag, Susan 158
sound environment 93–4
spaceship 66–9, 71
Spain 128–9
Spanish Flu (epidemic of 1918–19) 2, 52, 128–9
spatial boundaries 6, 103, 127, 129, 134
spatial science 37–40

stay home 3, 13, 181
  #stayathome policy, MAXXI 233–5
  Stay Home project 61, 183, 247, 259–60
staying-at-home situation 75–6, 85
  expectations about objects 84
  living room working space 79
  material changes/adjustments/reorganization 75, 77–82
  rechoreographing of home 83
  re-materialization 82–4
Stefancic, Jean 182
Stern, Nelly 39
Stewart, Susan 250
Strnad, Oskar, flexible spatial art (*Raumkunst*) 37
Sumi Oe 52
surveillance 22, 33, 133, 200, 202
Sweden 2, 5, 75–7, 84, 167
swine flu (2009 H1N1) epidemic 129
Swiss National Science Foundation 97 n.1
Switzerland 2, 5, 38, 97 n.1
symbolism 65, 149, 150, 157

Taubenfligel, Adam 187
Taylor, Claude, Twitter feed (@ratemyskyperoom) 217
Tehve, Karin 122
telehealth programme 4, 26, 61, 64, 67, 70
tele-therapy 61
temporary housing. *See* refugee camps
ten Oever, Hendrick 143, 145, 147, 149–50, 151 n.5
  The Slaughtered Pig 1670 143, 145
ter Borch, Gerard 144, 151 n.8
  Woman Reading a Letter 147, 149
ter Borch, Gesina 149
  Death at Ramshorst 1660 144
territorialization process 109
theatre-therapy space 70
therapeutic scenography 70
therapeutic space 69–70
three-dimensional spaces 167–9
Tianshi, Emily 187–9
Toobin, Jeffrey (in Zoom meeting) 31
#tradwife movement 187
transactional spaces 119

transgression 6, 91, 127, 134, 151
transitional justice 6, 114–15, 122–3.
    See also restorative justice
Tschumi, Bernard, *Manhattan Transcripts* 235
tuberculosis 36, 51
Turkle, Sherry 26
Twitter/Twitter feed 108
    @BCredibility 217–18
    @ratemyskyperoom 217

unemployment 14, 63
The United Kingdom 2, 8, 49
    lockdown portraits (*see* portrait/photographic portraiture)
The United States 2, 8, 27, 49, 209, 211
    Asian Americans 184, 188
    California 28
    Chinese American 227
    identity-making in (*see* identity-making)
    immigrants to (nineteenth century) 191 n.1
    middle-class home in 211–15
urban spaces 4, 7, 109, 155–6, 164

van der Schuer, Theodoor, *Pest Victims in a Pest House 1682* 142
van Hoogstraten, Samuel 151 n.8
    The Slippers 1658 145–50
vanitas objects 144, 146, 149–50
ventilation 2, 13–14, 36, 39, 52, 55, 57, 135
Vidler, Anthony 155–6, 198–9
    The Architectural Uncanny: Essays in the Modern Unhomely 156, 199
    mutual mechanization 200
Vienna, Austria
    designers/architects 35–7, 40
    flexible spatial art (*Raumkunst*) 37
    health/hygiene/well-being 36–8
    in confined space 40–4
    interior design and dwelling culture 35–7, 42–4
    municipal housing programme 36
    spatial science 38–40
Vienna, Red 4, 40

Viennese Spatial Artists/Viennese Interior Artists (*Wiener Raumkünstler*) exhibition 41
Vignelli, Massimo, *The Triennale of Leisure Time* (1964) 244
violence 50, 63, 113–14, 119–21, 123, 130, 187
virtual reality/space 26, 33, 101, 104, 108–9, 119, 157, 170, 176, 248
visual culture 7, 78, 212, 214
visual images 183, 209, 211, 213–14

Walters, Kylie 217–18
Wearing, Gillian 161, 163
well-being 3–4, 14–15, 22, 26, 35–9, 48–50, 56, 58, 132
    of children 61
    in confined spaces 40–4
    and hygienic homes (Confucian thought) 50–2, 57
West, Shearer 158
What is modern in Vienna. Modern Spatial Art: The Well-Used Corner (*Was in Wien Modern ist? Die wohlangewandte Ecke*) 41
white cube space 9, 224
white supremacy 182, 184, 186–91
Wilbur, Matika 187–90
Wilk, Richard 76
Wiseman, Eva 157
Woestyn, Omer 17
    vs. Daan 18–20
women
    burdens on 1, 37, 39
    domestic violence against 50
    emancipatory power of 87–8, 90
    housewives/homemakers 14–15, 36, 87
    independent home-based workers (*see* independence for women)
    paid work 87, 90
    self-employment 89
    self-realization 88, 90
    Stern's advise for 39–40
    women audience for radio 15, 18, 20
    working-class 39
Woolf, Virginia 66, 89

INDEX

closable room 91
domestic economy of women 89
habitation unit 92
A Room of One's Own 87, 90
workrooms for women 91–2
working-class 36, 39–40, 181–2, 241
working spaces (work from home) 2, 35, 44, 48–51, 76–7, 79–82, 85, 88, 92–3, 96, 101–2, 104–5, 109, 114, 118–23, 129, 157, 196, 241, 264

Ying Chang 254
Youjou-kun (*Youjou theory*), Kaibara 51, 57

Zardini, Mirko 195
Zimbler, Liane 40, 42–3
   Trennungswand in der Diele (partition wall in hallway of an apartment) 44

Zoom video conferencing platform 2, 9, 25–6, 29, 31, 76, 97 n.1, 157–8, 160, 209, 215
   backgrounds 4, 25–6, 32
   camera (on/off) 4, 22, 27–34
   Colonial Revival House, 1902 216
   modelling a hat after class 32
   multiple computer screens for teaching 29
   participants on one of many screens 30
   public performance, spaces for 209–11
   self-curation in 209, 215–19
   soundtrack (silent/mute) 33
Zoutman, Birgitta 160
Zumba fitness class 4, 27, 31–3
   Ketty (teacher) 27–31, 33
   living room transformed for 27–8